Red Delight

Liverpool's 150 Greatest Matches

David Plumbley

For my father, who took me to my first match and my companion for hundreds of subsequent matches

Table of Contents

Introduction

My first book, "Songs from a Quarantine", was written during the first Covid lockdown and featured reviews of my favourite 101 songs. I enjoyed the process and discipline of writing, so thought that I would like to write about my beloved Liverpool FC next. I liked the idea of their greatest matches, and the 75 years since the Second World War seemed like a suitable timeframe.

With such an illustrious past, I quickly knew that 101 would not be sufficient this time, so went for 150, but it still left some difficult choices and many great moments are missing. As Liverpool fans we are so lucky and blessed to have such a rich and glorious history. Obviously the 1960s to 1980s were so trophy laden, their matches spring to mind easily. But even in the "30 years of hurt" between title wins, there were still two Champions Leagues, a UEFA Cup, three FA Cups and four League Cups. There may have been few trophies in the 1990s, but Roy Evans' team could be thrilling. Likewise, only one trophy between 2007 and 2018 hides many delights of the later Benitez team, Brendan Rodgers' exciting title chase, and the early Klopp years.

Liverpool seem to have especially spoilt by a succession of special strikers; Liddell, Hunt, Keegan, Dalglish, Rush, Barnes / Beardsley / Aldridge, Fowler, Owen, Torres, Suarez / Sturridge and today's Mané / Salah / Firmino. This pattern can also be easily extended to other positions too, like the centre-backs Yeats, Hughes, Thompson, Hansen, Lawrenson, Hyppia, Carragher and van Dyke.

What makes a great match? It is hard to define, as there can be many different characteristics. It can be a stunning dominant team performance (5-0 Nottingham Forest or 7-0 Tottenham), or an end to end thriller (4-3 Newcastle). It may not even be that exciting, but the result is significant, like winning a final (Tottenham in 2019). Often it could be a personal achievement, and the book is littered with hat-tricks. Then there are notable moments in Liverpool's history with a debut or defining win. It may not even be a win, as one of my all-time favourites is the 1-1 draw at Bayern Munich in 1981. There is normally an element of drama, with Liverpool triumphing against the odds, reversing a seemingly insurmountable deficit or scoring a late winner.

I tried to avoid focussing too much on recent games, but failed as Klopp's achievements are too hard to ignore. However, I also wanted to pay tribute to the previous generations, and ensure that even the dark days of the 1950s Second Division could have some special moments.

You will find many special European nights included. I know many opposition fans take great delight in their "Where's your famous atmosphere?" taunts during a routine league match. But the frequency, often against the odds, that Liverpool triumph in such a unique atmosphere, makes it undeniable. As they are even decades apart, it feels like a collective DNA of fans and players is passed down the generations.

I attended my first Liverpool match in November 1974 (just missing Shankly, but ready for Paisley's glory). So this means that I can recall the subsequent matches, but those earlier require poring over old newspapers and books (see the bibliography for credits). I, and all Liverpool historians, are particularly indebted to the Liverpool Echo journalists, with pennames like Stork and Ranger from the 1950s. They filed meticulous and detailed reports of the afternoon's action, despite tight deadlines. I remember the joy of a Saturday night in the late 1970s, an era before Ceefax and the Internet, devouring the Football Echo and studying the league tables.

Today's fans and future generations are fortunate to be able to see the recent teams in all their glory with extensive (or oversaturated) television coverage. Going back further is problematic. It is such a pity that the skill of Billy Liddell is recorded by just the occasional Pathé news clip. They tended to focus on the FA Cup, so it is regrettable that the title showdown with Wolves in 1947 was not recorded. The Shankly era has more available, due to the introduction of BBC's "Match of the Day" and then ITV, but again it often relied on the luck of them selecting a single game. Even in the 1970s there were still quirks, such as the 1976 title decider against Wolves only has a short single-camera news clip of the goals and dressing room celebrations. It seems strange that the TV companies spent the whole season with weekly programmes, but did not cover the decisive finale. Thankfully, European matches had better coverage (although there is only a short black and white clip of Barcelona in 1976).

I have attempted to highlight where clips are available on YouTube or DVD. Since the Premier League era every match has been filmed and the LFCTV Go service has them all available. The LFCTV channel has made some interesting documentaries and includes a variety of excellent content.

It has been interesting to detect the evolution of football over seventy five years. From domestic players paid a maximum wage, on treacherous pitches with fans packed on to terraces, to today's all seater stadiums, with well-paid foreign players and high speed matches.

I also noticed that for all Liverpool's glory, there were many near misses too, especially the Shankly lean years or the post 1990 league title attempts. However by the same token, there were many moments when other rivals could have triumphed instead, so many twists of fate and "sliding door" moments.

It was inevitable that wins over Manchester United and Everton would feature prominently, as a win against a local rival feels even more significant and sweeter. However, it is amazing how often Newcastle United appear, as each generation seems to have inflicted a crushing victory. On the European scene, Roma or even Barcelona must be really sick of meeting Liverpool.

Generally, I have tried to provide a context for each match and then a description of the events that took place. I also wanted to include some of the trivia, as I always enjoy hearing about new records and feats. I am also intrigued by rival players and managers reappearing in the Liverpool story, or what happened to them next.

The only downside with the hastily filed newspaper reports is that discrepancies or mistakes can occur. These can be amplified by subsequent repetition or mistaken recollections in ghost-written player autobiographies. Hopefully, I have detected most of them, and hope this 90,000-word book will not include too many of its own.

I hope you enjoy reading, and that it will bring back happy memories for older fans, or introduce new matches for younger fans to investigate.

Notes

All information should be correct as of 1st July 2021.

The top league in English football was called the First Division until 1992 and is now known as the Premier League. Traditionally, this division had 42 matches, until the Premier League reduced it to 38 in 1995 (although it was briefly smaller between 1987 and 1991 too).

Two points were given for a win, and one for a draw until 1981, and since then, it has been three points for a win. Two teams were promoted from the Second Division until 1973/4, and now it is three teams.

If two teams had the same number of points, then goal average (goals scored divided by goals conceded) was used until 1976/77, and now it is goal difference (goals scored minus goals conceded).

The English domestic trophies, the FA Cup and League Cup, have been frequently renamed according to their current sponsors, but for consistency, I have not used them.

The European Cup was only open to national League winners until 1992, consisting of two-legged knockout ties, with a one-off final. The Champions League from 1992 allowed multiple teams from the same nation, with group stages and then a knockout format.

The Fairs Cup and its successor, the UEFA Cup, was a competition for teams that finished below the champions. It was renamed in 2009-10 as the Europa League and featured a group stage.

Substitutes were not possible in English football until 1965/66, and initially just for injuries. Over the subsequent years, the number of substitutes and substitutions has increased.

Football statisticians disagree whether the Charity Shield is a friendly, or should be included as an official competitive match on records for appearances and goals. I have chosen the latter.

1940s

Liverpool 7 Chelsea 4

07/09/1946 - First Division - Anfield

The Second World War devastated the careers of many aspiring footballers. Amongst those were two additions to Liverpool's 1939 squad; the 17-year old Billy Liddell and 20-year old Bob Paisley. They would need to wait seven long years to make their league debuts, and forge their indelible marks on Liverpool's history.

In the meantime, football carried on with regional leagues of makeshift teams, often featuring guests players. Both Liddell and Paisley combined their appearances with duties in the Royal Air Force and Royal Artillery respectively. Liddell quickly became one of the stars of wartime football, with 74 goals in 147 matches and Scotland international caps too. Paisley had less opportunity, as he was stationed overseas from 1941, serving in North Africa and playing a part in the liberation of Italy.

Although the FA Cup restarted as normal in January 1946, it was not until the end of August 1946 that the regular league format resumed. Liverpool won their first match, away to Sheffield United, but in midweek slumped to a lacklustre home defeat to Middlesbrough.

This did not dampen the enthusiasm of the fans at the prospect of the first Saturday home match, on a boiling September afternoon. The Main Stand gates were closed 30 minutes before the start, but fans could still pack onto the bulging terraces.

The squad assembled by manager George Kaye featured a mixture of first team players from before the war (Jack Balmer, Willie Fagan, "Nivvy" Nieuwenhuys, Phil Taylor, Jim Harley, Bernard Ramsden), former youth players (Paisley, Liddell, Cyril Done, Ray Lambert) and those recently acquired (Cyril Sidlow, Laurie Hughes, Billy Watkinson, Bob Priday)

For this match, Liverpool were boosted by the addition of Liddell and captain Fagan, after they had missed the first two matches through injury, and Paisley was also introduced in response to the midweek setback. Sidlow was injured, so Ashcroft made his debut in goal. The visitors, Chelsea, like their modern-day successors, had made several expensive purchases, the most eye-catching, the capture of England centre forward Tommy Lawton for £14,000 from Everton.

Liddell seemed determined to make up for lost time and nearly scored in the opening minute, with a typically powerful drive that flew just wide into the Kop. He only needed to wait another minute to make his mark. Paisley won a corner, and Liddell scored directly, as goalkeeper Bill Robertson could only help the cross into the net.

Spurred on by their perfect start, the home team swept forward, creating several chances, and Bill Jones scored twice; a quick shot on the turn after 24th minutes, and a header 6 minutes later, after Nieuwenhuys flicked on a Liddell cross. Lawton's only chance was safely tipped over by Ashcroft. Robertson also made two fine saves, but could not stop Fagan scoring off the post, for a commanding 4-0 half-time lead.

Half-time saw the gates finally closed, locking out an estimated 5,000, while hundreds of children were placed next to the touchline after suffering from the heat. Liverpool continued their domination after the restart, with another two quick goals. A shot from distance by Balmer was missed by Robertson, and Liddell scored after a powerful run, despite several strong challenges, which limited his involvement for the rest of the match.

6-0 after 50 minutes was surely unassailable. However, Chelsea clawed two back through Len Goulden and Jimmy Argue. Balmer then missed an easy chance, as two quick Alex Machin goals in the 70th and 72nd minute made it 6-4. An improbable comeback was now possible due to complacency or the returning players tiring. Ashcroft had to make a great stop to prevent Machin's hat-trick on 80 minutes. The nervous fans must have been relieved when Fagan finally sealed the win in the 87th minute, from a Nieuwenhuys' corner. There was still time for Balmer to hit the post, and the children swarmed on the pitch at the end to mob their new heroes.

League football was back with a stunning match, made even more significant as the formal start of two glorious Liverpool careers. Their contributions did not go unnoticed, as the Liverpool Echo headlined "Liddell and Paisley transformed Liverpool attack". It would only be the start for these legends.

- The official attendance of 49,995 (probably an underestimate) contributed to a total of over one million spectators for the English football leagues this Saturday.

- Admission costs were 1/3 for the ground, 2/9 for the stands, and 9d for boys and armed forces in uniform.

- Billy Liddell's two minute league debut goal puts him ahead of other legends like Keegan (12 minutes), Dalglish (7 minutes), Owen (16 minutes) and Suarez (16 minutes), but Paul Walsh holds the distinction of taking just 15 seconds on his home debut.

- Liverpool would lose their next match 5-0 to Manchester United and then promptly splashed out a club record £13,000 on centre forward Albert Stubbins from Newcastle United.

- Bill Jones was the grandfather of Rob Jones, who played for Liverpool in the 1990s.

- The first time Liverpool had scored seven goals in a league match since beating Grimsby Town 7 - 1 in September 1936.

- South African Berry Nieuwenhuys had made his Liverpool debut in September 1933 and scored his first goal against Everton later that month.

- Liverpool's strong start was attributed to a tour of the USA the previous May, which allowed the squad to gorge on foods currently rationed in the UK.

- Manager George Kay, from Manchester, was West Ham's captain in the first Wembley FA Cup final in 1923 and had taken over at Anfield in 1936.

- On Christmas Day 1940, Tommy Lawton played for Everton against Liverpool in the morning, and in the afternoon guested for Tranmere Rovers against Crewe.

Arsenal 1 Liverpool 2

24/05/1947 - First Division - Highbury

Expectations had been low at the start of the season, but a solid defence and regular supply of goals from Balmer, Stubbins and Done had seen Liverpool hover around the top all season. The harshest winter since 1910, had seen many matches postponed, so this landmark season was extended. After losing an FA Cup semi-final replay to Burnley, chances of silverware seemed slim, as they were fifth, but they responded with four wins and a draw. Although it only lifted them to fourth place, the title race was so close, that any of the top four could now win it. They knew they had to gain maximum points away at lowly Arsenal in their penultimate match, and put the pressure on the faltering leaders, Wolves.

However, there were injury concerns, as Taylor, Liddell (injured playing for a Great Britain team) and Paisley were all missing, so squad players Eddie Spicer, Watkinson and the South African Priday all appeared. Curiously, also missing from the travelling party was the manager George Kay ("business elsewhere"). It was a critical decision, as although the trainer Albert Shelley was nominally in charge, it was the Liverpool directors that would make a fateful decision.

In a scrappy match, Liverpool defended resolutely, but struggled to create much without Liddell, although deputy Priday was lively. The best chances of the half fell to Rooke and Mercer that were pushed wide by Sidlow. At half-time the directors discussed tactically switching Fagan and Jones' positions, to utilise more of Fagan's creativity. It might seem unusual for the directors to have such input, but in this era they exerted much more control, and even approved the team proposed by the manager.

Liverpool's season looked doomed as Arsenal deservedly took the lead after 61 minutes; a strike from winger Ian McPherson. A quick vote was taken in the stands, and Vice-Chairman Ronnie Williams was sent down to the touchline to relay the agreed change, as the Reds gambled.

The change may not have directly affected the outcome, but provided the necessary impetus. Liverpool were level on 76 minutes as

Balmer rose well to meet Watkinson's corner. Arsenal were stunned as the visitors then took the lead just 4 minutes later; Bob Priday beat his man, crossed hard and Balmer connected. The panicked Arsenal defender Barnes miscued and his clearance went in ("as unlucky as a woman looking for nylons" according to the Sunday People). There is some debate about the scorer, as the Liverpool Echo describes an "unmistakeable" own goal, but other reports and the Liverpool players, claimed the ball was already over the line before Barnes' intervention.

Liverpool held out for the final few minutes to secure the precious points. A win that sent them to the top of the league for the first time since December, because their rivals were not in action until two days later. It also set up a potential title decider in their last fixture away to Wolves.

- Liverpool's last four league games were all away from home.

- In the reverse fixture in November Balmer had scored a hat-trick, completing an unprecedented feat of hat-tricks in three successive matches.

- Arsenal's Reg Lewis and Joe Mercer would be the goals scorer and captain for the Arsenal team that beat Liverpool in the FA Cup final three years later.

- Leslie Compton missed this match for Arsenal because he was playing cricket for Middlesex.

- The excellently researched "At the End of the Storm" by Gary Shaw and Mark Platt gives a game by game description of this season.

- During this season Liverpool's next four managers, either played for Liverpool (Phil Taylor, Bob Paisley) or against them (Don Welsh, Bill Shankly). The opponents had mixed fortunes, as Welsh scored, but Shankly missed a penalty at Anfield !

Wolverhampton Wanderers 1 Liverpool 2

31/05/1947 - First Division - Molineux Stadium

Despite Liverpool's strong run, table toppers Wolves were still strong favourites to claim their first league title. Their experienced team, had agonisingly been second twice immediately before the war. They had been top since winning 5-1 at Anfield in December, thanks to Dennis Wescott netting four times in the first half. Their team featured stars like Bert Williams in goal, centre-half Billy Wright and the inspirational captain Stan Cullis. They were also the sentimental choice, as it was announced just before kick-off, that this would be Cullis' final appearance, as he was retiring at the age of 31.

Over 50,000 crowded into Molineux, including a sizeable contingent from Merseyside, and as the heat rose to over 90 degrees, many covered their heads with handkerchiefs.

Liverpool were encouraged by the return of Liddell, but Fagan had been injured, so Priday stayed as outside left, and Liddell moved to inside left. Incredibly, manager Kay was still missing, this time for a five day scouting trip in Ireland, that was deemed more important than a title decider. Wolves' recent form had been poor, and now they had suffered the blow of missing key strikers Wescott and Galley.

In spite of the intense heart, the start was frenetic, with Wolves dominating, but not creating any decent chances. So it was Liverpool who opened the scoring after 21 minutes; a slick interchange of passes involving five players, with Balmer striking home his 28th goal of the season.

The key moment of the match occurred in the 32nd minute. Wolves were pressing, and Sidlow saved well from Jimmy Dunn. From the corner, the ball was cleared to Priday, and he launched a long ball down the middle for Stubbins to chase. The striker outpaced Cullis, running half of the pitch and then coolly slotted past Williams (also his 28th league goal). Cullis could have probably fouled Stubbins, but later honourably revealed he did not want to win the league in that manner.

Liverpool withstood fierce Wolves pressure in the second half, as Wright was moved forward. The defenders, like Lambert and Hughes, provided a resolute screen, and when necessary ex-Wolves keeper Sidlow made some important saves. Liverpool were still dangerous on the break, with Stubbins denied by the keeper's legs, and Liddell had a goal disallowed for offside.

Dunn reduced the deficit in the 65th minute, setting up a nail-biting finish, but the defence was solid and offered few glimpses of goal. The away win sent Liverpool back to the top, and ended Wolves' chance.

They then endured a tense two-week wait, as Stoke City could still win the league at Sheffield United on 14th June. However, the Potters would lose 2-1, and the result was joyously relayed to Anfield, as Liverpool were beating Everton in the Liverpool Senior Cup. Although there were still ten minutes left in this match, the fans celebrated wildly with hundreds of hats being thrown in the air. A special day, as they clinched two trophies within 15 minutes.

The late charge of thirteen from a possible fourteen points, had secured a fifth league title, and the first in 24 years. An incredible achievement in an extraordinary season.

- This would be the only major club honour in Billy Liddell's distinguished career.

- Wolves striker Jimmy Dunn was the son of an Everton player, and a boyhood Liverpool fan.

- There was no ever present player in the league season, as the squad of 26 was utilised, but only 13 medals were awarded, so Liverpool requested four more.

- Although Stan Cullis missed out on the title in his playing career, he won three League Championships and two FA Cups as Wolves manager.

- Liverpool's squad shared a £275 bonus for the title win. At the time the maximum wage for players was £12 a week.

- Sadly there is very little footage of this team. YouTube only has a brief amateur colour clip of the match at Aston Villa and newsreel footage of two FA Cup matches.

- The popular and influential chairman Bill McConnell, who had joined the board in 1929, would be in hospital for the climax of the season, passing away in August 1947.

- This would be the first of four occasions that Liverpool would succeed Everton as the League champions, although this occasion had a seven year gap.

Liverpool 4 Everton 0

21/04/1948 - First Division - Anfield

After the unexpected success of 1946/7, the next season reverted to the normality of 1930's mid-table obscurity. In fact, after five successive defeats, Liverpool were in the bottom three at the end of February. They managed to regain their form, with a run of six wins and two draws, assuaging any worries.

There was still the matter of local pride in the derby match, with a 6.30 pm kick-off on an April evening. It had been a disappointment for the fans in the previous glorious season that Liverpool had not recorded a league win (or goal) against their local rivals. They put that right in September with a comfortable 3 - 0 at Goodison Park.

For the return match, Liverpool utilised the same team as the previous year, but the only new signing, Ken Brierley, had managed to secure a place at the end of the season. Everton were missing the creative spark of Wally Fielding.

Liverpool dominated the first half, but only led by Albert Stubbins' 14th minute chipped goal, after admirable work by Taylor and Balmer. This was chiefly because of the dramatics of the Everton goalkeeper, the 38-year old Ted Sagar, who made a remarkable array of saves from Paisley, Fagan, and Brierley, while Balmer also shot wide.

Everton improved in the second half, and although they could not get past the resilient Liverpool backline, they still harboured hope of a point. These hopes were shattered by a blitz of three goals in three minutes just after the 80 minute mark.

Even better for the Kop, all three of them were fine. Liddell scored first, running on to a flick from Balmer, and squeezing his shot into a tight gap. He turned provider for the next; with a perfect cross for a Brierley header. Balmer grabbed the last, smashing in a Brierley corner from close range. Sagar's heroics were for naught, as Liverpool had recorded a memorable crushing win.

The Liverpool newspapers extolled the quality of the match, and the friendliness with few fouls. Liverpool may not have recaptured the heights of the previous season, but the majority of the 55,000 fans this evening could celebrate their biggest league derby win since 1935.

- Ken Brierley scored his first goal in his eighth Liverpool appearance, and would later be joined by Brian Hall, John Toshack, Alan Waddle, Steve McMahon, Harry Kewell, Nicky Tanner, Virgil van Dyke, who all notched their first Liverpool goal against Everton.

- Cyril Sidlow's clean sheet was his seventh in a run of nine matches, conceding just two goals.

- Liverpool's first league derby double since 1924–25, and they would have to wait another 29 years for the next.

- The previous weekend Liverpool had drawn 1-1 with a Manchester City team featuring the future Liverpool manager, Joe Fagan.

- On May 3rd, Liverpool beat Everton again, a 2-0 win to retain the Liverpool Senior Cup.

- A photo of Albert Stubbins would appear on the cover of the 1967 Beatles album "Sgt Pepper's Lonely Hearts Club Band".

Liverpool 4 Sunderland 2

20/08/1949 - First Division - Anfield

After two mid-table seasons, 1949-50 provided another opportunity for Liverpool to reassert their title claims. Another bumper crowd of nearly 50,000 filled Anfield on a typical sunny opening day.

The Liverpool teamsheet still contained the spine of the 1947 title winning team, with Sidlow, Taylor, Paisley, Stubbins, Balmer and Liddell all present. There had been no big money transfers, as they relied on local youth in the form of winger Bill Shepherd, Jimmy Payne and Kevin Baron. Opponents Sunderland were now labelled the "Bank of England" team after a series of major transfers, and had broken the British record transfer record for Len Shackleton.

The teams traded early chances, Balmer for the Reds and Shackleton for the visitors. Balmer soon had the ball in the back of the net, but it was disallowed for offside, and he also missed two more opportunities.

Liverpool took the lead after 32 minutes through Paisley, after Robinson could not hold on to Payne's fierce shot. Liddell could have extended the lead, but missed a penalty, after a foul on Balmer. It looked like a costly mistake, as Sunderland equalised; Dickie Davis profiting while the defenders waited for an offside flag that didn't come. However, Liverpool replied within a minute, the energetic Balmer finally getting his deserved goal; heading in from Payne's cross. The latter had been injured early, limping for much of the match and so his impact would be severely limited.

In the second half, Sunderland started the brighter and levelled again through Ivor Broadis' sharp shot on 62 minutes. But again, it only took a minute for Liverpool to respond; this time a jinking run and shot by Baron. They finally clinched the win in the 73rd minute; Liddell put in a deep cross, and Stubbins rose to head past an uncertain Robinson.

The match tailed off, disrupted by a series of injuries, as in addition to Payne, Liddell went off with a bad cut, but returned, and Wright "went lame".

An exciting first match and it was just the beginning, as Liverpool's early form impressed, and hopes raised for more glory in the 1950s.

- Liverpool went undefeated in their first 19 league matches (ten wins and nine draws); the best top-flight start of this century so far.

- Jimmy Payne would play for both Liverpool and Everton.

- Dickie Davis would be the top scorer in the First Division this season, as Sunderland finished third.

- Len Shackleton was nicknamed the "Clown Prince of Soccer", and his popular autobiography famously contained a chapter entitled "The Average Director's Knowledge of Football", which consisted of a blank page.

1950s

Everton 0 Liverpool 2

25/03/1950 FA Cup Semi-final - Maine Road

Liverpool had never been to Wembley, so the 1950 cup semi-final provided the ideal opportunity, with also the bonus of avenging Everton's 1906 semi-final win.

Their early sparking form had dissipated, coming into the match with a poor run of just one point and one goal from the last five league matches. However, Everton were even worse, as they languished in 19th position with just two wins in the last twelve games. The rivals adopted different preparations; Everton spent several days in Buxton, while Liverpool just stayed overnight at Alderley Edge, but included a trip to the cinema.

As thousands descended on the city for the Grand National, 500 coaches and 36 trains departed for a sunny Manchester, and the 72,000 capacity Maine Road. The Liverpool team was still essentially the same as the previous years, but Laurie Hughes was injured, so the utility man Bill Jones stepped in.

The blues started very strongly, with shots from Fielding, Catterick and Wainwright, but Liverpool steadily grew into the match, as Payne forced two saves from Burnett. There were also appeals that a Stubbins' header had crossed the line before Moore cleared.

No goal was given, but it was only a short reprieve, as Liverpool went ahead 5 minutes later. Payne's cross was punched out by Burnett, and it fell to Paisley. He recalled the advice from his manager, and simply lofted the ball into the danger zone rather than shooting. Both Burnett and Liddell went up for the ball, but it sailed over their heads, and nestled in the back of the net. Eglington almost replied immediately, but missed, as Liverpool continued attacking, but couldn't force a second.

In the second half, Everton started well again with good passing moves, but could not create clear cut chances as Bill Jones excelled in the defence. After absorbing the early pressure, Liverpool went on top again, pinning them back and forcing a spate of corners. The second goal came in the 62nd minute and was a gift. In trying to prevent the ball from going out for a corner, Wainwright simply sent it straight to

Liddell, who duly punished him. Everton tried to rally, but could not beat a well-marshalled Liverpool defence, while Liddell was a constant threat, hitting the post from a corner.

It may not have been a classic footballing encounter, but the hard fought victory was celebrated keenly by the Liverpool fans as they looked forward to Wembley. The Liverpool Echo saluted the "finest Liverpool v Everton of all time", highlighting again the sporting nature of the action and cacophonous noise of 10,000 football rattles.

The semi-final win provided the catalyst for three consecutive league wins, to return to the top of the table. A league and cup double seemed possible, but dashed by a disastrous end of season run of form. Liverpool lost their first Wembley final, 2-0 to Arsenal, and only took one point from the possible ten, finishing a remote 8th, but just five points adrift from champions Portsmouth.

- There is Pathé newsreel film of the match available on YouTube

- This was the fifth of Bob Paisley's 13 goals in his Liverpool career of 277 matches. He missed four games in the run-in through injury and although fit again, was not selected for the FA Cup final, with Bill Jones winning a directors vote by 5-4.

- Everton would finish 18th in the league, but were relegated the following season, after finishing bottom.

- Striker Harry Catterick would return to Everton as manager from 1961 to 1973, winning two league titles and an FA Cup.

- The receipts for this match totalled £13,497.

- This was only Liverpool's second semi-final win in nine semi-finals matches, including replays.

- In the run up to the final, Hoylake-based Arsenal captain Joe Mercer trained at Anfield as normal.

- In the summer, Laurie Hughes became the first Liverpool player to feature in the World Cup, as he played in all of England's three matches, including the notorious 1-0 defeat by the USA.

Tottenham Hotspur 2 Liverpool 3

01/12/1951 - First Division - White Hart Line

After George Kay resigned from ill health, Don Welsh took over as manager in March 1951 and ensured a mid-table finish. He faced a difficult task as the team was aging, with few successful replacements, as Brian Jackson was the only signing in his first season.

By December Liverpool were meandering in 9th place, and facing a daunting trip to reigning champions Tottenham, who were in 3rd place, and had only dropped three points in nine home matches so far.

Jackson and Jack Smith bolstered the Liverpool attack, but the main attraction was still Billy Liddell. In an intriguing move, Welsh had been toying with the right footed Jimmy Payne on the left. The defence now had Ashcroft as the regular in goal, but still relied on Jones and Paisley (both in their 30s), skipper Hughes, with Heyden replacing the injured Taylor. For Spurs, Bill Nicholson was injured, so Harry Robshaw made his debut.

Again, for such an important match, the Liverpool manager was missing, as Don Welsh was busy scouting in Ireland. On a bright but crisp day, Liddell was again the focus, putting over two teasing crosses, and also needing treatment. Liverpool pressed more and earned their reward with the lead after 10 minutes; Payne stretched for a Baron pass, managed to connect, but it hit the post. Liddell was alert to follow up and score. Robshaw nearly scored on his debut, but overhit a rebound after Ashcroft saved.

Although Spurs were passing sweetly, Liverpool were more clinical. Liddell made it two after just 17 minutes with a fine drive on the run, after controlling Paisley's probing ball forward. The experiment of the two wingers on the left was causing Spurs problems, as another Liddell shot was off target. Tottenham finally found more penetration, fashioning chances from Ramsey's free-kicks, shots from Burgess and Duquemin, as Hughes needed to clear off the line.

It is uncertain whether the lack of half-time talk affected Liverpool, but Spurs went straight on the attack; Robshaw's 40 yard lob was tipped over and Jones had to clear from the line. Bennett squeezed the ball in after 50 minutes (some reports have it as a Hughes own goal, as it hit his shin), despite Liverpool protesting that it had not crossed the line. Inside another 10 minutes, Spurs were level, as Sonny Walters netted from a Medley cross.

The buoyant Tottenham now seemed more likely to win, but the Liverpool defence was resilient, especially the reliable Ashcroft. While at the other end, their threat grew again from the pacy forwards. Liddell was a constant menace, and it was he who was fouled for a penalty by Ramsey, just as he was about to shoot (Liverpool and London's press disagreed about whether it was a correct decision). Liddell stepped up to smash in the penalty, claiming his and Liverpool's third.

Spurs tried to respond again, but could not muster enough attacks, as they were too occupied by the Liverpool forward line, with Payne and Smith going close.

Liverpool registered a fine win in an enjoyable and exciting match that Stork in the Liverpool Echo described as "quite the best I have seen this season". Despite this upset, Tottenham would still finish second, and Liverpool a typical mid-table 11th.

- The first of five hat-tricks by Billy Liddell for Liverpool.

- Don Welsh mainly played for Charlton Athletic, captaining them to the 1947 FA Cup final, but he often guested for Liverpool during the war, and in December 1944, scored six goals in a 12 - 1 win over Southport.

- Tottenham manager Arthur Rowe had won the Second and First Division titles in successive seasons, with his pioneering "Push and Run" style.

- Tottenham's right-back Alf Ramsey would win the league as Ipswich manager and then the 1966 World Cup with England.

- Along with Paisley and Ramsey, Bill Nicholson also became a successful manager winning the League / FA Cup double in 1961.

- A month later, Anfield would record its largest attendance as 61,905 watched Liverpool beat Wolves 2-1 in the FA Cup.

Liverpool 5 Newcastle United 3

04/10/1952 - First Division - Anfield

Sidlow, Done and Fagan left in the summer of 1952, but again there were no major purchases of replacements, as the directors seemed content in the mid-table doldrums. Surprisingly then, Don Welsh managed to guide Liverpool to the top of the league after seven games, with five wins. Defeats against Tottenham and West Brom saw Liverpool slip to third, as reality hit, and the imminent visit of Newcastle United would be another stern test.

The Magpies had won the FA Cup for the last two years. This year, their early form was disappointing and they were missing the legendary centre forward Jackie Milburn due to an international call up, but the South American George Robledo was also a formidable threat. For Liverpool, Laurie Hughes was fit for his first start of the season, and Bryan Williams started in place of Jackson.

Both teams had reasonable chances in an open start, as Liddell headed over and Prior shot wide. An early goal was likely, and it was Newcastle who took the initiative through Robledo after Ashcroft could not hold Prior's shot. The lead only lasted a minute, as goalkeeper Simpson was confused by an inswinging corner from Liddell, and could only help it into the back of the net. He soon redeemed himself by saving a powerful Liddell free-kick, but then lucky to get away with mishandling another. In a breathless first half, Williams headed over from a corner, while Robledo scored, but it was disallowed for an earlier foul.

Liverpool took the lead for the first time on 36 minutes; and again Simpson was culpable, as a Smith shot from a tight angle went through his hands. Robledo should have equalised but headed over from just five yards out.

After resting at half-time, the second half was even more dramatic. Baron scored within 2 minutes of the restart, after Williams controlled a long ball from Paisley. Liverpool were now in control, with Baron's weak shot and Payne's free-kick was blocked. But in a topsy-turvy game, it was Newcastle who scored next, as Prior's chip made it 3-2.

Another Simpson fumble allowed Payne to head against the bar, before Smith grabbed his second after 69 minutes; firing in from Baron's setup. Liverpool were effectively reduced to ten men due to an injury to Williams, but the visitors could not take advantage. Bob Paisley notched the fifth in the 77th minute, following up after a Liddell header was not cleared. George Robledo converted a last minute penalty, but it was a mere consolation.

A wretched day for Simpson, but Liverpool delighted the 48,000 attendance by going back to the top of the league after an incredible match.

- This would be the last time Liverpool occupied top spot of the First Division until November 1963.

- Even with eight goals, this was not the highest scoring match of the season, as two weeks earlier, Blackpool had beaten Charlton Athletic 8-4.

- Paisley would have taken particular delight with his goal as a boyhood Sunderland fan.

- George Robledo had been the league's top scorer the previous season. Born in Chile, his family emigrated to the UK when he was five, but he appeared for Chile in the 1950 World Cup, despite not speaking Spanish. He had previously scored a five-minute hat-trick at Anfield in 1950.

- Ronnie Simpson would play in goal for Celtic against Liverpool in 1966, and won the European Cup in 1967.

- Cyril Done had transferred to Tranmere Rovers, but later moved to Port Vale, where he scored all four goals in a 4-3 victory against Liverpool in April 1955.

Liverpool 2 Chelsea 0

25/04/1953 - First Division - Anfield

In the 2000s Liverpool and Chelsea battled for European glory, but in April 1953, First Division survival was at stake, when they met on the final Saturday of the season.

After the fine start, Liverpool's form had disintegrated with no wins in twelve in the middle of the season. Seven defeats in the last nine had seen them in relegation contention, as injuries bit. Four teams faced the drop, but Liverpool knew a win would keep them safe.

The opponents Chelsea may have been in more danger, but had engineered unlikely escapes before (once by 0.044 goal average). They were also in better form, and the previous month had comprehensively beaten Liverpool 3-0 at Stamford Bridge.

The Liverpool Echo set the tone the day before, as they titled it their "match of the century", and urged the fans to "give them your support". The fans didn't disappoint, as a rowdy crowd of over 47,000 (up from 34,000 in the last home match) assembled with bells, rattles and passion.

Welsh went for experience, able to recall Laurie Hughes and Spicer after passing injury tests, prompting a rejig that pushed the versatile Bill Jones up front. The attack had also been reinforced by the December signing of Sammy Smyth, and bustling centre forward Louis Bimpson. Chelsea's main threat would be from Roy Bentley, an England international striker who had already scored 17 this season.

In a tense and fervid atmosphere, tackles flew in, and the vocal fans on the Kop twice appealed for early penalties, but neither was given. There were few clear cut chances with Chelsea edging it, as they threatened through Bentley, and Liverpool through Liddell. Liverpool broke the deadlock in the 33rd minute; Bimpson's perseverance paid off, as he managed to send over a cross, keeper Robertson spilled the ball under pressure from Jones, who then poked it in. A scrappy, but precious goal.

Into the second half, attacking the Kop end, Liverpool pressed for the knockout blow. A Bimpson "rasper" went close, and twice they had goals disallowed, Bimpson for offside and Paisley for handball.

The match became scrappy with injuries and the tension escalated. In the final ten minutes, the Reds finally managed the second goal; a clearance from a free-kick fell to Bimpson, who passed to Liddell, received the return, beat two men, and fired in (although the Robertson could have done better again).

Chelsea hit the bar almost immediately, and Payne did likewise in the last minute. Liverpool had survived, so Welsh and the players saluted the relieved fans for their efforts.

A close shave, but it merely delayed the inevitable.

- Liverpool's 17th place was their lowest since before the war.

- Billy Liddell was Liverpool's top scorer for the fourth consecutive season.

- The following midweek, Chelsea won their final league match, to avoid the drop, and won their first league title two years later.

- Liverpool would lose twenty successive away matches from March 1953 onwards.

- Sammy Smyth had scored for Wolves in the 1949 FA Cup final.

- Chelsea's centre-half, Ron Greenwood, would become West Ham manager, winning the FA Cup and European Cup Winners Cup, and later managed England from 1977 to 1982.

Liverpool 6 Aston Villa 1

10/10/1953 - First Division - Anfield

The aging squad and lack of investment finally took its toll in 1953/54, as Liverpool hit the bottom of the league in December and rarely looked like escaping, despite the belated panic buys of Dave Underwood, Geoff Twentyman, Frank Lock and John Evans. The statistics were appalling with one win in twenty attempts between November and March, and all of the first fourteen away games lost.

In mitigation, there were several key injuries, and using 31 players during the season affected any rhythm and cohesion. Strangely, amongst the carnage, there was some comfort at home, with seven victories of three goals or more, the most spectacular against Aston Villa.

The teamsheet still included veterans Jones, Spicer, Hughes, Paisley, Liddell, but now Russell Crossley was in goal and Roy Saunders added to defence. With Liverpool already in the relegation places and Aston Villa riding high in fifth, an onerous afternoon was anticipated.

These fears were confirmed within 5 minutes as Dave Walsh scored after Crossley parried Gilbson's shot. But Liverpool were not cowed, responding with a Bimpson header and Liddell's drive. The latter levelled in the 14th minute, heading in from a Payne corner that Smyth had flicked on. Bimpson and Liddell both missed great chances before half-time, while Villa seemed neat and tidy, but afraid to shoot.

Few could have anticipated the second half deluge. It started slowly, and although Liverpool were the superior team, it took until the 69th minute for them to take the lead, with a Smyth shot from distance flying into the top corner. Villa suddenly seemed to cave, as Paisley scored from distance too after 72 minutes. Liverpool were rampant, as Keith Jones had to make a fine save to deny Bimpson and Liddell's "whizzbang shot" was deflected for a corner. The corner was cleared, but it fell to Paisley, he passed to Payne to slot in the fourth, while Villa were expecting offside.

Smyth scored his second after 84 minutes, with another stunning drive from 35 yards. Villa's misery was complete 2 minutes from the end, when Bimpson crossed, Baron missed it, but the unfortunate

Danny Blanchflower diverted it in.

Five goals in less than 20 minutes gave Liverpool a stunning and implausible victory, although The Birmingham Sport Argos churlishly headlined "Villa sunk on the Mersey - but some of the six were lucky".

Liverpool jumped to 15th position, but it was a season high, as the decline accelerated and relegation beckoned.

- Roy Saunders is the father of Dean Saunders who played for Liverpool in the 1990s.

- Manager Don Welsh was again not at the game, instead scouting Charlie Fleming, an East Fife forward, who moved to Sunderland two years later.

- Danny Blanchflower, would move to Tottenham the following year, and captain them to the league and FA Cup double in 1960/61.

- Liverpool's eventual relegation was even more galling, as Everton were promoted to replace them. At least it preserved the unique record of the city always having a top-flight team.

- Fittingly Billy Liddell scored Liverpool's last goal in the First Division.

- Liverpool actually scored more than any of the seasons since the league title win, but it was the club record of 97 against that did the damage.

Liverpool 6 Ipswich Town 2

25/12/1954 - 2nd Division - Anfield

After relegation, Don Welsh kept his position, but Taylor and Paisley retired, both going into coaching roles. Any illusion that Liverpool would quickly bounce back were soon shattered as they lost five of the first seven. They recovered slightly, but December started with 9-1 (a club record) and 4-1 reverses to Birmingham City and Doncaster Rovers, as the Reds slipped to 15th place.

Hopefully Christmas would bring some cheer. The team that met Ipswich on Christmas Day, was a mishmash of former league winners (Lambert, Hughes, Liddell), recent signings (Doug Rudham, Twentyman, Evans), and promising youths (Ronnie Moran, Alan A'Court). The loyal Billy Liddell had moved to centre forward, and was so synonymous with the team that the term "Liddellpool" was affectionately coined.

Barely 24,000 attended, but at least the 11.15 am kick-off allowed them to return home in time for a late Christmas lunch. It was worth the trip, as they witnessed one of 32-year old Liddell's finest performances.

The details are scarce, with little newspaper coverage, but Liverpool scored four times in 19 minutes of the first half. Liddell seized a hat-trick, and also set up another for Bimpson. It seems that Liddell's movement and pace terrorised Len Fletcher, who was deputising in an unfamiliar centre-half role.

Ipswich reduced the deficit with a Garneys header, and in the 83rd minute Parker scored too after a Rudham mistake.

But nothing could spoil Liddell's Christmas show. He won a penalty after being brought down during a strong run, and converted it himself. Finally Evans rounded off the scoring, with another Liddell assist.

So four goals and two assists for the Anfield legend. A very happy Christmas from Billy Liddell after a very difficult year for the Liverpool fans.

- Ronnie Moran and Geoff Twentyman would later become part of the famous Liverpool coaching bootroom. Moran served over 30 years, as reserve coach, physio, assistant, and caretaker manager. Twentyman would be the main scout responsible for the recruitment of most of the 1970s and 1980s stars.

- On the same day, ex Liverpool striker Kevin Baron scored a hat trick for Southend.

- This was the first time Liverpool had ever met Ipswich.

- As was common at the time, the reverse fixture was played at Portman Road two days later, and Ipswich triumphed 2-0.

- Liverpool's last Christmas Day match was in 1957, when they lost 3-1 away at Grimsby Town.

- 1954/5 was Billy Liddell's best season for league goals with 30. However, John Evans was the top scorer with 33 in all competitions, including five in a match against Bristol Rovers in September.

- Liverpool's 11th place finish in Division Two remains their lowest ever position. Scoring 92 league goals matched champions Birmingham City's total, but conceding an astonishing 96, was the worst in the whole league.

Everton 0 Liverpool 4

29/01/1955 - FA Cup 4th round - Goodison Park

Both rivals eagerly anticipated another FA Cup derby meeting. For Everton the chance to erase the memory of the semi-final defeat five years earlier, and for Liverpool the opportunity to forget their Second Division travails and restore some pride against their higher division opposition. With home advantage and residing in a lofty 7th place in the First Division, Everton would be strong favourites, but as the clichés stated, the derby and the Cup were a great leveller. Liverpool were encouraged by three wins in the last four matches, and had spent the week preparing in Blackpool.

Everton had five survivors from the semi-final, and had added Dave Hickson as striker. Liverpool had just two (Lambert and Liddell), but had to make changes from the recent mauling of Ipswich, as Payne and Bimpson (flu) were out, so Jackson and Anderson came in.

The first Goodison FA Cup meeting since 1932 was the hottest ticket in town, but only 72,000 could be lucky to attend. Like the semi-final, Everton dominated the first 15 minutes, as Eglington, Fielding, Potts, and Wainwright all tried efforts, but Rudham only had to make one save. Against the run of play, Liverpool took the lead in the 18th minute. Jackson fed Liddell who flicked the ball over Jones, and quickly fired a left foot drive across O'Neil. He would later recall "I cannot think of a goal that gave me a bigger thrill".

Everton tried to respond through Fielding, but it was Liverpool who were growing stronger, and doubled their lead after 29 minutes, with a well worked set piece. As Twentyman took a free-kick, the Everton players rushed forward to catch the visitors offside. However, Evans' late run foiled this plan, as he went past the keeper, Anderson touched the ball on to A'Court who tapped in. The move had been planned on the training ground, after a group of fans wrote to Don Welsh warning about Everton's offside trap.

Liddell should have grabbed a third, but slipped at the vital moment, while Everton had a goal disallowed for offside, so Liverpool went in two up at half-time. Everton's second half onslaught did not materialise, as Liverpool were comfortable.

The only disruption was an injury to skipper Hughes, which led to a reshuffle, as he moved to outside left (barely touching the ball), Twentyman moved back, and Liddell went to left half. It did not affect Liverpool's momentum too much, and they added their third after 57th minutes; O'Neil could not hold Jackson's fierce 20 yard drive, and Evans finished easily.

Everton finally exerted some pressure with several corners, with chances for Potts and Hickson, but the makeshift Liverpool defence was determined to preserve their lead. In the 75th minute, from a breakaway, Liverpool sealed a famous victory; Evans heading a Jackson cross (his third assist).

Happy Liverpool fans swarmed on the pitch at the end, relishing facing their Blue workmates on Monday. Local pride had been restored, even if they were a division apart.

- A two minute newsreel film of the game is on the Pathé YouTube channel.

- Referee Arthur Ellis, was acknowledged as England's top referee, taking charge of World Cup and European Cup matches, and later became even more famous as the adjudicator on "It's a Knockout".

- Liverpool's biggest win at Goodison Park so far, and the first time they had scored four there since 1907.

- The only previous time Liverpool had beaten a team from a higher division was Preston North End in 1894.

- This was Liverpool's first away win since April 1954, and only the third away win in 41 attempts.

- David Hickson, would have two spells at Everton, before signing for Liverpool in November 1959, where he scored 38 goals in two seasons.

Liverpool 7 Fulham 0

26/11/1955 - Second Division - Anfield

Liverpool were more acclimated to the Second Division the following year, and although they improved, they struggled to claim the second promotion slot in a tight race.

For this match, Dave Underwood made his first appearance in over a year, replacing the dropped Rudham in goal, while John Molyneux and Alan Arnell were now regulars. Fourth placed Fulham were renowned for their fearsome forward line that had scored 44 in 18 games, with Johnny Haynes the jewel in the crown, so the Liverpool Echo predicted "a stiff test for the home defence".

However, it would be the Liverpool strike force that shone. Within the opening minute, Payne and Twentyman supplied A'Court, he beat one man, and crossed for Evans to head in (his first since the opening day, due to a serious collarbone injury). Evans nearly scored again a minute later, as Liverpool were laying siege to the Fulham goal, as Twentyman, Evans again, and Arnell all went close.

Fulham were struggling to even get out of their half, until Robson and Haynes forced stops from Underwood. The saves were crucial, as soon Liverpool scored twice in a minute. The Fulham defenders could not handle the winger play of A'Court, and his tempting crosses were headed in by Arnell and Liddell.

Five minutes into the second half, it was A'Court again causing the damage, as his centre was headed on by Arnell, for Liddell to claim his second. Twentyman made it 5-0 with a shot in the 55th minute after a defensive mistake. After creating four goals, A'Court fittingly scored one himself; firing in, after shots from Arnell and Evans had been blocked. Jimmy Payne rounded things off with the seventh in the 82nd minute, to seal a wonderful win.

The speed and dazzling trickery of the 22-year old A'Court, and Liverpool's striking prowess had devastated one of the best teams in the Second Division. It could not be sustained enough, successive losses in early April doomed their promotion aspirations, and manager Don Welsh departed at the end of the season.

- Liverpool's biggest league win since an 8-0 win against Burnley on Boxing Day 1928.

- The Fulham team contained two future England managers (Ron Greenwood and Bobby Robson) and TV pundit, Jimmy Hill.

- Johnny Haynes would play 594 matches for Fulham, appear in two England World Cup squads, and be the first player to be paid £100 a week.

- Fulham won the return fixture 3-1 in April, as Elton John's cousin, Roy Dwight scored a hat-trick.

- 1955/56 was the first time Liverpool had consecutive seasons in the Second Division, as the previous three times they had won promotion immediately.

Liverpool 4 Notts County 0

9/11/1957 - Second Division - Anfield

The board turned to former captain Phil Taylor, and he achieved a creditable third place in his first season, missing out on promotion by a single point. After finishing with nine wins in twelve matches, hopes and expectations rose for the next season, but again no summer purchases. Early results were mixed with too many draws, but Liverpool were second by the time of this November fixture.

The teamsheet included the Taylor purchases Tommy Younger in goal and midfielder Johnny Wheeler, along with other recent additions like Jimmy Melia, Dick White, Bobby Campbell and Tony Rowley.

It was due to be a landmark day, as Billy Liddell was poised to break Elisha Scott's record of 429 league matches for Liverpool. The Scotsman was widely lauded as not just a model footballer, teetotal and non smoking, but also a pillar of the community, soon becoming a Justice of the Peace. The Liverpool Echo marked the occasion with a four page special, and the Notts County players lined up to shake his hand before the kick-off.

With County next to bottom, it was expected to be an easy afternoon, and hopefully Billy would mark the occasion with a goal. He tried a header early on, but it was County who had the best chances, requiring Moran to clear off the line twice within seconds. Slowly Liverpool found their rhythm, creating chances for Rowley and Melia, while Liddell twice went close with a shot and a header.

The visitors were still dangerous though, and had a goal disallowed for offside. Their attacking proved their undoing, as Liverpool took the lead from a swift breakaway just before half-time; Wheeler released Melia, who ran through and coolly fired in.

The second half was more one-sided, as Liverpool exerted pressure from the restart, as Liddell had a penalty claim rejected and Rowley missed a sitter. Two goals came quickly, starting in the 49th minute; A'Court intercepted a short back pass, and went around the goalkeeper to finish. Liddell nearly got his goal, with a left foot strike, but Linton saved well. From the corner, Melia found Liddell, and he scored via a deflection on his special day.

Notts County provided some token resistance with attempts from Lane, but Rowley wrapped it with the fourth with 7 minutes remaining. A rueful Liddell remarked to The People "I don't know when we missed so many sitters. But the packed Notts defence took some breaking open". The party atmosphere was enhanced with the news of Blackburn's draw meaning Liverpool went to the top of the table on goal difference.

Sadly it was another false dawn, as although they were in contention for most of the season, Liverpool missed out on promotion by two points.

- The celebrations were premature, as modern records, like Lfchistory.com, show that Scott actually played 430 league matches, so Liddell would break the record the following week. Both players could have played more official league matches, but their careers were affected by World Wars.

- Tommy Lawton was manager of Notts County. He had signed for them in 1947 for a British record fee of £20,000 when they were in the Third Division, and returned as manager in 1957 but was sacked after they were relegated.

- Liverpool conceded only one goal at Anfield in the first nine home matches.

- This would be the fourth and final consecutive season that Liddell scored over 20 goals in all competitions.

- This was the first league match at Anfield to be played under floodlights, as they were turned on at half-time. They had been inaugurated earlier in the week, with a two-legged tie against Everton for the Floodlight Challenge Cup.

- Bob Paisley had been promoted to a first team chief coach role after guiding the reserve team to the Central League title for the first time in Liverpool's history. He was also studying physiotherapy to assist with players' injuries.

- Jimmy Melia would manage the Brighton team that knocked Liverpool out of the FA Cup in 1983.

Liverpool 5 Brighton & Hove Albion 0

3/9/1958 - Second Division - Anfield

Another season, and another attempt at promotion, but again just one point from the opening two games left Liverpool playing catch-up.

For this match, Taylor was able to give a debut to winger Fred Morris, a recent £7,000 signing, available now after a suspension, and 19-year old local (he lived 200 yards from the ground), Alan Banks, described as a "goer" by the Echo. Arnell replaced Liddell after he failed an injury test. The visitors Brighton also had a single point, after a shocking 9-0 reverse at Middlesbrough on the opening day. Almost 40,000 attended on the Wednesday evening.

The recall of Arnell made an immediate impact, as he scored twice in the first 18 minutes; one of them a poacher's goal from close range. Harrower made it three just two minutes later, as Brighton feared the worst again. Things looked even bleaker when Dennis Foreman suffered an injury, and could not play any significant part for the remaining hour.

On the half-hour Banks marked his debut with a goal, and just before half-time Molyneux, scored the fifth, a stunning strike from at least 35 yards. Liverpool could not add to the score in the second half, but not for the lack of trying, as they spurned several opportunities and hit the woodwork twice (Wheeler and Twentyman). The Liverpool Echo were impressed with Morris' lively debut, with a hand in some of the goals, accurate deep crosses, and his own headers and shots.

Five straight wins in the autumn and six around Christmas pushed Liverpool up to second at the start of 1959. Typically the form tailed off in the new year as they finished 4th, seven points from promotion. There was even the ignominy of an FA Cup exit at non-league Worcester City.

A low point, but salvation was on the way.

- The first time Liverpool had scored five in the first half since 1927.

- Alan Banks would only play a further seven matches for Liverpool, but had a more successful career at Exeter City.

- John Molyneux's first goal for Liverpool, and the defender would only score two in his 228 appearances.

- Brighton's Dave Sexton later managed Manchester United and QPR to second place in the First Division, both times being pipped by Liverpool.

- Alan A'Court had been in England's 1958 World Cup squad, despite playing in the Second Division.

- Centre-half Dick White was the only ever present this season, and would only miss two matches between 1957 to 1961.

- Jimmy Melia was the top scorer with a career best 21 league goals.

Liverpool 2 Charlton Athletic 0
28/12/1959 - Second Division - Anfield

The poet Phillip Larkin claimed the 1960s started in 1963, but for Liverpool FC they started in December 1959, with the arrival of Bill Shankly. His managerial record amongst the lower divisions had not been that spectacular, but at Huddersfield, despite financial constraints, he had built a young exciting team, reflecting his infectious enthusiasm. He just needed a bigger stage now, and a slumbering giant he could inspire would be ideal. As he memorably recalled "Liverpool was made for me and I was made for Liverpool".

The effect wasn't immediate with a 4 - 0 home defeat to Cardiff City, and a 3-0 defeat at Charlton on Boxing Day. The busy Christmas schedule provided an immediate chance to put things right, with a Charlton rematch on a Monday evening. The mood was indifferent, as only 25,658 turned out. Although Liverpool had slipped to 12th, they were only two points behind sixth placed Charlton.

The team Shankly inherited was a combination of experienced Taylor regulars like Moran, White and Melia, recent signing Hickson, and emerging local youth Roger Hunt. Another recent acquisition Tommy Leishman would make his Liverpool debut in place of Bobby Campbell.

It was a drab and uninspiring encounter, with the Liverpool Echo describing it as "one of the dullest seen on the ground for a long time", and another opined that the fans should have stayed home and watched "Wagon Train" on TV. Apparently one of the most enjoyable moments was when a fan caught a wayward ball and refused to return it.

The defences were on top, with few clear cut chances, perhaps because the players were too anxious to please their new boss. The best chance in the first half was a fierce shot from Moran that went wide. Shankly was experimenting with Melia in the outside right position, but it was not proving successful.

The deadlock was broken just before the hour mark. The visiting keeper Duff was penalised for running with the ball. Harrower knocked the indirect free-kick to Leishman, who crossed for A'Court to score from close range. Within five minutes Liverpool doubled their lead, Leishman releasing Hunt to fire home. Little of consequence occurred afterwards.

A disappointing and inauspicious encounter, but it was the first win and goals for the Shankly team, sparking a nine league match unbeaten run with seven wins.

- Bill Shankly came from a family of five brothers who all played professional football. He had previously worked in a pit, before moving to Preston and winning the F A Cup. He had guested once for Liverpool during the war, in a 4-1 win over Everton in May 1942.

- Shankly says he was unsuccessfully interviewed for the Liverpool job in 1951, and also lists failed interest at Middlesbrough, Leeds United, Bradford Park Avenue and West Brom.

- One of his first acts was to keep the current coaching staff of Bob Paisley, Joe Fagan and Reuben Bennett, the basis of the legendary Boot Room coaching brains for the next three decades.

- Shankly's first transfer, Sammy Reid, never made a first team appearance.

- Liverpool never broke their transfer record during the 1950s, as the 1946 purchase of Albert Stubbins remained the record for over 14 years.

- Charlton centre-back Gordon Jago would later manage QPR, Millwall, Tampa Bay Rowdies and Dallas Sidekicks.

- Bobby Campbell would manage Chelsea, Fulham, Portsmouth and two teams in Kuwait.

1960s

Liverpool 5 Stoke City 1
05/03/1960 - Second Division - Anfield

Two months later, Shankly had ditched the Melia experiment, and brought back Billy Liddell for a final flourish in his illustrious career. Hickson and Hunt had formed a potent striking partnership, and would relish the visit of Stoke City, who had been in the top six recently, but were falling fast.

Liverpool started strongly with chances for Hickson and Harrower, before Hunt opened the scoring in the 14th minute with a header from an A'Court corner. Five minutes later, it was two; a scramble from another A'Court corner and Harrower fired in from a tight angle.

On the stroke of half-time, Liddell netted for the first time since his return, a header after a short corner had been worked between A'Court and Moran. Stoke had offered little threat, with their only chance from a goal mouth scramble.

Hickson had two chances early in the second half, but it was third time lucky after 51 minutes as he side-footed in an A'Court cross, set up by a devastating Hunt's dribble. Harrower got his second just before the hour, after another melee, as Hunt, Liddell and Hickson efforts were all blocked. Liverpool didn't score again, missing several more chances, and Bentley scored a consolation for Stoke near the end.

Although it would have been a thrill to see Liddell score again, it was Hunt that caught the eye, with the Liverpool Echo stating it was his best performance yet. However, The People still had a grudging headline of "5-goal yawn for Kop", attributing the result to Stoke's mediocrity than Liverpool superiority.

The form was still inconsistent, with no wins in the next four matches, but Shankly ensured a creditable third place finish, and raised hope for his first full season.

- This would be Liddell's 228th and last goal for Liverpool. At the time, he was the second all-time Liverpool top scorer, and today is fourth. He would make seven more appearances that season and a solitary start in September 1960, before retiring.

- Liddell is still Liverpool's oldest goalscorer being over 38 at the time of this goal.

- The 21-year old Roger Hunt had only made his debut in September, but would end the season as joint top scorer with Dave Hickson on 21 league goals each.

- Left-back Tony Allen made over 400 league appearances for Stoke. He played three times for England before his 20th birthday, but never afterwards.

- Three weeks later, Liverpool were winning 4-0 at Aston Villa after an hour, but conceded four in 20 minutes as Villa forced a draw.

Huddersfield Town 2 Liverpool 4

22/10/1960 - Second Division - Leeds Road

Shankly's first full season, typical of Liverpool in the Second Division, had started badly with a meagre two wins in eight matches. So he changed the formation to a 3-3-4, with Harrower moving back, to gain more control of midfield. The team was enhanced by the signings of Gordon Milne and Kevin Lewis, while Gerry Byrne was now a fixture at left-back. Slowly the Shankly revolution had begun, with four league wins and a draw.

Huddersfield Town were Liverpool's Second Division bogey team, with no win in six and three straight defeats at Leeds Road. Shankly had inflicted two of them, including a crushing 5-0. Now on his first return, could he break the jinx?

Liverpool were unchanged from their winning run, but Huddersfield brought back captain Bill McGarry, making his 500th career appearance, contrasting with Oliver Conmy, a 20-year old winger making his debut.

Liverpool needed to weather an initial storm, as Stokes and Conmy went close. Despite this momentum, the visitors went in front in the 20th minute; A'Court's powerful free-kick was headed in by Lewis. The goal helped galvanise the new Shankly team, as A'Court put a shot past the post and Hickson shot over. This intense spell of pressure resulted in a second goal only 5 minutes later; a low cross from Lewis was finished clinically by Hunt. It could have been more, as Hunt shot wide and A'Court brought a good save from Wood.

After being outplayed, Huddersfield pulled one back on 37 minutes through Les Massie, and Slater needed to make excellent saves either side of half-time to maintain Liverpool's lead. Having absorbing this pressure, Liverpool struck back again; A'Court beat a defender and scored at the near post. 3 -1 up, Liverpool seemed comfortable again, but Ken Taylor scored a rebound after 76 minutes, so tense finale ensued. They prevailed in the penultimate minute, as Leishman assisted Hickson to wrap up the two points.

A clinical and resilient away day performance against tricky opponents augured well for the future. Liverpool were second at

Christmas, but regular defeats in the New Year, meant they had to settle for 3rd again, six points adrift. Shankly was disillusioned with the lack of signings, and the fans fatigued, as barely 13,000 attended the final home match. But help was coming.

- Huddersfield goalkeeper Ray Wood helped Manchester United to two league title wins in the 1950s.

- Huddersfield have not beaten Liverpool in the 12 encounters since this meeting, and not scored in the last nine.

- Gerry Byrne had been on the transfer list when Shankly arrived after playing only twice in two seasons.

- Bill McGarry was Ipswich manager for four years and Wolves for eight years.

- Kevin Lewis would finish as top scorer with 22 goals; the only player to outscore Hunt in ten seasons.

- On the same day, Tommy Lawrence, Ian Callaghan, Gordon Milne and Billy Liddell were playing for the reserves against Sheffield United.

- Gordon Milne was the son of a Preston team mate of Shankly, who could recall seeing him as a baby.

Liverpool 5 Leeds United 0

26/08/1961 - Second Division - Anfield

Littlewoods' owner John Moores had invested in both Merseyside clubs, but preferred Everton, so took a seat on their board. of directors. He was not permitted to do the same at Anfield, so nominated Eric Sawyer, a Littlewoods' executive. Sawyer would become Shankly's ally, persuading reluctant fellow directors into costly signings; striker Ian St John from Motherwell and centre-back Ron Yeats from Dundee.

Hopes were raised again, as 42,000 attended the first Saturday home match, after the first two matches had been won without conceding. The opponents, Leeds United had recently appointed Don Revie as their new manager, and this would be the first encounter in a thirteen year span of rivalry, as they jostled for honours.

There were some signs of the future classic Liverpool lineup as Hunt and St John were partnered in attack, while Yeats and Byrne provided security at back. But there were still many of the established Division Two players like A'Court, Melia and captain White. Leeds showed few indications of their future, but Jack Charlton and Billy Bremner were already in place.

An ebullient Liverpool took the lead after just 6 minutes; Byrne passed to Leishman, who created the chance for Hunt to slot past the advancing keeper. Although the home team were on top for the majority of the half, they could not find a second. Bremner excelled for Leeds, but Slater was rarely troubled.

The second goal finally came within three minutes of the restart; a Lewis' shot was spilled by Humphreys, and Hunt finished assuredly. Within another 5 minutes, it was three as Hunt was fouled and Lewis converted the penalty. There was a brief lull, followed by another two goals in six minutes. Hunt created a goal for Melia, and then the young striker deservedly grabbed his hat-trick (as well as the two assists) after an A'Court cross was not cleared.

Winning eight of the first nine matches, saw Liverpool leading from the front. and they would not relinquish top spot for the whole season.

- Shankly had attempted to sign Jack Charlton as one of his first signings at the start of the 1960/61 season, but the directors could not agree a fee.

- It cost 3 shillings to stand on the Kop for this match.

- Leeds would win the return fixture 1-0 with a Billy Bremner goal. They would narrowly avoid relegation this season, but would be promoted as champions in 1963/4.

- Four Liverpool and three Leeds players in this match would contest the 1965 FA Cup Final.

- Ian St John had signed in May, immediately scoring a hat-trick in the Liverpool Senior Cup final against Everton, which Liverpool lost 4-3.

- Ron Yeats would be captain by December, replacing Dick White, who only made one league appearance after Christmas.

Liverpool 2 Southampton 0
21/04/1962 - Second Division - Anfield

By the spring of 1962 it was case of when not if Liverpool would clinch promotion back to the First Division. With only one league loss after December, they had built up an eight point leader, so with six matches remaining a home game against Southampton provided the first opportunity.

The team had continued to evolve, as Jim Furnell was now preferred in goal, and Ian Callaghan, who had just celebrated his 20th birthday, was a regular winger, dislodging Lewis. The latter returned for this match as St John was suspended. Southampton had won their last four fixtures against Liverpool, so two points could not be guaranteed.

The attendance was lower than expected, due to torrential rain, but still in excess of 40,000 were present, primed to celebrate. Shankly's team seemed determined to finish the job quickly, as A'Court hit the woodwork while Lewis, Callaghan and Milne all peppered the Southampton goal. The opener came in 19 minutes after a goalmouth scramble; a blocked Hunt shot fell to Lewis, but his shot on the turn was also blocked, before he poked it in off the post.

Southampton fought to reply, hitting the post and Byrne cleared a rebound from the line. Lewis settled any nerves with his second just before the half-hour; a header after Callaghan's deep cross was headed back by Hunt. Furnell had to make two fine saves as Southampton battled to stay in the match, but Melia, Hunt and Lewis all had chances too in this exciting and open game.

The second half was much quieter, as the conditions worsened. Liverpool were happy to preserve their lead, and Southampton could not create anything meaningful. The final whistle brought delight for the Liverpool fans, as their eight year ordeal was over.

Southampton gallantly formed a guard, while Liverpool trooped off. The jubilant Liverpool fans would not leave, chanting "We want the Reds!", despite speeches from the chairman and Shankly, and being informed that they players were in bath. Finally, their heroes returned for another rousing reception, but those that ventured too far were mobbed and had to beat a hasty retreat.

With a young team, Shankly predicted "I believe we are on the threshold of great things." The promotion was not the end goal, but just the start.

- Liverpool were presented with the Second Division title at the last home match, against Charlton; a nice symmetry with Shankly's first win.

- Roger Hunt hit a still club record of 41 league goals, including five hat-tricks, and earned a place in England's 1962 World Cup squad.

- This was the first time Liverpool had been unbeaten at Anfield since 1904/05, and they also recorded a record 68 home goals too.

- After the previous season's disappointments, the average attendance now topped 40,000.

- The Southampton party contained two Saints legends, as manager Ted Bates would occupy the role for 18 years and Terry Paine still holds the appearance record with 815 games.

Liverpool 2 Arsenal 1

14/11/1962 - First Division - Anfield

Oh to be alive in Liverpool in autumn 1962, with two top-flight teams again, the Beatles had just released their first single, and soon the whole country would be enthralled by the Merseybeat. Shankly's team struggled initially in the First Division, winning just four of the first sixteen games, barely two points from the bottom. Some of the players, too used to the Second Division, could not adapt to the pressures of the new league. Shankly responded decisively with two key changes, Tommy Lawrence replaced Furnell in goal, and Willie Stevenson (another Scot) was bought from Rangers to replace Leishman.

A late Johnny Giles goal had denied Liverpool victory at Old Trafford, but they still had a game in hand, the midweek clash with Arsenal. They were now a mid-table team, but had purchased Joe Baker (back from Torino) and included forward George Eastham, who would soon be capped by England.

Liverpool started with typical drive and pace, creating several chances, but again could not finish. Hunt twice, A'Court and Stevenson all went close as they dominated. At the other end, Arsenal provided little threat, as Yeats managed Baker well.

Arsenal were severely restricted by an injury to winger Skirton at the start of the second half, so Liverpool had even more licence to attack the Kop goal. Hunt had a shot cleared off the line by Magill, but a goal was coming on 52 minutes. Inevitably it was Hunt that broke the deadlock, after a slick passing move involving four players. The goal seemed to give Liverpool the extra confidence, and within three minutes, St John won a penalty, after being fouled by Brown. Moran smashed it home. Effectively playing against ten men, Liverpool were in total control, and could have extended the lead through Hunt, Callaghan or A'Court.

Against this tide, Geoff Strong pulled one back after 81 minutes to ensure a nervous finish. Liverpool looked tense, but managed to see out the remaining minutes, to claim a crucial victory and a welcome two points.

This win, and the two Shankly changes, inspired Liverpool to commence a run of nine straight league wins, leaping up to fifth place. Liverpool had found their feet in the First Division and would now thrive.

- George Eastham was an England squad player for the 1962 and 1966 World Cup, and contested the landmark "freedom to move" case. His uncle, Harry Eastham, played 62 games for Liverpool in a career restricted by the war.

- Arsenal, managed by Billy Wright, would finish 7th this season, qualifying for Europe for the first time.

- Geoff Strong would sign for Liverpool in November 1964, and be used in a variety of roles.

- Although the spine was Scottish (Lawrence, Yeats, Stevenson, St John), five of Liverpool's team were born locally, and Hunt from nearby Culcheth.

- Affectionately known as the "flying pig", Lawrence would be one of just three main goalkeepers over the next thirty years, and pioneered the "sweeper-keeper" role.

Liverpool 5 Tottenham Hotspur 2

12/4/63 - First Division - Anfield

Shankly kept faith in the same team for the rest of the season, with only Lewis replacing A'Court. Suffering just one defeat in 21 matches in all competitions, Liverpool were now a constant in the top six. The league title might be too far, but there were still hopes for the FA Cup as they reached the semi-final.

Easter would see three tough matches in four days; a difficult double header against league favourites Tottenham, who were well placed in second with a game in hand. They had been the most formidable team of the early 1960s, guided by Bill Nicholson, the first team to win the league and FA Cup double this century, and retaining the FA Cup a year later. To the devastating attack they had even added the prolific Jimmy Greaves, returning from AC Milan.

Tottenham oozed class, completely governing the first half, confidently racing into a two goal lead through Dyson (20 minutes) and Jones (33 minutes). Passing with speed and precision, Liverpool looked lost, chasing shadows. It could have been worse, as Spurs spurned several excellent chances, the best falling to Allen just before half-time.

Harsh words were spoken in the dressing room at half-time, and it was a completely different Liverpool that emerged in the second half. The change was seismic, with the Reds level within just 10 minutes. Stevenson scored with a half volley rocket from 25 yards, and then Melia managed to force the ball over the line from close range, after Hunt and St John shots had been blocked. Greaves would rue missing a glorious opportunity in between these goals.

The momentum was all with the home team, as the Kop roared them on, searching for a turnaround victory. The hard working St John scored the pivotal goal, after he had dispossessed Norman. Tottenham rallied to save the match, but the tide had turned. Lewis made it four, after a pass from Melia. In the 89th minute, Moran supplied St John, he went round the keeper Brown and gave Melia a simple tap-in.

The rapturous crowd of over 54,000, broke into a chorus of "London Bridge is falling down", as Liverpool's power had beat the

Spurs artistry. They had waited eight years to face the best, and this was a compelling statement of intent.

Spurs gained swift and brutal revenge, winning the return 7-2 on Bank Holiday Monday, with four goals for Greaves. Liverpool would run out of steam, winning just one of the last ten matches, losing seven, including a heart-breaking FA Cup semi-final defeat to Leicester City. Everton would win the league title, but Liverpool and Shankly had learnt much from their first season back. Next year they would surely be even closer to silverware.

- Liverpool finished 8th in the league, starting an incredible consecutive run of top half finishes that is still maintained today after 58 years. In comparison, Manchester United, Arsenal and Chelsea's most recent bottom half finishes were in the 1990s.

- A month later, Tottenham would win the European Cup Winners Cup, the first European trophy by a British side.

- Leicester City established their credentials as Shankly's bogey team, beating Liverpool three times this season, and would win on three consecutive Anfield visits, often due to the brilliance of Gordon Banks.

- Roger Hunt scored an impressive 24 league goals in his first top-flight season, and St John was not far behind on 19.

- Ian St John and Jimmy Greaves would host a popular football show on ITV from 1985 to 1992.

Liverpool 6 Wolverhampton Wanderers 0

16/09/1963 - First Division - Anfield

The1963/4 season started bizarrely, with three away wins and three home defeats. After the weekend's 2-1 Anfield reverse to West Ham, there was a quick chance to redeem themselves, with the visit of Wolves on the Monday evening. Liverpool had already won away at Molineux the previous Monday. Wolves' glory days were now a distant memory, and after four successive defeats, manager Stan Cullis spent a club record £50,000 on the striker Ray Crawford. He would make an immediate debut, amongst ten changes, following a 5-1 loss on Saturday.

Liverpool had two enforced changes due to injuries. Furnell was in goal, and Alf Arrowsmith replaced St John. However, Stevenson was fit again, and new signing Peter Thompson, the thrilling winger from Preston was seen as the final piece in the Shankly jigsaw.

With so many changes, Wolves were inevitably disjointed, while Liverpool settled and clinical. It took only 45 seconds for the difference to show; Callaghan crossed low and hard for Arrowsmith to finish. The Wolves' goal was bombarded with efforts; an Arrowsmith header, a Stevenson shot and goalkeeper Finlayson denied Hunt when he was clean through. It was merely delaying the inevitable, as just after the half-hour, Thompson pounced on a cross from Milne that had not been cleared.

The only surprise was that it took until the 57th minute, before Liverpool extended their lead further. Ian Callaghan took a short corner, and his resulting cross curled into the net, despite protests that he had kicked it twice. 10 minutes later it was four; Hunt netted from an Arrowsmith centre. Wolves offered little with Crawford starved of service, but Crowe did hit the post.

Wolves' plight worsened as Finlayson was injured saving a Thompson shot, so inside right Murray took over in goal for the remaining 19 minutes. He was helpless to prevent two more; a sublime chip from man of the match Milne, and Hunt again, this time from a Thompson cross.

Even though Wolves were wretched, Liverpool were excellent, playing again with pace and power. The brief home jinx was over, and the autumn form was superb again, winning seven out of eight (although four consecutive home games helped).

- The previous week's fixture had an even quicker goal with Roger Hunt scoring after 30 seconds.

- The first Liverpool goals for both Alf Arrowsmith and Peter Thompson.

- Jim Furnell's last Liverpool appearance as he was transferred to Arsenal in November.

- The match was played on a Monday, as Everton hosted their first European Cup fixture against Inter Milan on Wednesday.

- Wolves would avoid relegation, but Cullis was sacked the following September.

- Ron Flowers had won three league titles in the 1950s, playing over 500 times for Wolves and would be the oldest member of England's 1966 World Cup squad.

- This was the first win in front of the newly rebuilt Kemlyn Road stand of 6,700 seats; the first major change since the Kop was roofed in the 1920s, and the first new stand since 1906.

- A month later, "You'll Never Walk Alone" by Gerry & the Pacemakers was number one in the pop charts, and thus began a tradition of its playing before every home match, with the Kop singing along in unison.

- After a slow start, Liverpool would score 60 league goals at home (hitting six on three other occasions).

Manchester United 0 Liverpool 1

23/11/1963 - First Division - Old Trafford

A visit to Old Trafford was always difficult, even if they were still rebuilding after the Munich disaster. Dennis Law and Bobby Charlton were now in place, but George Best was still in the reserves. They had won the FA Cup the previous season, but also narrowly avoided relegation in 19th place. This season United had started better, in sixth place, just a point behind second placed Liverpool. Shankly had just one change, the versatile Phil Ferns replacing the injured Byrne.

There was a typical United barrage in the opening minutes, with three shots from Albert Quixall, while Yeats blocked a Charlton shot. But Liverpool were not overawed, and soon created their own threats through Stevenson and Melia. Hunt even pushed the ball past Harry Gregg, but the goalkeeper recovered to save it.

The key incident occurred on the stroke of half-time; Yeats accidentally crashed into Gregg, while winning a towering header from a corner, that required Setters to clear off the line. Setters was hurt in the clearance, but recovered quickly. However, Gregg was more seriously injured, leaving the pitch, so striker David Herd went in goal.

In the second half, against ten men, Liverpool tried to force the issue, Thompson blazed over a great opportunity, Melia shot wide, and then forced Herd to make his first save. Hunt missed his kick after being put clear by St John. United tried to offer some attacks and Quixall was always dangerous.

Liverpool finally scored with 15 minutes left; Callaghan's corner was met powerfully by Yeats again, and Herd had no chance. Thompson and St John both then missed chances to secure the win. Gregg valiantly reappeared with nine minutes left, even though he had a broken collarbone, playing at outside right. He could not affect the result, as Liverpool controlled the remaining minutes.

Another two points claimed, Liverpool went top of the league, for the first time since their return, after Sheffield United lost. Although it was a slender lead on goal average, as three other teams had the same number of points, this was another milestone in the Shankly era.

Liverpool's defence was resilient now, with the best record in the league, and with St John and Hunt up front, supplied by Callaghan and Thompson, there was always the probability of a goal. The signs for the rest of the season were very promising.

- Liverpool first away win at Manchester United since 1936, and in the previous four visits had conceded 15 goals.

- Ron Yeats' first goal for Liverpool.

- Matt Busby played 122 matches for Liverpool, but the war ended his playing career. He was offered a coaching role at Anfield, but preferred the manager's job at Old Trafford.

- President John F Kennedy had been assassinated the day before, which may explain the lower than expected attendance.

Tottenham Hotspur 1 Liverpool 3

18/04/1964 - First Division - Anfield

Although Liverpool soon lost the leadership, they were always in the top four in a tight race, with the fading Blackburn, defending champions Everton, Tottenham, and a late charge from Manchester United. Liverpool always seemed to have at least one game in hand, and although home form had been excellent, the away form was now a concern. They had not won away in the league since Christmas, often being criticised as being too conservative. They would need to improve it quickly, as six of the last nine would be away. Easter would be crucial, consisting of another four day double header with Spurs, who were level on points, and a trip to bogey team Leicester City in between.

Unfortunately, Ron Yeats had been given a 14 day ban after being sent off at Arsenal in the FA Cup, so Chris Lawler deputised, and Alf Arrowsmith had replaced Jimmy Melia. Tottenham still had the prodigious front line of Jones, White, Greaves and Dyson, with Alan Mullery added to defence.

Liverpool were determined to put on a team performance to banish memories of last year's 7-2 humiliation. They were dominant from the start, as Lawler impressively kept Greaves quiet, Stevenson passed well, and the Hunt / St John partnership a constant threat.

Hunt nearly scored twice in the first ten minutes, being denied by the keeper and shooting wide. The first came after 28 minutes; Stevenson's long ball found Arrowsmith, Henry could not clear his cross, so Hunt pounced to give a justified advantage. Spurs were second best, and Lawrence was only called into action to save from Jones, after he beat three men.

Hunt could have scored again after the hour, but Hollowbread saved with his legs. The match was wrapped up in three second half minutes. On the 67th minute, St John put Hunt through, and he finished supremely, chipping the advancing keeper. Hunt clinched his hat-trick with a header from a Callaghan cross. The scoreline could have been even more emphatic, as Arrowsmith missed two good chances. Norman scored near the end, but it was a mere consolation for a well beaten team

Liverpool moved two points above Spurs, and with Everton surprisingly held at home, it left Shankly's men a point from the summit with two games in hand. They completed a fine Easter with a 2-0 win at Leicester and another 3-1 defeat of Tottenham. The Spurs glory days were fading and Liverpool were ready to usher in a new era.

- Hunt's third top-flight hat-trick, and he would accumulate twelve hat-tricks for Liverpool.

- Liverpool's first win at White Hart Lane since the Liddell hat-trick in 1951.

- St John would score twice and Arrowsmith in the return game.

- Tottenham's third home defeat in a row.

- Tottenham's John White would be killed by lightning in July.

- For more on this season, read "We Love You Yeah, Yeah, Yeah!" by Steven Horton.

Liverpool 5 Arsenal 0
18/04/1964 - First Division - Anfield

Including the Easter extravaganza, Liverpool strung together six league wins, leaving their faltering rivals behind. They were on verge of the league title, with four matches left, almost exactly two years to the day since they clinched promotion.

Shankly could chose his strongest team, as Hunt returned after missing the previous match with injury. The opponents, Arsenal put out a similar team to the previous year, but captain for the day, Jim Furnell, aimed to stop his former teammates. In an echo of the previous title decider, the visitors were still managed by Billy Wright.

As a few fans queued overnight to guarantee their entry, this led to a rapid increase during the morning, so much so that the gates were opened early at 12.30, and the crowd was full by 2 pm. The massed ranks were expectant and ready to celebrate.

Liverpool tore into Arsenal from the first whistle, Hunt had an early header over, and it took barely six minutes to register the first goal; Hunt came forward, passed it to Arrowsmith, he touched it on to St John, who slotted home. Arrowsmith nearly scored twice (one a great save from Furnell) and Hunt went close.

After the early assault waned, Arsenal tried to attack, with Byrne clearing on the line. They were awarded a penalty on 29 minutes, but Lawrence preserved the lead, diving to make a great save from Eastham's kick.

Liverpool renewed their dominance, as Arrowsmith and Milne both had efforts that did not trouble Furnell, while Hunt's shot was well saved. As half-time loomed, Liverpool scored their second; Thompson after beating two men, floated a cross that St John headed back, and Arrowsmith headed in from close range.

Into the second half Liverpool attempted to kill the game off with a third goal, as Furnell made a special double save; tipping Arrowsmith's effort onto the bar, and blocking the rebound from Hunt. His efforts would be in vain, as Thompson scored twice in five minutes, both powerful shots from distance. Hunt got on the scoresheet after Milne and man of the match Thompson had combined. They were cruising to the title; and there could have been a sixth, but Callaghan's penalty was well saved by Furnell.

The final minutes played out in a party atmosphere, the champions elect, serenaded by a range of Kop chants. The final whistle brought a small pitch invasion, but the players managed a lap of honour, (which Shankly modestly declined to join), and celebrations in front of the Kop. The league trophy was not present, but it didn't matter as a fan thrust a paper mache copy into Yeats' hand. After pleas, the champions reappeared in the Directors' Box, with Shankly present, as the hand clapped "Liverpool" filled the air.

- YouTube has a four minute clip from BBC's Panorama, that shows all five goals, but mainly focussing on packed swaying Kop singing "She Loves You " and "Anyone Who Had a Heart".

- This victory equalled Liverpool biggest ever win over Arsenal.

- Liverpool sixth league title, and first for 17 years.

- There were three ever presents in the league (Milne, Callaghan, Thompson) and three other players made 40 or 41 appearances.

- Only two of this team (Moran and Byrne) had made their Liverpool debuts before Shankly arrived.

- The paper mache replica, now known as the Curlett Cup, is in the Anfield museum. The real trophy was only handed over at the Football League AGM on 6th June.

- At this stage of the season, Liverpool had lost five at home, but only four away.

- Liverpool would embark on another post-season tour of America, including a 14-0 win over a San Franciscan Select team, and attending a recording of the Ed Sullivan Show featuring Gerry & the Pacemakers.

- Liverpool would beat Arsenal 3-2 in the opening match of the following season; which featured in the first ever edition of the BBC's "Match of the Day".

Liverpool 3 Anderlecht 0

25/11/1964 - European Cup 1st Round 1st   leg - Anfield

The league win ensured Liverpool's first entry into European football, and the start of a great love affair. An unusual and glamorous distraction, as the early league form was concerning, residing in 16th place with just one win in the last eight.

Reykjavik had been easily dismissed, but Anderlecht, the Belgium champions, were a very different proposition. A skilful, stylish and modern team, included seven of the Belgium players (including captain Paul Van Himst) from an impressive 2-2 draw with England at Wembley recently. Shankly had attended the match and was very worried, but faked bravado, dismissing the Belgians abilities. He had a psychological plan, by choosing this moment to switch Liverpool to an all red kit for the first time. As modelled by the imposing Yeats, it appeared even more intimidating.

Shankly would also make a virtue of injury problems of the forwards Arrowsmith and Wallace, by selecting 19-year old Tommy Smith, in only his sixth appearance. Although he would wear the number ten shirt, his role would be defensive, helping Yeats neutralise any Anderlecht threat, and allow more freedom for the Liverpool midfield

The plan worked perfectly, as the English champions took a 10th minute lead, and it was actually Smith in a creative role, that put Hunt through. Trappeniers parried his shot, but St John buried the rebound. Anderlecht were overwhelmed and unable to cope with Liverpool's pace and intensity. Their only solution was a rigid offside trap, with Hunt the main victim. But frequent chances still came, Thompson hit the bar and St John's header went wide. St John then robbed Verbiest to set up Hunt for a clinical second just before half-time.

Liverpool resumed with the same control and passion after the break, as Yeats made it three on 50th minutes, meeting a Stevenson free-kick. Anderlecht now could only resort to fouling, and were indebted to keeper Trappeniers, with stunning saves from Hunt twice and St John. 3-0 was the least Liverpool deserved.

Although the Belgians were easy on the eye, and confident passing the ball, the Liverpool Echo damned a "midfield melange of nothingness", which didn't trouble the Liverpool defence. Typically Shankly now proclaimed to the players that they had just beaten one of the best teams in Europe !

After weathering an early onslaught in Brussels, Liverpool eased to a 1-0 away win too. Europe provided a catalyst, as Liverpool embarked on a twenty match unbeaten run, and entered the top six.

- No film seems to exist for this match. The BBC filmed it, but only for continental sale, although some of the away match is on YouTube.

- Yeats' second goal for Liverpool and his first at Anfield.

- Bill Shankly had also consulted with his brother Bob, who had also beaten Anderlecht as manager of Dundee in 1963, and had even reached the semi-final of the European Cup.

- A ticket for a 36-seater plane for the second leg cost £14.

- Paul Van Himst would win eight Belgian league titles in a sixteen year Anderlecht career, and would later manage them to a UEFA Cup win, and also Belgium in the 1994 World Cup.

- In the next round Liverpool drew both legs and a replay with Cologne, so a disc was flipped (twice, as the first stuck in the mud) and Liverpool went through.

Chelsea 0 Liverpool 2

27/03/1965 - FA Cup Semi-final - Villa Park

Come March, retaining the league was unlikely, but they were pursuing cup glory on two fronts. On a Wednesday evening, Liverpool had contested the gruelling replay with Cologne in Rotterdam. They had requested that Saturday's FA Cup semi-final be delayed, but the FA refused.

Also in Rotterdam, on a spying trip, was Chelsea manager, Tommy Docherty, revelling in the exhausting extra time. His young team were enjoying an excellent season with the likes of Peter Bonetti, Terry Venables, George Graham, John Hollins and Bobby Tambling. They were currently second in the league and were enjoying other cup success, as they held a lead after the first leg of the League Cup final.

Shankly opted for the same team as midweek, with local youngsters Chris Lawler and Tommy Smith now defensive regulars. The newspapers rated Chelsea as favourites, as their youthful spirit would overcome Liverpool's fatigue, with the Liverpool Echo claiming in these circumstances, a victory would be their greatest ever.

The pundits were wrong. Liverpool didn't look tired, and started with a zest, with early chances for Milne and St John, the latter after Bonetti spilled from a Thompson shot. As the half wore on, play became more scrappy, Chelsea had a goal from Mortimere disallowed for a foul on Lawrence.

In the second half, Liverpool defied the odds again, and were even stronger. Shankly prided himself on being the fittest team due to their pre-season preparation. St John missed an easy cross, and Gerry Byrne went closest with a shot off the post. The deadlock was broken just after the hour; St John laid the ball to Thompson on the wing, and instead of heading for the byline, he cut inside, past two defenders, and unleashed a fierce left foot shot inside the near post.

The young Chelsea team tried to reply, but created little, and it was Liverpool who assured the win on 79 minutes after a "Chopper" Harris foul on St John in the area. Although Milne had been the nominated penalty taker, Stevenson stepped up, and after a slight slip on the muddy pitch, saw the ball fly perfectly into the top corner.

Liverpool saw out the last few minutes, retaining the ball to chants of "easy, easy", securing a place in their third FA Cup final. Many of the 20,000 travelling Liverpool fans invaded the pitch on the final whistle, to acclaim their heroes after an exhausting but successful week.

- A Pathé news clip including the goals is available on YouTube.

- Receipts from the 67,686 attendance at Villa Park totalled £28,143.

- While playing for Preston North End, Peter Thompson scored the goal that knocked Liverpool out of the FA Cup in 1962.

- Liverpool had not scored from the penalty spot since November 1963, missing six in the meantime (Milne had missed the previous week).

- Tommy Docherty had succeeded Shankly in the right half position at Preston, and Shankly had joked "the shirt will know where to go".

- George Graham had regular memorable encounters with Liverpool during his career. He scored against them in debut for Aston Villa, won the 1971 FA Cup final with Arsenal, and managed Arsenal for the dramatic 1989 league title triumph at Anfield.

- In addition to Graham, Terry Venables won the FA Cup as a manager with Tottenham, and McCredie and Holllins would both manage Chelsea.

- Chelsea would knock Liverpool out in the third round at Anfield the following year, and Docherty would manage Manchester United in their FA Cup final win over Liverpool in 1977.

Leeds United 1 Liverpool 2

01/05/1965 - FA Cup Final - Wembley Stadium

Liverpool fans and Bill Shankly were embarrassed that such a big club had never won the FA Cup, and had to endure the taunts from Everton fans about their two triumphs. Finally there was an opportunity to put that right

Shankly had rotated his team for the remaining league games, losing several, as they packed in ten matches in under a month. Despite the changes, he had injury concerns for Callaghan, St John and Milne. The squad only travelled to their Weybridge hotel on the Thursday and attended a Ken Dodd show at the London Palladium on the Friday evening. It was a relief to be there, after the stress of demands for tickets. Liverpool had only been allocated 15,000 in the 100,000 stadium, and touts were extracting a fortune. Still thousands descended on London, with a fleet of cars, buses, trains and even an aeroplane

The opposition were Leeds United, also aiming for their first FA Cup win. A "War of the Roses" between the Reds and Whites. They had enjoyed a remarkable season after promotion, just missing out on the league title on goal average, finishing a whopping 17 points ahead of the Reds. Their team included such talent as Paul Reaney, Charlton, Bremner, Norman Hunter, Johnny Giles, and the 35-year old ex-Everton and new Footballer of the Year, Bobby Collins.

St John and Callaghan were passed fit, but Milne was ruled out by midweek. Strong was the reliable replacement, and would be charged with stopping the influential Collins. The day was wet and cold, but it did not dampen the spirits of the congregated Liverpool fans, as they bellowed "God save our gracious team" during the National Anthem.

The first half was a dour battle, littered with fouls and few chances. Leeds were more nervous and rigid, but Liverpool could not break them down. Strong and Callaghan had shots blocked, and Hunt put one over the bar, followed by Smith, with the keepers not being tested yet. The most significant incident occurred after only three minutes, as Collins crashed into Byrne. The Liverpool left-back's collarbone was actually broken, but he hid his agony to protect his team.

The rain was even heavier in the second half, as Leeds defended deeper. Liverpool had plenty of possession, but struggled to fashion any major chances. Callaghan hit the side netting, and a St John flick header went past the post. Sprake was finally called into action with saves from Thompson and Byrne.

Extra time was required for the first time in eighteen years, as Wembley's energy-sapping wide spaces took their toll, and Byrne's agony continued. The stalemate was broken in the third minute; Stevenson played the ball forward to the fearless Byrne, he crossed for Hunt to stoop and score with a header. Liverpool players jumped for joy, as surely the below-par Leeds could not respond. The joy was short-lived as Bremner soon equalised on the volley from a Charlton knock-down.

In the second period of extra time, Bremner and Strong had shots, and St John put a lob on to the roof of the net. In the 111th minute, Callaghan broke down the wing, and crossed. It was a little behind St John, but throwing himself backward, he managed to make contact, and couldn't miss, as he described "the goalmouth looked as big as the Mersey tunnel".

Liverpool held out for the final minutes, and the fans were ecstatic to hear the final whistle, which ended their long wait. Ron Yeats collected the trophy from the Queen who remarked that the match "looked hard". The lap of honour was accompanied by delirious chants of "Ee Y Adio We Won the Cup".

The press were less impressed by the match as a spectacle. Headlines such as "Drab Deadlock" and "Bore of the Roses", as Tommy Finney summarised "defences are the final ruin". A little harsh as Liverpool had tried to attack, but it mattered little to the 250,000 Liverpool fans who welcomed the team back on Sunday, with an open bus tour to a Town Hall reception.

- The whole match is available for purchase on DVD, and there is a six minute colour version on the Pathé YouTube channel.

- Liverpool were the 37th team to win the FA Cup in the 84th final.

- Hunt's goal was Liverpool's first in an FA Cup Final after 4 hours and 33 minutes.

- Gordon Milne missed the final through damaged knee ligaments, and his father had also missed the 1938 final with a broken collarbone.

- Geoff Strong's first FA Cup appearance for Liverpool.

- Bill Shankly was the seventh person to win the FA Cup as a player and manager.

- Shankly was the guest on Desert Island Discs earlier that week, and, of course, chose "You'll Never Walk Alone", and his luxury was a football.

- For more information on this FA Cup campaign and some wonderful black and white photos, read "Cup Kings Liverpool 1965" by Mark Platt.

- Leeds' Albert Johanneson was the first black player in an FA Cup final.

- Five of this Leeds team would win the FA Cup in 1972, their only win to date.

Liverpool 3 Inter Milan 1

04/05/1965 - European Cup Semi-final 1st leg - Anfield

There was little time for recovery, as on Tuesday, the Italian giants Inter Milan came to Anfield for the first leg of the European Cup semi-final. The defending European Champions (beating Everton on the way), Inter had a star-studded team including captain Armando Picchi, Giacinto Facchetti, Mario Corso, Sandro Mazzola, and Luis Suarez (a £200,000 signing from Barcelona). Their respected manager Helenio Herrera had pioneered a counter attacking system, known as "catenaccio" with an impregnable five man defence.

The match was not all ticket, so the ground had to open at an unprecedented 3.30 pm to accommodate the rising queues, and closed at least an hour before the kick-off, producing an excited and celebratory atmosphere. Milne was still out, and veteran Moran replaced Byrne after his Wembley heroics. Shankly deliberately invited Inter to go out first, and then sent out the Liverpool team followed by Milne and Byrne (with his arm in a sling), to parade the FA Cup, heightening the crowd to an even more frenzied and intimidating roar. Legend has it, they could be heard as far away as the city centre.

With this fervid background, Liverpool tried to take the game to Inter with an early goal. Actually, the first goal after 4 minutes, came from a counter attack after Inter won a corner. The ball was cleared up to Strong, who passed on to Callaghan, and his cross was met first time by Hunt, firing into the net. Inter did not buckle, and soon Mazzola equalised after Yeats had been dispossessed.

Inter were more relaxed now, passing the ball sweetly, and fending off any attacks as Liverpool tried again. They were undone in the 34th minute with a well worked free-kick. Callaghan ran over the ball, as Stevenson passed to Hunt, and his flick found Callaghan, who had not stopped running, and he slotted in coolly. A priceless reward for a training ground routine, that had never worked in the league. The goal spurred on the Reds, as Smith shot over from a free-kick, Lawler had a superb goal harshly disallowed for offside, and Yeats hit the bar.

In the second half, Liverpool were dominant and the ruffled Inter were clinging on. Yeats caused panic in their area, St John headed wide, and Stevenson shot twice. They had to wait until the 75th minute for the third; Callaghan to Smith, on to Hunt, Sarti saved his shot, but St John netted the simple rebound, despite suggestions of offside. The Kop celebrated with a chant of "Oh Inter, 1, 2, 3, Go back to Italy" to the tune of Santa Lucia. Sarti added to his collection of fine saves from St John and Hunt near the end, to keep Inter in the tie.

Fans and writers could only admire Liverpool's fitness and intensity in their 58th match of the season, and just days after the Wembley extra time. Even the great Herrera conceded "We have lost before, but never been defeated. Tonight we were defeated"

The second leg would be lost 3-0, but Shankly would always rue some questionable refereeing decisions. A poignant end to a thrilling and historic cup season.

- An eight minute video of the BBC coverage is on YouTube. There is also a brief amateur colour film of the FA Cup being paraded, and a little action on the Unofficial Liverpool Football Club Museum Facebook page.

- Chris Lawler managed to squeeze in his wedding on the Monday; but spent his wedding night sharing a room in a Blackpool hotel with Tommy Smith.

- Admission for the Kop was 5 shillings and for the Main Stand £1 and 10 shillings.

- Inter Milan would beat Benfica 1-0 in the final to retain the trophy.

- An 11-year old Phil Thompson was sitting in the front row of the Kemlyn Road stand.

- Helenio Herrera is one of the most influential managers of the modern game. An Argentine who won two European Cups and three Serie A titles with Inter Milan, but also four La Liga titles with Atlético Madrid and Barcelona.

- Giacinto Facchetti and Sandro Mazzola would both become Inter Milan legends, as single club men, with 634 and 566 appearances in lengthy careers, in addition to 94 and 70 caps for Italy respectively.

Liverpool 5 Everton 0

25/09/1965 - First Division - Anfield

"Same again" was Shankly's mantra for 1965/66, with no major transfers, as he trusted the same eleven key players and Geoff Strong to step in anywhere required. Liverpool were a now a well-oiled machine, and Shankly would claim he only needed to discuss tactics once at the start of the season, as everyone understood his role.

Liverpool's start was solid, but not spectacular, and they had lost their most recent outing to Tottenham before the derby match loomed. Everton were level on the same number of points, but the Reds could still remember the previous year's 4-0 humiliation at home. Everton were establishing their classic 1960s side, with Gordon West, Ray Wilson, Jimmy Gabriel, Brian Labone, Alex Young and Colin Harvey all playing, but Derek Temple was out with flu. For Liverpool, typically Strong was in for the injured Lawler, so Smith moved to right-back. Again the gates were opened at noon, to allow the eager 53,000 crowd to safely assemble.

Liverpool went straight at Everton from the kick-off; Byrne's free-kick was tipped over, and from the resulting corner Hunt's shot hit West and Yeats shot hit the post. They totally controlled this fast and furious encounter. West was overworked saving next from Thompson, and then Smith's free-kick, while Milne and Yeats went close, and a Hunt effort was cleared on the line. It took until the 34th minute before Liverpool's command was reflected; Smith threw himself forward to connect to a Thompson free-kick, and it flew past West. At the other end, Lawrence had been a virtual spectator, with only Young testing him.

At half-time, there was the novelty of substitutions due to injuries, Labone going off for Everton, and Arrowsmith replacing Milne. The extra striker did not affect Liverpool's control, but actually gave them more attacking options. Within 4 minutes of the restart, Hunt grabbed the second from an Arrowsmith pass, managing to squeeze the ball into the Kop goal, despite an acute angle. The third was just three minutes later; Thompson's cross reached Stevenson, who confidently chipped West.

The Everton goalkeeper again helped them avoid an even larger reverse, saving from Smith, Hunt and Callaghan. After 73 minutes, Stevenson's cross deflected and Hunt stooped to head in. The delighted Kop mocked "Ee I Addio we are going home" and "We want five", and St John duly obliged in the final minute with a header from a Callaghan cross.

A rampant Liverpool had exceeded Everton's previous victory, and also proved that they would be serious challengers again for the title.

- Substitutes were introduced in the league for this season, but only for injuries. Geoff Strong was Liverpool's first league substitution, and even scored against West Ham in September.

- Liverpool's biggest derby win since 1935.

- Johnny Morrissey played 37 games for Liverpool, and was sold to Everton, without Shankly's knowledge.

- Although Liverpool frequently beat Everton at Anfield, Shankly only won two of his first twelve visits to Goodison Park.

- Everton's left-back Ray Wilson had been coached by Shankly at Huddersfield Town, and would play in the 1966 World Cup final.

Liverpool 2 Manchester United 0

01/01/1966 - First Division - Anfield

A now customary late autumn surge of ten wins in eleven matches saw Liverpool progress in Europe and hit the top of the league. Christmas would be critical, with matches against their closest rivals. Back to back matches were split 1-0 each with Leeds before Manchester United's visit on New Year's Day.

Liverpool were still top, but United, the defending champions, were well poised at third, five points behind, but two games in hand. They still had some 1950s stars like Gregg and Bill Foulkes, but now had the combative Stiles and the formidable forward combination of Charlton, Law and Best. Liverpool were unchanged again with their regular lineup, and Strong on the bench. A bumper holiday crowd swelled the attendance, with all gates shut by 2.10 pm, and an estimated 10,000 locked outside.

United took the early lead, from a long kick from Gregg, Law shook off Yeats and rounded Lawrence, to calmly place it in the empty net. Liverpool were struggling in a scrappy start, as Smith and St John's efforts were off target. Gradually they found their rhythm, and exerted more sustained pressure. Gregg saved from St John and then Smith's free-kick. But he was helpless to prevent Smith's equaliser just before half-time, as the shot from the edge of the area, crept in at the near post.

In the second half, Law had another early shot, but then Liverpool dominated. They were quicker and stronger, as they forced the visitors to defend, as their goal was bombarded. Hunt shot over, Foulkes nearly scored an own goal, St John hit the bar, but Stevenson could not follow up.

Liverpool pressed and pressed, roared on as they attacked the Kop, but Gregg was stopping everything, and a superb late save from St John, seemed to ensure a point. However, Liverpool were relentless, and in the 88th minute they snatched a late winner; the ball was cleared after a scramble, Byrne fired it back in, and it flew into the net to the Kop's elation. Although the late Liverpool Echo gave the headline to Byrne (and most fans agreed), the goal was subsequently credited to

Milne, as the shot had taken a sizeable deflection off his head.

A vital two points secured, it increased the gap over United to seven points, with a richly deserved result after the second half domination. On the first day of the year, Liverpool had taken a major step to the title, and would not relinquish the lead for the rest of the season.

- The third in a run of eight matches when Liverpool were unchanged.

- Dora Bryan, star of "A Taste of Honey" was guest of honour, as she was currently starring at the Royal Court Theatre.

- Bill Shankly coached the 16-year old Dennis Law, when he was in charge of Huddersfield reserves, and then when he was promoted to manager.

- In April 1964 Phil Chisnall transferred from Manchester United to Liverpool. He only made eight Liverpool appearances, but remains the last player to be transferred directly between these teams.

- Two years later, six of this Manchester United team would win a European Cup final.

Liverpool 2 Celtic 0

19/04/1966 European Cup Winners Cup Semi-final 2nd leg - Anfield

During the spring Liverpool had extended their lead to nine points, and also progressed in Europe, with Honved going the same way as Juventus and Standard Liege. Another European semi-final beckoned and this time Celtic awaited, managed by Jock Stein. Along with Busby and Shankly, they formed a trio of friends and iconic 1960s Scottish managers. Stein had barely been back at the struggling Celtic for a year, but he had already recorded their first Scottish Cup since 1954 and were now on their way to their first league since 1954 too.

Celtic won 1-0 in the first leg at Parkhead on Thursday night with over 76,000 attending, but should have had a larger lead, as Liverpool were very poor

For the Anfield return leg on the Tuesday, Liverpool were still missing Hunt, so Strong was preferred to Chisnall this time, and Byrne played, despite dislocating his elbow in the first leg. Stein's selection surprised many by leaving out the mercurial winger Jimmy Johnstone. Celtic were allocated 5,000 tickets, but far more Glaswegians descended on the city, and this time the gates had to be opened at 4.45 pm.

There was heavy rain throughout the day, which made the pitch treacherous for good football, and also produced steam on the packed Kop. Liverpool attacked from the first whistle, eager to wipe out the deficit, and Celtic were forced into desperate defending. The speedy Callaghan and Thompson on the wings supplied quality crosses for the head of Strong. The two went wide, and two were well saved by Simpson. Smith shot from long range twice, once hitting the bar.

Celtic only had one real chance, as McBride hit the bar too. Lawler then unbelievably put the ball over the bar, from five yards out. Liverpool then suffered a major blow, as Strong suffered a knee injury, but like Byrne in the FA Cup final, he battled on, limping throughout the match (as no European substitutes were allowed yet). This gave Celtic an advantage, as Hughes and Lennox started to venture forward, but Callaghan still forced another good save on the stroke of half-time.

Attacking the Kop in the second half, Liverpool renewed their bombardment. Smith finally broke through just after the hour. He won a free-kick, Stevenson dummied, so Smith struck it hard and low through the wall, which deceived Simpson. Within five minutes Liverpool were ahead in the tie, as Callaghan's cross was met perfectly by Strong's header, using his good leg to launch himself.

Celtic tried to rescue the match, with Hughes and Gemmell shots, and Lennox had the ball in the back of the net, three minutes from the end. However, the linesman had already put his flag up for offside, thus provoking a hail of bottles descending from the Celtic fans. Over 100 fans needed medical attention, as the match was temporarily delayed. Shankly later reputedly asked his friend Stein, "Jock, do you want your share of the gate money or shall we just return the empties?"

The players returned, with little incident, and the referee blew early for safety. Liverpool had reached their first European final, and another trip to Glasgow, but they were beaten 2-1 by Borussia Dortmund after extra time.

- Although the highlights of the match were shown on BBC TV, it seems that only the goals are on YouTube.

- Celtic would win the European Cup the following season, beating Inter Milan in Lisbon in the final, with eight of their players from this match. Shankly attended the match, and greeted Stein afterwards "John, you're immortal now".

- These were the only two occasions that Stein and Shankly managed opposing teams in a competitive match.

- In 1974, Liverpool and Celtic met twice in testimonials for their long serving captains, Ron Yeats and Billy McNeil, and they would meet again for Jock Stein's benefit match in 1978.

Liverpool 2 Chelsea 1

30/04/1966 - First Division - Anfield

Four days after the intense Celtic match, Liverpool had the chance to clinch the league title at second place Burnley, but they lost 2-0. However, it set up the following week's home match against Chelsea. It was really just a mathematical confirmation, as Leeds United would need to win their remaining five matches by very large margins, so just a point was required.

Chelsea were in fourth place and had already won at Anfield in January in the FA Cup, but their season was collapsing, having lost an FA Cup semi-final, and then a European semi-final in Barcelona in midweek. They were also without Venables (about to depart), Bonetti and Graham, while Liverpool were at full strength, with Hunt returning from injury.

A carnival mood ensued in the hot sunshine, as a sense of a formality prevailed, with a fan placing a trophy replica on the centre spot. Even the Chelsea players lined up to applaud Liverpool on to the pitch.

In an open start, Osgood looked dangerous for Chelsea, and Dunn made a good save from St John's header. Liverpool pressed more, with two Smith shots, and Hunt hit the post, but they could not score before half-time.

It only took three minutes after the restart, as they attacked the Kop goal; Byrne passed forward long to Hunt, he managed to retrieve it on the line and squeezed in a shot from a tight angle (although Dunn got a hand). Liverpool were on top now, and pressed for the important second. St John had a shot deflected wide, Yeats header was saved, and both St John and Stevenson went close.

Against the run of play, Chelsea were level, as Murray outpaced Yeats and shot in. Liverpool were not discouraged, and regained the lead 7 minutes later, Callaghan crossed to Hunt, he feinted and then fired in, despite another hand from the keeper. Milne celebrated by swinging on the goal netting.

Liverpool coasted through the remainder of the game with chances to seal it for St John and Milne, but Chelsea were already a beaten team. At full time, there were the now customary celebrations and a lap of honour from the eleven players, with Geoff Strong rightly appearing, after a chant from the Kop. Three trophies in three years, the first Shankly team had hit its peak.

- A twelve-minute clip of the "Match of the Day" highlights is on YouTube.

- Shankly only used fourteen players in the entire league campaign, even more remarkable in that Bobby Graham only played once (the final match) and Arrowsmith five times. Nine players made 40 or more league appearances.

- Liverpool had the best defence in the league, with 34 conceded, and Roger Hunt was joint highest scorer in the First Division with 29 goals.

- Home attendances soared again, with just one match below 40,000, and the aggregate totalling a new record of 975,000.

- In the summer of 1966, Roger Hunt would be the first Liverpool player to win a World Cup final, while Callaghan and Byrne were also in the squad.

Liverpool 5 Leeds United 0
19/11/1966 - First Division - Anfield

With no major summer signings again, Shankly again relied on his trusted charges to go the distance again. The initial signs were promising, as Liverpool lost only three matches in the first 16. When Don Revie and normal rivals, Leeds visited Anfield in November, Liverpool were second, after three straight wins without conceding.

Leeds' start had been disappointing, but they had won four of the last five matches, although they suffered a shock 7-0 league cup defeat at West Ham the previous week. Sprake had missed that game, but now returned from injury, while Johanneson was not fit. Liverpool were at full strength, as Shankly would often announce his team selection was "same as last year".

Liverpool commanded from the off, with quick passing and shooting on sight. Sprake single-handedly kept Leeds level; saving from a Hunt header, Thompson (twice), St John, and Callaghan. Milne had the ball in the net, but it was disallowed for offside. The breakthrough finally came just before half-time; Yeats won a header from a Stevenson free-kick, it dropped to Lawler, but as he was facing away from goal, he quickly back heeled the ball into the net.

After such a defensive first half, Leeds restarted on the offensive, with chances for O'Grady and Madeley. But it was Liverpool who scored the second, as a St John shot deflected in off Charlton. The visitors battled to get back into the match with further chances for Bremner and Madeley, but then the hosts took over again, with St John, Thompson, and Strong going close.

The win was secured, with a third after 75 minutes; Strong played a one-two with Milne and rifled the ball in from over 25 yards. St John also scored from a similar distance, hitting the bar on the way in. Hunt and St John both missed good opportunities for the fifth, but Strong scored it with another fierce shot in the last minute.

Leeds had not played that badly, with Sprake outstanding, but they had met a Liverpool team in sparkling form. As the Liverpool Echo wrote, "On this form Liverpool looked what they are - the champions". Even Don Revie concurred that "We shall now have to seriously think of Liverpool as one of the greats of all time".

Liverpool looked set for another league triumph as they were top at the start of March, but uncharacteristically won just two of the last twelve, sliding down to fifth, nine points behind the winners. Perhaps the "same again" had failed this time, even with the addition of Emlyn Hughes in February.

- Rinus Michels, the coach of Ajax, was at this match to watch Liverpool before the forthcoming European Cup match, but had to leave at half-time for his flight home. It made little difference as Ajax won 5-1 in the first leg.

- Although Hunt scored his lowest total of 14 league goals, Thompson and Strong (now a regular) would both hit double figures.

- Leeds' Jimmy Greenhoff would score the winner of the 1977 FA Cup final against Liverpool.

- A year later, on a snowy day Gary Sprake accidentally threw the ball into his own net, and the Kop responded with a chorus of the popular song "Careless Hands", and the half-time music also included "Thank You Very Much".

- Bill Shankly claimed he attended Emlyn Hughes' league debut for Blackpool in 1966 and immediately tried to sign him, but had to wait until their manager Ron Suart was sacked in 1967.

Liverpool 6 Newcastle United 0

26/08/1967 - First Division - Anfield

After the disappointing end of the previous season Shankly broke the club's transfer record with a £96,000 fee for robust centre forward Tony Hateley from Chelsea. He had already scored four times against the Reds while playing for Aston Villa, but his spell of less than a year at Chelsea was unhappy with only six goals.

Liverpool had a good start with a draw at Manchester City, and a win against Arsenal, without conceding. Hateley had not scored yet, but it was hoped that the first Saturday home match would provide the perfect opportunity. Opponents Newcastle had struggled the previous season, but now had started well, due to three goals from Albert Bennett and centre forward Wyn Davies, a recent £85,000 signing.

Hateley made the ideal start, scoring after 9 minutes; Smith crossed and Hunt laid it back to him to shoot in. The fans were impressed as he also created chances for Thompson and Lawler too. They thought he had his second on 21 minutes, but it was ruled out for offside. Hateley would have a hand in the second though, knocking down a long ball from Smith, to Hughes who fired in from 30 yards. Thompson was also lively, with a dangerous cross, and a shot well saved. The third came just before half-time, the keeper spilled a Thompson free-kick, and Callaghan squared for an easy Hunt conversion.

Liverpool were quickly on the attack in the second half; Hughes beating two men, and Hateley smashed in his second. Hunt hit the post soon after, but Hateley claimed his hat-trick on 75th minutes; meeting a Callaghan free-kick with a powerful header. The Kop had a new hero, but no one could replace their love for "Sir Roger", as he scored the sixth. Again Hateley was involved, striding forward, swapping passes with St John, and then on to Hunt's head. The three Hs - Hunt, Hughes, and Hateley had won it.

It seemed that the new look potent attack would help Liverpool to more honours, as they hit first place in November, but again they faded and finished third, three points behind champions Manchester City.

- Emlyn Hughes' first goal for Liverpool.

- Newcastle manager Joe Harvey and left-back Frank Clark, would lose to Liverpool in the 1974 FA Cup final.

- Despite scoring an impressive 27 goals in his first season, Hateley was sold early the next season, as it was felt that he forced Liverpool into playing too many long balls. Hateley's five transfers in six years, led to Tommy Smith's quip, that "Tony didn't buy a new car every year, but a Pickfords' van".

- Hunt would still be top scorer with 30 goals, but St John suffered with Hateley's inclusion, only scoring six all season.

- Former Liverpool player, and Shankly player at Carlisle United, Geoff Twentyman returned in this month as chief scout. A role he would keep until 1988, seeking players on modest fees with a "Northern Soul" that could pass well and be moulded in the Liverpool way.

Wolverhampton Wanderers 0 Liverpool 6

28/09/1968 - First Division - Molineux Stadium

Hateley's replacement would be an 18 year-old blonde Beatle-haired striker from Wolves, Alun Evans, the first £100,000 teenager. He scored on his debut against Leicester, and his next league match would be a return to Molineux. The only other change to the established 60s team was Peter Wall coming in, as Byrne was being eased out.

Although Wolves started brightly, Liverpool took the lead after 15 minutes, when Hunt's low shot was deflected by Woodfield, and past Boswell in goal. The lead was soon extended with a quick fire two goals in four minutes. Thompson made it 2-0, as he cut in and shot low from 25 yards. He also assisted the third, a through ball for the unmarked Evans to run in and slot past the keeper. It was a sweet response for Evans, who had been barracked by the Wolves fans in his last match there, and been relegated to the reserve team.

Liverpool were in total control, with only a Farmington chance for Wolves. Surprisingly it took another 30 minutes for the fourth; Evans again haunting his old club, with a glancing header from a Hunt cross.

The travelling Kop were infatuated, chanting "Thank you very much for Alun Evans" as they enjoyed their day in the Black Country. It seemed like the Reds could score with every attack. Hunt would make it five with a header from a Callaghan centre after 74 minutes and Thompson claimed his second 6 minutes later with a powerful drive.

A stunning away win, and so pleasing how Evans fitted in. Unfortunately, his bright start would fade, with only two goals in the last 30 games. But Liverpool flourished, as they were top from October to February. They could not shake off the relentless Leeds United who kept winning, and ended with a record 67 points. Liverpool had 61 points, equal to or more than the previous eight league champions' totals. Close again, but a third year without silverware.

- Alun Evans marked his 19th birthday, two days later.

- Wolves biggest home defeat since the Second World War, and Liverpool biggest top-flight away win so far.

- Liverpool lost only six times in the league, less than Shankly's two title winning teams.

- Leeds clinched the title at Anfield after a 0-0 draw. Don Revie instructed the Leeds players to salute the Kop, and they received a huge reception.

- 1968 would see the arrival of Tom Saunders as the Youth Development Officer, and he would also be entrusted on scouting opposition, especially in Europe. He was held in such high regard that he became a Liverpool director in 1993.

- This season Liverpool reserves would win the Central League, the first of three successive wins under Joe Fagan, assisted by Ronnie Moran.

- In January, Hunt would be credited with breaking Gordon Hodgson club record of 233 league goals. It was actually two weeks later, as LFCHistory found he had erroneously been given an extra goal. When he left in 1970, he had accumulated the current record of 244 league goals and 285 in all competitions.

Liverpool 10 Dundalk 0

16/09/1969 European Fairs Cup - 1st round 1st leg - Anfield

Alec Lindsay and Larry Lloyd joined in 1969, but could not break into the first team, as Shankly still chose the same trusted players. Again his faith was initially rewarded as Liverpool made a superb start with eight wins from the first ten fixtures, and briefly topped the table. The first defeat of the season came away to Manchester United in September, before attentions turned to European football, and the visit of Irish part-timers Dundalk.

Shankly had suggested changes would be made to rest players after the hectic start, but eight players kept their places. Reserve goalkeeper Ray Clemence made his second Liverpool start after Lawrence had a stomach complaint, and the attack was refreshed with Alun Evans (only his second game this season) and Lindsay making his debut (wearing the number 9 shirt). Dundalk arrived with four former Irish internationals, including goalkeeper Swan, and three had English league experience.

Alun Evans started the avalanche in the first minute, with a header from a Callaghan cross, and Lawler made it two with another header after 10 minutes. A fierce Tommy Smith free-kick was the next goal after 24 minutes, followed by two quick goals from Graham (a volley) and Evans again to give Liverpool a 5-0 half-time lead.

They did not ease up in the second half, with waves of assaults laying siege to the Dundalk goal, and Lindsay marked his debut, with a fine strike. There was another rapid double just after the hour mark; Smith from 30 yards and Thompson with a low drive. Callaghan made it nine in the 76th minute with a shot from 25 yards, and Graham rounded off the evening with his second and Liverpool's tenth

A record breaking win, with the double figures coming from seven different scorers. The Irish team received sympathetic applause at the end, but had been completely outclassed. It could have been even worse as Smith had a goal disallowed, Strong hit the post, and Swan made some excellent saves, while several shots sailed wide.

The Liverpool Echo described it as "wasn't so much a football match, as an exhibition of torture". Dundalk manager William Tuohy wasn't too downcast, as he thought such an impressive scoreline would increase the gate for the second leg, as the Irish fans would be curious to see such a devastating team.

A brief happy moment, as Liverpool would be knocked out in the next round by Vitoria Setubal and finished 15 points behind champions Everton. A shock FA Cup exit away at Watford in February 1970, signalled the end of the era and for several of 1960s stars, as Shankly finally realised he needed to build again.

- This victory broke Liverpool's largest win ever record, and the first time they had scored ten goals, since 1896.

- Liverpool won the second leg 4-0, and the 14-0 aggregate remains Liverpool's biggest European margin.

- Ray Clemence had been signed from Scunthorpe United for £18,000, but had also worked as a deck chair attendant on Skegness beach during the summers.

- Dundalk would visit Anfield again in the European Cup in 1982, losing only 1-0, but 5-1 on aggregate.

- A French placement teacher at Alsop Comprehensive school, Gerard Houllier, attended this match on the Kop with his visiting friend Patrice Bergues.

1970s

Liverpool 3 Everton 2

21/11/1970 - First Division - Anfield

It was a new-look team that emerged to play Everton in November 1970. Clemence was now a regular in goal, Lloyd at centre-back and Lindsay converted to a left-back. The flanks saw Brian Hall and Steve Heighway, supplying crosses for the new £110,000 six-foot centre forward, John Toshack. There were also starts for John McLaughlin and Ian Ross, as Graham, Thompson, Callaghan, and Evans were all out injured. Only the captain Tommy Smith and Lawler survived from the title winning teams as Lawrence, Yeats, Hunt and St John, had either departed or soon would.

The early signs were promising with no defeats in the first eleven, but by November, three losses and too many draws saw Liverpool in 8th place. The reigning title holders, Everton now had the celebrated midfield of Alan Ball / Howard Kendall / Colin Harvey with Joe Royle as centre forward. With both teams short of goals, the Liverpool Echo's preview headline predicted "It's odds on a goalless derby game".

The first half fulfilled this prophesy, being scrappy, with lots of commitment and forceful tackles, with 25 fouls, but few chances. Everton edged possession, as Royle and Toshack both went close with headers. Although Liverpool started the second half better, they fell behind around the hour mark to two quick Everton goals; a Whittle lob and a Royle header.

The young Reds could have folded, but quickly pulled one back within six minutes. Heighway, running down the wing, skipped past a lunge, evaded two defenders and squeezed the ball from an acute angle. The Everton defenders would not be the last to be deceived by the illusion that Heighway had played the ball too far, but then surprised as he burst past them.

He also had a hand in the equaliser on the 76th minute, turning his man, and putting in an inviting cross. that Toshack rose to power in. Everton nearly retook the lead, but Clemence made a fine save. Attacking the Kop, Liverpool completed a remarkable turnaround with six minutes left. A deep Lindsay cross, was nodded on by Toshack and Lawler came around the back unmarked to finish decisively. It wasn't over, as Clemence had to make another crucial save, this time from Newton.

The young players, seven making their derby debuts, had played with courage and resilience. The win was an encouraging indication, and a key milestone had been recorded.

- YouTube has a three-minute clip of the goals from ITV coverage with Gerald Stinstadt commentating.

- Heighway and Hall were both university graduates, so were nicknamed Big and Little Bamber, after the "University Challenge" host, Bamber Gascoigne.

- On the same day, Lawrence, Yeats and St John were playing out a 1-1 draw in the mini reserve derby at Goodison Park.

- Kendall, Harvey and Royle would all later manage Everton, while Ball managed Southampton and Manchester City.

Liverpool 3 Bayern Munich 0

10/03/1971 - European Fairs Cup 4th round 1st leg - Anfield

Liverpool were up to fourth by March, but the cup competitions were the best shot at a trophy. However, a European quarter-final against Bayern Munich was a daunting task. Germany would win the 1972 European Championship and the 1974 World Cup final, with a spine of Munich stars; Sepp Maier in goal, Franz Beckenbauer, Paul Breitner, and Gerd Muller (38-goal golden boot winner the previous season). They were top of the Bundesliga, but at a disadvantage, as they had not played for three weeks due to heavy snow in Germany.

After not scoring in their previous three matches, Liverpool were relieved to welcome back Alun Evans for his first start after a cartilage operation in October. His replacement Phil Boersma stayed in, at the expense of John McLaughlin. The kick-off was delayed by 15 minutes, as a power cut at 6.30 pm blocked the electronic turnstiles, and also plunged the Bayern dressing room into darkness.

The Germans set up defensively, as Liverpool attacked with power and pace, with Toshack a domineering fulcrum, winning most balls in the air. At the other end, Clemence had little to do, as Lloyd shackled Muller. Actually Lloyd was able to be a threat in the opposition box, as he hit the post. on 18 minutes. The pressure paid off on the half-hour, with Heighway beating his man, crossing, Evans controlled and accurately fired into the corner of the goal.

Evans would double the advantage, just after the interval, as he deflected a Lloyd header from Lindsay's free-kick. Evans' and Liverpool's third came after 73 minutes; another from close range, as he pounced when Maier could not hold Hughes' weak shot. It was Evans' first hat-trick and a timely return.

Munich made substitutions, attacking with a purpose to seize an important away goal, and Roth hit the post. Liverpool thoroughly deserved the result, and it could have been more in the closing minutes, as Lawler had a goal disallowed and Maier had saved from Evans. Shankly was delighted, and hailed the success due to the "whippets ", the pace of the mobile strikers.

- Colour footage of the goals is on the "Liverpool in Europe" video on YouTube.

- Tickets for European matches were more expensive, so the stand prices for the match ranged from 75p to £1.50.

- Alun Evans was the first Liverpool player to score a hat-trick in a European match.

- The second leg was a comfortable 1-1 draw with Shankly bringing in Ian Ross to effectively man mark Beckenbauer.

- The two teams would meet again, later in the year, in an early round of the European Cup Winners Cup, with Bayern winning 3-1 on aggregate. They would win the European Cup for three successive seasons from 1974.

- Manager Udo Lattek would win all three European club competitions, but with three different teams; European Cup (Bayern Munich), European Cup Winners Cup (Barcelona), and UEFA Cup (Borussia Moenchengladbach), and would also amass eight German league titles.

Everton 1 Liverpool 2

27/03/1971 - FA Cup Semi-final - Old Trafford

Three days after the second leg in Munich, Liverpool faced Everton in the FA Cup semi-final, at Old Trafford. Everton had also been in European action too, going out to Panathinaikos on away goals in the European Cup. Over 50,000 Liverpudlians again descended on Manchester, to see if the established champions or callow youth would triumph.

Callaghan was fit again to add his experience, now in central midfield. Everton were missing Newton and Husband, but also manager Harry Catterick, due to illness, so coach Wilf Dixon took charge. Shankly joked that even if he was dead, he would even have attended in a coffin !

In a thrilling encounter, Everton took the lead after 10 minutes, with Alan Ball (in his white boots) getting on the end of a cross, after a flick on from Whittle beat Clemence. Callaghan seemed to have equalised within a minute, but the referee detected a handball. Lawler, Heighway and Evans all had shots blocked, while Toshack and Lloyd both headed wide. Everton were defending stoutly, relying on their experience and seemed composed up to half-time. Shankly told his players that they were rushing too much with too many aimless long balls to Toshack.

Everton were dealt an early blow after the restart, as the injured Labone needed to be replaced. Liverpool attacked with even more vigour and utilised the midfield more. After concerted pressure they were level by the hour mark; Heighway, drew three Everton players to him, but quickly released, to put Evans through to calmly slot in. Soon they had turned the game around and taken the lead. Rankin could not clear an Evans cross under pressure from Toshack and his own defender, so Hall hit a rising shot into the empty net, and then celebrated in front of the travelling Liverpool fans hosted in the Stretford End.

Everton tried to reply, with Ball the key focus, but the new Liverpool defence was solid. There was also always the threat on the counter attack with Heighway nearly creating a third and Rankin saving twice from Toshack.

Liverpool saw out the remaining time, and clinched another famous semi-final victory over their closest rivals, as the evening Echo headline simply read "It's the Reds". Veteran correspondent Michael Charters would extol the spectacle, stating it was the best derby he had ever seen in his years of reporting.

Unfortunately, Arsenal repeated their 1950 win in the final, and Leeds United knocked Liverpool out in the Fairs Cup semi-final. No trophies again, but the new young team had impressed, and would only get better.

- There doesn't seem any footage on YouTube, but the goals can be found on Twitter.

- Brian Hall's first goal for Liverpool.

- Any replay would have been at Burden Park, Bolton.

- Despite missing a large part of the season, Evans was still top scorer, with 15 goals, the only players to reach double figures, with 16 different scorers during this transitional season. The league total of 42 was Liverpool's lowest ever and the 5th lowest in the league, but they also had the best defensive record.

- With two critical defeats in a week, Everton went into decline, with Ball leaving in December and Catterick suffered a heart attack in January.

Liverpool 3 Nottingham Forest 1

14/08/1971 - First Division - Anfield

Addressing the lack of goals, Shankly spent £35,000 in the week of the 1971 FA Cup final on a Fourth Division striker, the 20-year old Kevin Keegan from Scunthorpe United. He had not been selected for the pre-season tour, but a lively appearance in a training match saw him tapped for the opening day, wearing what would become his iconic number seven shirt. Liverpool could also welcome back Peter Thompson after missing much of the previous season with an injury, and McLaughlin started as Hall had a minor injury, so Callaghan and Evans would miss out.

Keegan's match day preparations were not ideal, as he was stuck in traffic, after driving himself to the ground, and only arrived at 2.15 pm. It did not affect his performance as he was immediately in the action, creating chances for Toshack and McLaughlin. It took just 12 minutes for his first goal; Thompson's pressure forced a defensive mistake and Toshack presented Keegan a gift, as he scuffed in from 12 yards into the Kop goal; the start of a fruitful partnership.

Four minutes later Keegan robbed O'Kane and was brought down as he was preparing to shoot. Smith converted, sending the keeper the wrong way. Liverpool were buzzing, and overrunning Forest, with Keegan catching the eye with his style of perpetual motion.

Forest survived a Thompson shot and potential own goal, and started to mount their own attacks, with Clemence saving from Moore. Just before half-time an incisive Cormack pass, forced Clemence to bring down Martin, and Moore converted the penalty.

Into the second half, Liverpool restored their control, and there was only going to be one winner. Hughes had been denied from 25 yards, but then deflected in a Smith shot to make it 3-1 after 55 minutes. Toshack had a goal disallowed, Keegan shot inches wide, and then both were also denied by Barron saves, preventing an opening day hammering.

Shankly was delighted with their first win and the Kop already had a new idol.

- The goals do not seem to be on YouTube, but are on some videos and DVDs

- Andy Beattie recommended Keegan very highly, to his ex-teammate and friend, Shankly, and scout Twentyman agreed. Newspapers reports had previously linked Keegan to Everton, Leicester City and Newcastle United.

- Peter Cormack would sign for Liverpool in July 1972.

- This match was also the debut of George Sephton as stadium announcer, a role he still occupies 50 years later.

- In a summer reshuffle, Bob Paisley was now designated assistant manager, Joe Fagan promoted to the first team coach, and Ronnie Moran took over the reserves.

- The following Friday, Manchester United beat Arsenal 3-1 in a "home" league match staged at Anfield because United had a home ban due to crowd incidents in the previous season.

Liverpool 3 Derby County 2
11/12/1971 - First Division - Anfield

Even with the addition of Keegan, goal scoring was still a worry as indifferent form culminated in a November defeat at Goodison. Shankly turned to Jack Whitham, a forgotten man, who had signed for £57,000 in April 1970 but barely played for the first team, despite scoring plenty for the reserves. He scored twice at Coventry, and kept his place in the next two wins and a draw.

Brian Clough's Derby County would provide a stiffer test, as they were in second place, two points ahead of Liverpool. Clough had assembled a dynamic blend of youth and experience with Roy McFarland, Colin Todd, Archie Gemmill and Kevin Hector

After a rousing start, Liverpool went ahead on 14 minutes; Whitham latched on to a long ball from Hall, and although his initial touch was saved by Boulton, the ball spun into the air, allowing him to head in. Liverpool were inspired, applying pressure and forcing corners, with Heighway putting one on the bar, and Smith having a good run stopped.

Clemence had to save at the feet of Durban, but was helpless after 42 minutes, as Hinton's shot was deflected over the line by O'Hare. Their parity was short-lived; Ross won the ball in midfield, and found Callaghan, he played it up to Whitham, who controlled and hit a fine strike.

He nearly scored again after the interval, beating Boulton to a cross, but his header went over. Whitham did manage to complete his hat-trick on 53 minutes, after a good passing move involving Ross, Smith, Hall and Keegan. The ball was pushed out to Heighway, and his pinpoint cross was finished by Whitham Derby were not finished, as on the hour Clemence pushed a McFarland header on to the bar, and O'Hare was on hand to stab it home.

The action flowed end to end, a Durban long shot was well saved, while Whitham, Heighway, Keegan and Callaghan went close. Despite Derby's spirit, the home win was fully merited. It was also an incredible moment for Whitham, but his revival was short-lived, and Toshack soon returned.

A storming run of twelve wins in thirteen matches, put Liverpool on the brink of a title. However, a defeat at Derby, and a goalless draw at Arsenal (including a late disallowed goal), meant more heartbreak for the young team, but joy for Derby and Clough. Shankly's second team had gone so close again, but were learning all the time, and next season would be different.

- There is a four minute colour clip of the goals on YouTube.

- Whitham would only score one further Liverpool goal, and would leave in 1974.

- Toshack would be the top scorer with 13 league goals, with Keegan on nine. Evans would only play six league games and was sold to Aston Villa in the summer.

- Gemmill, O'Hare, and McGovern would be reunited with Clough at Nottingham Forest, winning the 1977/78 league title and the European Cup twice.

Leeds United 1 Liverpool 2

30/09/1972 - First Division - Elland Road

After an encouraging start, Liverpool were top by the end of September 1972, but an away trip to serial challengers Leeds would provide the litmus test. Revie's team were only a point behind in the early table, retaining Giles, Bremner and Charlton, but now complemented by 1970s mainstays Trevor Cherry, Allan Clarke and Peter Lorimer. Liverpool had added Cormack to midfield, but with injury concerns, Boersma replaced Toshack, and Trevor Storton would make his debut, instead of Tommy Smith.

In a niggly and tense first half, fouls were plentiful, with bookings for Keegan and Giles, as Liverpool looked uncertain without the influence of captain Smith. Clemence had to save from Madeley and a curling shot from Bates. The goal on the half-hour was overdue; a Lorimer free-kick was flicked on by Clarke to Jones, who scored with a spectacular overhead kick.

It was not all one way traffic though, as Callaghan had a free-kick over the bar and Boersma went close after a good run. The equaliser came just before the interval. Liverpool's first corner was floated in by Boersma, and Lloyd's looping header evaded Harvey in goal.

The goal changed the match, as Liverpool started to take control in the second half through Cormack in the midfield, and Heighway a constant danger on the wing. However, the best chances fell to Leeds, and Clemence saved again from Giles and Lorimer. The decisive goal came from a calamitous mistake by Charlton. He fell over, gifting possession to Boersma, who went past Hunter and calmly chipped the ball over the advancing Harvey.

Leeds threw men forward to respond. but could not break the well organised Reds defence, with the impressive Storton, making several clearances, and Clemence saved from Charlton. Leeds had the ball in the net near the end, but the offside flag had already been raised for a while.

An important and psychological win at the home of their perennial rivals was recorded, and a sparkling run of form ensued.

- A forty-minute video of the ITV coverage is on YouTube.

- This was the eighth match of an eighteen match unbeaten run.

- Liverpool had not scored against Leeds in the last six encounters in all competitions.

- Only Lloyd's second goal for Liverpool, and it meant that already ten different players had scored by the end of September.

- In January 1972, Liverpool would start a run of 21 successive home league wins.

- Trevor Storton was a Leeds fan, born in Keighley, and signed from Tranmere. He would only start four more league games for Liverpool, but play 468 games for Chester, scoring in a famous giant-killing of Leeds in 1974.

- In the absence of Tommy Smith, Emlyn Hughes captained Liverpool for the first time.

Liverpool 2 Leeds United 0

23/04/1973 - First Division - Anfield

Apart from a brief blip in February, Liverpool were always top, holding off the pursuit from Arsenal and inevitably Leeds United A loss at Newcastle on the Saturday had delayed their coronation, but a win against Leeds on Easter Monday would almost certainly secure the title; a nice symmetry after Leeds claimed the title at Anfield four years earlier.

Shankly included local starlet Phil Thompson, in place of the injured Lindsay, and Hall instead of Toshack. Leeds were again fighting for multiple trophies, so were enduring their normal end of season fixture congestion. Joe Jordan and Terry Yorath came in place of the injured Mick Jones and Giles. The Anfield gates were shut at 2 pm, as the capacity crowd waited, expectantly for the end of the seven barren years.

In a thrilling and high quality match, Liverpool pressed for most of the first half, but could not break down a stubborn and well marshalled Leeds defence. Heighway and Smith were the major threats, as the Leeds goal was under intense pressure. Leeds were dangerous on the counter attack, with Lorimer going close twice, and Clemence saved well from Jordan in a three minute spell.

Liverpool renewed their assault immediately in the second half, Harvey tipping over a long range Smith shot. The defence would finally be breached by the corner; it was only cleared to Lawler, who lobbed it back into the area, Keegan headed on, and Cormack finished with a left foot half volley.

Leeds could only muster a Clarke shot, while Liverpool created several more. The match was wrapped up with five minutes remaining, Cormack crossed, Harvey mishandled, so Keegan nipped to score.

Leeds had fought bravely, given no inch, but Liverpool were the deserved victors, and now so very close to the title. Sportingly Leeds accepted their fate, and lined up to applaud Liverpool off the pitch. The mathematical confirmation arrived on the Saturday after a 0-0 draw against Leicester City, and the waiting trophy was paraded.

- There is a black and white news clip on YouTube, but colour version of the goals on DVDs.

- Bill Shankly was the first manager to win three league titles with Liverpool (although Tom Watson could claim a total of five, as he also won three with Sunderland too).

- Liverpool were top goal scorers and had the best defence in the league.

- Leeds had not lost at Anfield in their previous seven visits.

- In a major shock, Leeds would lose the FA Cup final in May to Second Division Sunderland, and also lose the final of the European Cup Winners Cup.

- The new extended Main Stand had been officially opened the month before, and helped set a new average high of over 48,000, and the cup matches meant Liverpool exceeded a one million aggregate for the first time.

- Larry Lloyd would later also win the League title, and two European Cups with Nottingham Forest.

- Liverpool reserves also won the Central League under Ronnie Moran, the first of five successive wins.

Liverpool 3 Borussia Moenchengladbach 0

10/05/1973 - UEFA Cup Final 1st leg - Anfield

After a marathon season, Liverpool had ten days to prepare for the 65th game, the first leg of the UEFA Cup final. They had already beaten the defending champions Tottenham, but Borussia Moenchengladbach would be an intriguing challenge featuring German internationals such as Berti Vogts, Günter Netzer and Jupp Heynckes. Liverpool were at full strength, with Hall preferred to Toshack, so Keegan would lead the attack.

In echoes of Inter semi-final, the league championship trophy was displayed before the kick-off, but conditions were atrocious after two hours of torrential rain. They only played a goalless 27 minutes, before the referee took the players off and soon abandoned proceedings for the day.

It was rescheduled for the following day, and as the ground had not been fully ticketed, the admission was reduced to a bargain ten pence (previously it had been sixty pence), and over 41,000 attended again. Shankly had learned from the abortive exercise, spotting Netzer playing sweeper and a vulnerability to high balls. He dropped Hall, and brought in the height of Toshack for his first start in two months.

Liverpool went straight on the attack at the Kop end, with the best opportunity for Lawler, who missed from close range. Keegan, although closely marked by Vogts, was pivotal in the early stages, and scored the opening goal after 21 minutes; a diving header after Toshack knocked down a Lawler cross. He should have made it a double 2 minutes later, but Kleff got down to save his scuffed penalty.

Borussia were struggling to cope with Toshack's aerial power, and Keegan profited from another layoff, as he struck home the second on 33 minutes. Although Borussia had been outplayed, they still posed a threat on the break, and Danner hit the post. The aerial superiority paid dividends again just after the hour, as a Keegan corner was headed home by the unmarked Lloyd.

Borussia had to come forward more to seek a precious away goal, and had a great opportunity from the penalty spot. However, Clemence's superb save denied Heynckes (he recalled watching a previous penalty on television). Borussia pressed more with no impact, and Toshack came closest, with a disallowed goal.

An exciting and dramatic match had been decided by Shankly's tactical switch. Afterwards he applauded the performance of both teams, but his despondent counterpart, Johannes Weisweiler confessed "I can't say I fancy our chances now".

Borussia tore into Liverpool in the second leg, and were 2-0 up by half-time. However, into the second half, Shankly was confident that they had blown themselves out. Liverpool saw out the match, and Tommy Smith collected Liverpool's first European trophy.

- YouTube has a six minute clip of both games.

- Liverpool were the first English team to win a double of a domestic and European trophy.

- Six Borussia and five Liverpool players would contest the European Cup final four years later.

- Despite playing 66 matches, Shankly only used 17 players, as Callaghan, Lawler and Lloyd were ever present and four others played over 60.

- Ten British clubs won European honours before Liverpool. The Fairs Cup / UEFA Cup had now been won by British teams for the last five years.

- Liverpool played four German teams in this year's UEFA Cup, two from the East and two from the West

- Borussia Moenchengladbach would win the UEFA Cup in 1975.

- Keegan claimed the bonus for the double was £2,000, but they only received £400 after supertax.

- Liverpool returned to parade both trophies and were joined by local boxer John Conteh, who had just retained the European light-heavyweight title.

Liverpool 3 Newcastle United 0

04/05/1974 - FA Cup Final - Wembley Stadium

Leeds United made a tremendous start to the 1973/74 season, so even with twenty unbeaten matches after Christmas, Liverpool could not retain their league title. However, the good form did propel them to their fifth FA Cup final.

They still had the majority of the league winning team, but the injured Lloyd had been replaced at centre-back by Phil Thompson forming a solid partnership with the new captain Hughes, while Smith, had moved to right-back, after Lawler's cartilage operation. The latter had now recovered to earn a place on the bench, but Boersma was so incensed that he walked out of the team hotel.

Newcastle United seemed supremely confident, especially their brash striker Malcolm MacDonald, who boasted in newspapers and television about his expected exploits. He had scored in every round so far, and had also recorded a hat-trick against Liverpool on his Newcastle home debut.

Liverpool were far superior in the first half, with the midfield dominant, especially Cormack, the irrepressible Keegan up front, and Thompson shackling McDonald. Keegan, Lindsay and Toshack all had chances saved. Going off at half-time, MacDonald reassured his teammate "At least we can't play as bad in the second half".

He was wrong again, as the second half was even more one-sided. Lindsay soon scored with a sweet strike, but it was harshly adjudged for offside against Keegan. A Liverpool goal was inevitable, and the breakthrough came just before the hour. Smith crossed, Hall ducked, Keegan had time to control, and fire into the corner, even though McFaul got a hand to it. BBC commentator David Coleman proclaimed "Goals pay the rent, and Keegan pays his share".

Waves of attacks continued on the Newcastle goal, with a Hughes free-kick and Heighway shot going narrowly wide. The only surprise was that it took Liverpool until 75 minutes to increase their lead. A long kick from Clemence was headed on by Toshack, and Heighway swerved around a defender and hit low into the corner.

McDonald finally had a shot, but wildly off target, earning the crowd's derision, as Liverpool played out the final minutes as an exhibition. Shankly on the bench was seen extorting the players to pass the ball about. Such a passing move resulted in the third goal, as seven players kept the demoralised Newcastle at bay. Smith injected some pace, with a one-two, and his low cross was turned in on the stretch from Keegan at the far post, as Coleman again purred "Newcastle were undressed".

One of the most one-sided Cup finals ever, the biggest winning margin in 14 years, was a fitting farewell from Shankly.

- The whole match is available on DVD.

- Newcastle's Terry McDermott and Alan Kennedy would never win the FA Cup, but both would score in and win European Cup finals with Liverpool.

- Liverpool had been held 2-2 at home by Fourth Division Doncaster Rovers in the third round, but it proved a lucky omen as they had also drawn against lowly Stockport County in 1965.

- This was not actually Shankly's last competitive match as manager, as there was still a rearranged league match with Tottenham on the following Wednesday.

- Newcastle's first Wembley defeat after winning their first five finals there.

- Two players from the 1965 FA Cup final team played, Smith and Callaghan, with Lawler also on the bench.

- This year Ian Callaghan was the first Liverpool player to win the Writers Player of the Season award.

- Left-back Roy Evans made the final of his eleven appearances in this season, but was soon offered a coaching role, at the age of 25.

- Malcolm MacDonald would be top scorer in the First Division the following season and would score twice in a 4-1 win over Liverpool.

Liverpool 11 Strømsgodset 0

17/09/1974 - European Cup Winners Cup 1st Round 1st leg - Anfield

To the shock and disbelief of his devoted fans (check out the Tony Wilson clip on YouTube), Bill Shankly retired in June 1974, and Bob Paisley reluctantly took over. Initially he was seen as the continuity option, keeping the same backroom staff and training routines, but would soon forge his own path. He learnt from the previous year's humbling European Cup exit to Red Star Belgrade, masterminded by Miljan Miljanić. They needed to be more patient, building from the back with players who were comfortable on the ball, like the former midfielders Hughes and Thompson.

Barely a month after his first match, Paisley had broken Liverpool's record victory. They even achieved it without Keegan, serving a six week suspension, and Toshack, who was recovering from a virus. The victims, Strømsgodset, were Norwegian part-timers, who had rarely played under floodlights. They had managed to hold Leeds United 1-1 in Norway last year, but it was not an attractive fixture, so less than 25,000 tuned up.

Liverpool commenced the rout after 3 minutes; Lindsay from the penalty spot after Smith had been pushed over, and Boersma slid in after 13 minutes from a Heighway cross. Phil Thompson scored the goal of the night, after 30 minutes, running 50 yards to receive a long Lindsay pass, and slotting in. There were two more goals before half-time, from Boersma and Heighway, for both of which it seems that the shell-shocked goalkeeper should have done better

It took 20 minutes of the second half before the goals flowed again; Cormack, with a rebound from a Kennedy shot, while Thompson and Hughes netted from crosses for an 8 -0 lead In the final five minutes Tommy Smith was responsible for putting the match in the record books. He smashed in a half volley from outside the area after a long Clemence punt. His low shot was deflected in by Callaghan and another of his efforts was put in by Kennedy on the rebound. Olsen missed Strømsgodset's best chance, shooting wide in the final minute.

Even though Thun in goal had made mistakes, he had also made several saves to prevent an even greater hammering. The Liverpool

Echo was pretty damning, describing the visitors as "hopeless and hapless".

The record win did not help Paisley collect any major honours that year, as they finished second in the league, just two points behind. At least he had gained the experience, and was moulding his own team.

- Liverpool record win, and in Paisley's first European match as manager.

- Nine different players scored, with Brian Hall being the only outfield exception, as Paisley joked afterwards "I have given a rocket to Brian Hall".

- The final 20 minutes were also enlivened by a black cat appearing on the pitch, and the Kop singing "Pussy for England" and "When the cat goes marching in".

- Despite adding Keegan, Liverpool only won the return leg 1-0.

- Ray Kennedy had played against Liverpool in the 1971 FA Cup final, and a key member of the Arsenal double winning team. He was signed on the day that Shankly's retirement was announced.

- 1974 was the end of an football era, as along with Shankly's retirement; Alf Ramsey was sacked by England and replaced by Don Revie from Leeds, while Bill Nicholson left Spurs. Manchester United were also relegated to the Second Division.

Liverpool 3 Manchester United 1

08/11/1975 - First Division - Anfield

Quietly Paisley undertook his own transformation, keeping the core Shankly players like Clemence, Smith, Hughes, Keegan, Toshack, but adding new full-backs Phil Neal and Joey Jones, midfielder Terry McDermott and Ray Kennedy, converted to a left midfield role.

Results were more consistent during autumn 1975, and although fifth before this match, they were only two points behind leaders Manchester United. Tommy Docherty had helped them bounce back with a young and exciting team with Jimmy Nicholl, Brian Greenwood. Steve Coppell, Lou Macari and Stuart Pearson.

The attendance was less than 50,000, probably though due to the reputation of the 6,000 visiting fans, that had necessitated the £5,000 expenditure on a separation divide at the Anfield Road end.

In a lively and fast-paced match, the action flowed end to end. Roche had to save from Toshack, Clemence from Sammy McIlroy, and Neal shot wide. Liverpool 's 12th minute lead was a gift, as Roche came for a Callaghan cross, collided with Greenhoff, spilled the ball to a grateful Heighway to tap in. United's best opportunity to reply fell to Coppell after a Macari run, but he miskicked in front of goal. Roche redeemed himself by saving well from Heighway twice.

The second half continued in a similar fashion, and it took just a minute for the home team to double their lead. Keegan beat the United offside trap, and squared to Toshack for an easy finish Clemence saved brilliantly from McIlroy, but shortly after he could not hold a Houston cross, and Coppell pounced. Both teams chased the crucial next goal with Heighway and Keegan always a threat, and it was the latter who grabbed it A Hall cross was headed on by Toshack and Keegan stooped low to head in from close range.

Clemence and Roche both made late saves, as Liverpool clinched a defining win. United may have performed well, but Liverpool were more clinical. By Christmas, they were top, as QPR and Manchester United emerged as the main rivals.

- YouTube has the six minutes of ITV highlights

- Keegan's first goal in eleven matches.

- Phil Neal, Paisley's first signing, would be a mainstay of his team, playing 365 consecutive league games from December 1974 to Sept 1983, and only missing one cup game too.

- Neal and Keegan were born six days apart in February 1951 (and Kenny Dalglish two weeks later).

- Steve Coppell was born in Liverpool, going to John Lennon's old school, Quarry Bank High School. He had been signed for Tranmere Rovers by Ron Yeats and also studied at Liverpool University; before Docherty signed him in 1975.

- Shankly had tried to sign Lou Macari in 1973 from Celtic, but he chose to join Manchester United instead.

Barcelona 0 Liverpool 1

30/03/1976 - UEFA Cup Semi-final 1st leg - Camp Nou

Liverpool were still well placed in March, as they discovered their best form, and had also progressed to the semi-final of the UEFA Cup. They would meet the mighty Barcelona for the first time, with the first leg in the intimidating 70,000 Camp Nou stadium.

Paisley now had a stable lineup, as Phil Neal had moved to left-back to allow Tommy Smith to return at right-back, and 21-year old Jimmy Case had earned a place in midfield due to his fierce tackling and powerful shooting.

Barcelona included the £920,000 Dutch pair of Johan Cruyff and Johan Neeskins, and were managed by Johannes Weisweiler, the former manager of Borussia Moenchengladbach. He was under pressure as they were well off the pace in the Spanish league, six points behind Real Madrid after losing at lowly Las Palmas at the weekend.

Liverpool, in an unusual all white away kit, didn't go to defend, and were keen to seek an early away goal. It came after 13 minutes, a long kick from Clemence was headed on by Toshack to Keegan, who quickly returned it, to allow Toshack to hold off the defender and fire in, silencing the huge arena.

Paisley's team were confident and patient, knocking the ball around, as the excellent Callaghan controlled the midfield, while the vaunted Neeskins and Cruyff were rarely seen. Barcelona could not get past the well structured backline, ably supported by the tenacious midfield, and the selfless, willing runs of Toshack and Keegan. Clemence only had to save from Marcial and Rexach

In the second half, Liverpool should have increased their lead, as both Keegan and Case had two chances each, and Smith another. Barcelona still created little, to the fury of their fans, with frequent jeers, and their cushions cascaded down in the dying minutes. Substitute Joey Jones began hurling them back until he was restrained

It was undoubtedly Liverpool's finest away European performances so far, as the Liverpool Echo gushed, "Skill and teamwork of high quality", adding "They were a credit to themselves, to their club, and the good name of English football"

Weisweiler resigned two days later, but assistant coach Laureano Ruiz could not inspire Barcelona to overhaul Liverpool's lead, as the return leg was drawn 1-1, and Liverpool reached their second UEFA Cup final in four years.

- Strangely, there only seems to be a very brief black and white film of this match on YouTube.

- Liverpool were the first English team to beat Barcelona in the Camp Nou stadium.

- John Toshack would enjoy a successful management career in Spain, with Real Madrid twice and Real Sociedad three times (including coaching a young Xabi Alonso).

- He published a book of poetry, "Gosh, It's Tosh", with a whole poem devoted to the Barcelona victory.

- The return leg saw Liverpool's biggest ever home attendance for a European night.

- Barcelona were undefeated in the league at home winning 15 out of 17, but only won three away.

- Johann Cruyff had scored in Liverpool's record European defeat, Ajax's 5-1 in 1965. He had already won the European Player of the Year three times in the 1970s.

Liverpool 3 Club Brugge 2
28/04/1976 - UEFA Cup Final 1st leg - Anfield

Liverpool's season raced to a thrilling and nail-biting climax with three matches to determine their fate. First up was the first leg of the UEFA Cup final, against Bruges. Although relatively unknown, en route to the final they had disposed of Ipswich Town, Roma, AC Milan and Hamburg. They has already won that year's Belgian league that year; and were managed by the highly regarded Austrian, Ernst Happel, who managed Feyenoord to the European Cup triumph in 1970.

With a fully fit squad, Paisley selected an attacking lineup of Keegan, Toshack, Heighway, in addition to the 19-year old striker David Fairclough, rewarded for six vital goals in the closing weeks of the season.

Any ideas that Bruges would initially defend in the away leg, were dispelled inside 12 minutes as they raced into a shock 2-0 lead. In the 5th minute, Lambert intercepted Neal's short headed back pass and looped it over the stranded Clemence. Then midfielder Cools unleashed a stunning half volley in from a Lambert header back.

Liverpool looked out of sorts, unsure with the formation, and passed poorly, barely created anything. A Keegan free-kick and a Kennedy shot saved by Jensen were the only chances of note. Bruges still looked so dangerous, especially down their left wing But like the 1973 UEFA Cup final, it was a switch of Toshack that made a difference. Paisley brought him off and put on Case. He added more stability to the midfield, protected the full-back Smith, and allowed Keegan to revert to his more familiar forward role.

Attacking the Kop, a classic European night unfolded. Liverpool were immediately more threatening as Case and Keegan both could have scored. It took until the hour mark for the changes to dramatically alter the scoreline. Heighway played a square ball, and Kennedy crashed a shot into the top corner. It only took 2 more minutes for the tie to be levelled. Keegan turned well, fed Kennedy, his shot beat the keeper, came back off the post, but Case followed up to tap into the empty net.

The Kop were now in full cry, roaring the team on, as Bruges were rocking. Three more minutes, and Bastijns brought down Heighway for a penalty. Keegan stepped up, and made it 3-2. They pressed to extend their first leg lead, but Volders cleared a stooping Keegan header off the line, and Jensen saved a Fairclough header. Bruges could also have scored near the end with Lambert and Van Gool

3-2 wasn't the ideal score, but a precious lead after the disastrous start, setting up an intriguing second leg.

- A seven-minute clip of the ITV coverage is on YouTube.

- Jimmy Case was the first substitute to score for Liverpool in a major final.

- Ticket prices were raised to £3 for the Main Stand and £1 for the Kop.

- Keegan took the important penalty, even though Phil Neal had scored with five of Liverpool's last six penalties.

- The following night, the reserve team, managed by Roy Evans, was presented with the Central League trophy, their seventh in eight years, the last two by Roy Evans.

Wolverhampton Wanderers 1 Liverpool 3

04/05/1976 - First Division - Molineux Stadium

QPR had gone back to the top of the league by winning their final match, but Liverpool's was delayed due to Wales playing a European Championship match. Liverpool had put themselves in a strong position by winning eight of their last nine league fixtures. It set up a fascinating match at Molineux, 29 years after the title decider; Liverpool knew a low scoring draw (2-2 or less) would clinch the title, but Wolves needed a win (and a favourable result in another match) to avoid relegation

A week after the dramatic Bruges first leg, Paisley brought in Toshack in place of Fairclough, and Case started in midfield. Thousands of Liverpool fans travelled, and with loyal Wolves fans keen to support their team, an estimated 7,000 fans were locked outside.

Liverpool started nervously, and Wolves led after 15 minutes; a clever ball from John Richards freed Steve Kindon who beat Clemence. It took 30 minutes for the visitors to steady, with a probing Heighway run before Toshack's shot was blocked and Kennedy forced an excellent save from Pierce. Clemence then had to make an important save from Carr, but it would be his last action, as the match descended to one way traffic.

In the second half Liverpool totally dominated and bombarded the Wolves goal. Pierce saved from Kennedy and Toshack, who also shot wide, as did Keegan. Fairclough was introduced on the hour as Liverpool sought the decisive goal. He did not directly contribute to it, but his pace always worried Wolves and created more space for Keegan and Toshack. The breakthrough came with only 15 minutes left. A Smith cross was deftly flicked on by Toshack, Keegan controlled, and stabbed under Pierce, to the delight of the travelling fans behind the goal.

The dispirited Wolves collapsed and there would only be one winner now, as Heighway, Fairclough and Kennedy all had shots saved. On the 85th minute, a Heighway cross was touched on by Kennedy, Toshack (probably offside) controlled, went one way, then back, then shot in. Many Liverpool fans ran on the pitch to celebrate, as the league win was certain now. In the final minute, Keegan fed Kennedy who rode a challenge and fired in, prompting another mass pitch invasion from the fans now camped on the touchline. The three goals in the last 15 minutes of the league season had secured Paisley's first trophy.

They had to wait (or play international football), before the return match with Bruges on 19th May. Liverpool managed a 1-1 draw, with Keegan scoring the important first half equaliser. Paisley had equalled Shankly's feat of the First Division and UEFA Cup double, and it also allowed him a shot at the European Cup.

- The only film seems to be a one-minute clip of the goals and brief dressing room celebrations from the TV news coverage.

- The front page of the programme is designed to resemble a theatre programme, with the title of "The Great First Division Drama".

- Elton John was performing a concert in Liverpool this evening, going off stage at 9.15 pm and returned with a board displaying the final score.

- Liverpool's 9th league title and they now had recorded the most. The five defeats were the fewest in Liverpool's top-flight history.

- Liverpool used 21 players in a 59 match season, with only Clemence and Neal as ever presents.

- John Toshack was top scorer with 23 goals, 16 of them in the league. His best ever goal scoring season at Liverpool, and surprising turnaround. as he had been set to join Leicester in 1974, but failed a medical.

Liverpool 5 Leicester City 1
16/10/1976 - First Division - Anfield

The pursuit of the 1977 championship was less dramatic, as the champions hit the top by September, and had opened up a three point lead in November. Paisley had sold the 1973 heroes Cormack and Hall, and broke the club record to sign striker David Johnson from Ipswich. The only future concern was that Keegan had announced he would be pursuing his career with a European club the following season. However, Leicester endured a classic performance before his departure.

The teams had met two weeks earlier at Filbert Street, and Liverpool eased to a comfortable 1-0 victory, the first of four straight wins with clean sheets in each. Liverpool were missing Johnson, Smith and McDermott, but Paisley's squad had more depth and flexibility now.

Leicester could not be underestimated, as they were in sixth place, and provided early scares as Frank Worthington shot over and Rofe's effort was tipped over. Keegan seemed to have opened the scoring after 18 minutes, but it was harshly chalked off, as Toshack was standing offside. This was compounded 2 minutes later as Worthington gave Leicester the lead, despite hints of offside too.

Liverpool harnessed any feelings of injustice, and were soon level. A Keegan free-kick, headed on by Toshack and Kennedy before Heighway finished. Keegan might have made it two, but Wallington made a fine save. It soon came anyway from a Toshack header, created by a Keegan cross. The impish striker seemed irresistible, typically buzzing around, a constant nuisance for defenders. He forced another good save by Wallington and had another effort cleared off the line just before the interval. Clemence was now quiet, but kept his concentration to save well from Weller.

Leicester started the second period better, and Neal cleared off the line, as they attempted to get back in the game. It was a forlorn hope, as Liverpool soon raised their game again, and put the game beyond their reach in the 70th minute. Neal scored from the penalty spot, after Keegan had been felled, and Jones made it 4-1 two minutes later via a deflection.

124

Case was brought down for another penalty near the end, this time Neal let Keegan take it, and he finally appeared on the scoresheet. A fitting reward after his excellent performance, instrumental in three of the goals, even though he had been a doubt beforehand because of a toe injury.

A resounding victory against a good team and even the experienced Michael Charters in the Liverpool Echo wrote "I felt privileged to be there". Leicester manager Bloomfield also conceded "I have never seen them better." Liverpool had now built up a sizeable five point lead, though Ipswich had played two less.

Could anyone stop Liverpool? How could they replace Keegan?

- Joey Jones' first Liverpool goal, and he would only score a further two more.

- Bill Shankly tried to sign Frank Worthington in 1972, but he failed a medical.

- Keegan would score 12 in the league this year, being the top scorer for the third time, despite never scoring more than 13. However, he created many more, as LFC History credits him with 18 assists for this season.

- The match was immediately before an international break, when England lost an important World Cup qualifier in Italy despite selecting Clemence, Hughes, and Keegan.

Liverpool 3 Saint-Étienne 1

16/03/1977 - European Cup Quarter-final 2nd leg - Anfield

Saint-Étienne are one of the finest and highly regarded teams to grace Anfield, but sadly for them, the Liverpool team they met were very special. French champions for the last three years, St-Étienne were very unlucky to lose the previous year's final 1-0 to Bayern Munich; the only goal they had conceded in their last eight European matches.

They had secured a slender 1-0 victory in France two weeks earlier, with a late goal from Dominique Bathenay, but would be lack of an away goal be critical? Phil Thompson was in hospital for a season-ending operation. Tommy Smith, who had decided to retire at the end of the season, now came into the centre of defence. St Étienne were missing the suspended Argentine defender Osvaldo Piazza, but still contained plenty of quality players like Gérard Janvion, Christian Lopez, Jacques Santini, Patrick Revelli and flamboyant winger Dominique Rocheteau.

The passionate French fans arrived en masse in thirty aircraft, bedecked in green and white, chanting "Allez les verts". The Liverpool supporters were equally enthusiastic with the gates closing early, as over 6,000 fans were locked outside. The Kop was packed, adorned with scarves, flags and one prominent banner hailing the emerging cult hero, left-back "Joey eats frogs legs".

Paisley preached patience, but almost immediately, St Étienne's advantage was wiped out. A short corner from Heighway was tapped to Keegan, he floated a cross (or shot) to the far post, which sailed over Ivan Curkovic and into the net. The keeper was also lucky to survive another misjudgement, as his poor punch was lobbed back over by Kennedy.

The visitors soon gathered their composure and impressed with their passing, technique and ball control. Rocheteau scored, but was offside, while Clemence (in an unusual yellow shirt) had to save quickly twice from a Synaegel header and Rocheteau, and then later Larque. At the other end, the French offside trap was effective, but still Callaghan shot over after good work from Keegan, Toshack put a free header over and Case also had a goal disallowed for a foul.

The game was delicately poised at half-time, but Étienne knew if they scored an away goal, Liverpool would require two. In the early exchanges, Clemence again saved well from Rocheteau, and Kennedy was close from a well-worked free-kick. In the 51st minute, Bathenay hit an unstoppable swerving shot from 30 yards that gave St Étienne their desired advantage. It could have been even more as Rocheteau headed wide from a corner.

Liverpool rallied in search of the two goals, and Kennedy scored 8 minutes later; a sweet left foot strike after a clever layoff from Toshack. The later also created a great chance for Keegan, but unusually he miscontrolled.

With 15 minutes left, Toshack had to leave after a kick on the heel, but it allowed the addition of Fairclough, who had earned the "supersub" tag after frequently scoring crucial late goals. Time was running out and there were few decent chances. Six minutes were left when Kennedy, in midfield lofted a speculative ball over the defence. The rapid Fairclough won the race, controlled the ball, and holding off the defenders he calmly slotted it past the keeper. Fairclough sprinted off, leaping in the air, but was brought down by his mobbing teammates, as the Kop went wild. There were still a few tense minutes as the visitors tried desperately to reply, but Liverpool held on.

As the game finished the Kop chanted, "We shall not be moved" and the European Cup was a step closer, after disposing of one of the favourites. There was also a sense of belief that the impossible treble of the European Cup, league title and FA Cup might just be possible.

- YouTube has 10 minutes of highlights from the Granada coverage with Gerald Stinstadt commentating, and also the entire match with French commentary. In 2001, the entire match was released to Liverpool Fan Club members on video.

- Fairclough scored 18 times from the bench, with three of them doubles.

- Tommy Smith had not featured in the Liverpool first team between November and February.

- Toshack's injury would prevent him from playing for the rest of the season.

- Saint-Étienne would only win one more championship in 1981 (the team included Michel Platini), and would be relegated in 1983.

- Jacques Santini would later manage Saint-Étienne, France and Tottenham (for 13 matches).

- Dominique Rocheteau would score for France in the 1978, 1982 and 1986 World Cup finals, but his career would be dogged by injuries.

- On the same evening, Borussia Moenchengladbach won away at Bruges to book a semi-final place, along with Zurich and Dynamo Kiev, who had ended Bayern Munich's three year reign. Everton also drew a League Cup final replay with Aston Villa.

Liverpool 2 Ipswich Town 1

30/04/1977 - First Division - Anfield

The Saint-Étienne match provided the spurt for the end of the season, with seven victories and three draws in a packed schedule, reaching their first European Cup final, and the FA Cup final, after another derby semi-final triumph. The unprecedented treble was still on!

Back in league action for the first time in two weeks, there was a top of the table clash against Ipswich Town. The visitors had been top, three weeks ago, but their form had deteriorated. Liverpool were now ahead of Manchester City, only on goal average, but with the cushion of a game in hand. Paul Mariner was back, but Ipswich were missing Kevin Beattie after a bonfire accident. Without Toshack, Paisley opted for Ipswich old boy Johnson, and Heighway returned after a brief injury.

Anfield was packed full again as the excited fans revelled in a remarkable season. Mariner had an early chance with a header, which Clemence tipped over, and Cooper saved McDermott's half volley. The match then became very scrappy, with too many fouls, trainers on for treatment, bookings and an unpopular referee, Mr Willis. Heighway had to leave on a stretcher after Mills' reckless challenge with his elbow. Substitute Fairclough was then booked for coming on without permission, and ten minutes of injury time were required. Mr Willis was quickly becoming a very unpopular figure, as the Kop chanted "We want a ref", and a fan ran on to even offer him a pair of glasses.

Fortunately, the second half was tamer, and more football was possible. Fairclough shot wide, and also smashed a left foot shot against the post. Wark's header glanced off the Liverpool bar. Liverpool thought they had scored after a scramble, but it was disallowed for a foul by Keegan.

The deadlock was broken in the 70th minute, with a well-worked goal. Smith intercepted the ball well in defence, came forward, passed to Case, and he ran from the halfway line. He could not fashion a shooting opportunity, so instead lifted the ball to Kennedy, who controlled and angled a shot in. Within three, minute it was two; Johnson crossed from the left, and Keegan's looping header went in.

In the closing minutes, Kennedy handled on the line, and Wark scored, once he found the penalty spot in the mud. There was still time for Willis to resume his unpopularity, as he awarded an indirect free-kick for too many steps by Clemence, but Liverpool survived. The police sensibly escorted the referee off the pitch, and not just to protect him from the fans, as Paisley had to restrain an irate Clemence.

With Manchester City losing 4-0 ("Derby 4 City 0, Hallelujah" the Kop sang), it was a pivotal moment in the title race, as Liverpool won their game in hand in midweek, and could play out three draws to retain the Championship.

- There are nine minutes of highlights on YouTube.

- John Wark played against Liverpool 27 times, but only won four times.

- Bob Paisley was the first manager to retain the First Division title in eighteen years, and this was the first Liverpool side to retain it since 1923.

- Surprisingly as champions, Liverpool only won five away matches, scoring just 15 times (even bottom place Tottenham scored more), but at home they were invincible, winning 18, and scoring 47.

- Peter Willis' controversial performance did not affect his career, as he would referee the 1982 League Cup final, and sent off the first player, in the 1985 FA Cup final.

Borussia Moenchengladbach 1 Liverpool 3

25/05/1977 - European Cup Final - Stadio Olimpico, Rome

The treble fell at Wembley, with a deflected goal on a hot day. Paisley blamed himself, as he played an extra striker, worried about the replay date of June 27th The players had to lift themselves for the midweek European Cup final in Rome, but a delay on the train back, led to a drunken party and the defeat was soon forgotten.

It would Liverpool's 62nd and final match of another epic season. Thousands of Liverpool fans descended on the Eternal City, despite the meagre 16,000 allocation. Some went on 24 chartered flights (£90 - £100), others by road and over 5000 by twelve special football trains (£59 - £72). The latter involved a particularly tortuous journey of three days, via Belgium, due to a French rail strike.

The squad flew out the day before, but opted to stay in the downtown Holiday Inn, even though it would be besieged by fans and reporters. For Paisley it was a sentimental return, as he pointed out his previous visit to Rome had been on a tank in 1944! He made one change, reversing his FA Cup mistake, bringing in the veteran midfielder Ian Callaghan instead of Johnson.

Since the last meeting, two of the Borussia players had won the World Cup (Bonhoff and Vogts), while ex-Bayern Munich Uddo Lattek had become manager. They had also added striker Allan Simonsen, the European Footballer of the Year 1977. Having won the last three Bundesliga, spy Tom Saunders rated them even better than St Étienne.

For Liverpool, Toshack broke down again in training, but Paisley had already opted to play without a target man, and utilise the pace of Keegan and Heighway. It would also be the end of an era, with the final appearances of Keegan (leaving for Europe) and Tommy Smith (retirement).

Arriving on the pitch, the players were greeted with thousands of red and white chequered flags, on a warm evening. The banner from the quarter-final stage had now been expanded "Joey ate the frogs legs, made the Swiss role and now he's munching Gladbach"

Ray Kennedy had the first shot, but it was tipped over, and Bonhoff hit the post. The prepared tactics of Keegan and Heighway dragging their markers all over the pitch, led to the first well-worked team goal (Paisley joked that Keegan had Vogts selling programmes to the crowd). Callaghan won the ball in midfield, passed to Heighway, who guided it on to a perfectly timed McDermott run into space in the centre, and he clipped the ball over the diving keeper. Liverpool looked assured for the rest of the first half, dominating the midfield, and Kieff had to save from Smith.

Borussia finally showed their threat in the second half. In the 51st minute, Simonsen seized on a loose pass by Case and flashed the ball past Clemence. The Germans were on top; a header went over from Simonsen and Clemence made a vital save rushing out when Uli Stielike was clean through.

Liverpool recovered, and Hughes won a corner from a long shot, after 64th minutes. Heighway fired in the corner, which was met by the head of Tommy Smith, and it flew in. Barry Davies exclaimed in surprise as much as excitement "Oh what a delighted scorer. It's Tommy Smith !"

Liverpool didn't rest on the lead this time. Case's free-kick was saved by Knieff, as was Heighway's cross shot. Keegan had been torturing his marker Vogts all evening. He picked the ball up in midfield, ran at the defence, and Vogts had no option but to pull him down in the area. Neal sent the goalkeeper the wrong way, sending the Liverpool bench and fans into delirium. As Davies now observed "With such simplicity, the European Cup is surely won"

All that was left was for Hughes to collect the trophy, and the players celebrated long into the night with a party. Paisley didn't drink, wanting to savour the moment, his mission accomplished. Tommy Smith, after his fairytale heroics, decided not to retire, but had a testimonial days after, and thousands lined the homecoming route from Speke Airport to the Picton library.

- The entire match is available on DVD, and 12 minute of British Movietone highlights are on YouTube.

- Match tickets cost £3, £6, £7 or £9.

- Tommy Smith's first goal since November 1974.

- The most common match programme was actually printed in Manchester. The most available Italian programme was an expensive history of the stadium.

- Bob Paisley was the first English-born manager to win the European Cup.

- Ian Callaghan was the only survivor from the first European match, thirteen years ago. Ian Callaghan and Tommy Smith played in both the first FA and European Cup victories.

- Liverpool were the tenth different team to win the European Cup.

- Reserve goalkeeper, Peter McDonnell, would collect a European Cup medal without ever playing for the first team.

- The Liverpool team consisted of nine Englishmen, one Welsh and one Irish, and bought for a total of just over £600,000.

- For more information on this European campaign, then read "Cup Kings Liverpool 1977" by Mark Platt, as it includes some wonderful colour photos.

- There was a lasting friendship between the players (Emlyn Hughes invited them for his testimonial opponents) and fans (with yearly exchange trips).

Liverpool 6 Hamburg SV 0

6/12/77 - European Super Cup Second leg - Anfield

Keegan moved to Hamburg SV in the summer for £500,00, and as a replacement in the seminal number seven shirt, Paisley opted for Kenny Dalglish from Celtic for £440,000. Keegan was due to make a quick return, as the two teams would meet in UEFA Super Cup. Liverpool managed a 1-1 draw in the first leg thanks to a Fairclough equaliser.

The return match at Anfield was not that attractive to the public, as less than 35,000 attended, and the £3 main stand tickets available at the gate. Ian Callaghan went down with flu, so Jimmy Case deputised, while Hamburg were boosted by the return of their captain Peter Nogly

Early on Liverpool were the better team, carving several good opportunities; McDermott was off target and Fairclough's effort was saved after a fine Heighway run. The deserved lead came from Thompson's shot, after a poor clearance from a corner. Hamburg's best effort was a shot from distance by Volkert. McDermott was denied again by a save, before he scored the second after 40 minutes; a well-timed run to meet Kennedy's through ball, and firing in.

Hamburg tried to rectify their position at the start of the second half, but Magath's shot was over. Their hopes were smashed within 10 minutes, as McDermott claimed a loose ball in midfield, charged forward, and blasted the ball into the roof of the Kop net. A minute later he had his hat-trick; Kennedy again threaded a ball through and the running McDermott finished with his left foot.

Hamburg collapsed as efforts rained down on their goal; Smith headed wide, Dalglish's shot was saved, Kennedy shot was blocked, but McDermott missed the rebound. Two further goals came at the end. Fairclough headed in a Case cross, and he also had a shot saved from a corner, but Dalglish netted the rebound from close range.

A match designed as a glamorous showpiece, between two of the best teams in Europe, had resulted in a one-sided procession, as the Kop teased their former hero "Keegan, Keegan, what's the score?".

- Twelve minutes of ITV highlights are on YouTube.

- Kenny Dalglish had played a trial match for the Liverpool B team in 1966, but never received any response. He also had a trial at West Ham, but then preferred to stay in his native Glasgow and sign for Celtic.

- Rademal Falcao is the only other player to score a hat-trick in the Super Cup.

- Kirkby-born Terry McDermott had only scored 10 goals before this for Liverpool, but would finish with a total of 81.

- Keegan and Hamburg would lose the 1980 European Cup final, but without Keegan, they would win the 1983 European Cup with Felix Magath's goal.

Club Brugge 0 Liverpool 1

10/05/1978 - European Cup Final - Wembley Stadium

It was always going to be difficult to follow such an incredible season. Inconsistent form allowed the newly promoted Nottingham Forest, managed by Brian Clough, to surprisingly run away in the league, and also beat Liverpool in a League Cup final replay. Form was more consistent at the tail end of the season, winning eight out of the last eleven, securing second place, and a back to back European Cup final (after beating Borussia Moenchengladbach again).

As well as Dalglish, fellow Scots Alan Hansen had joined in May 1977, and Graeme Souness in January. Thus, the spine of the team would be Scottish for the next glorious six years. Rome hero Smith was injured, while Jones, Heighway and Callaghan were all on the bench, so Hansen filled in at left-back, as Thompson, Souness, Dalglish and Fairclough all started

Bruges contained the majority of the players from the encounter two years prior, but were struggling with injuries, missing Belgium international Paul Courant and veteran striker Lambert. No one could doubt their credentials, as they had knocked out Italian champions Juventus and Spanish champions Atlético Madrid.

For the match at Wembley, Liverpool received 23,000 tickets, but the fans found many more from a variety of sources, including even going to Belgium, where they could buy ten each from the Bruges ticket office.

Possibly due to their missing stars, Bruges came to defend, with a rigid offside trap and proved difficult to break down. The match effectively resembled a training exercise of attack versus defence. Case was denied by a last-ditch tackle, Kennedy shot across the goal, Souness volleyed over, while Jensen had to save a Hansen header and Case's powerful free-kick.

The second half followed the same pattern. Dalglish just missed a cross, and Jensen blocked McDermott's low shot when he had burst through the middle. Sorenson had the only Bruges' chance in a rare foray upfield. Just after the hour mark, Paisley chose the pace and trickery of Heighway from the bench, and coincidentally they were ahead within the minute.

Dalglish's overhead ball from the byline was headed clear to Souness on edge of the area, he controlled and threaded a precise pass to Dalglish. Recalling how Jensen had gone down early to thwart McDermott, Dalglish feigned to shoot, but instead paused and then exquisitely lifted the ball over the prone Jensen, and into the net. A jubilant Dalglish ran off to celebrate in front of the Liverpool fans, hurdling an advertising hoarding on the way.

Liverpool kept attacking, but with only a one goal margin, were always susceptible to a counter attack. A short back pass by Hansen left Clemence was stranded, but Thompson managed to clear Simoen's shot off the line. It was Bruges' last chance as Liverpool then retained possession to retain the trophy.

An incredible achievement, although Happel ungraciously claimed that Liverpool were "not a patch on the team of two years ago".

- There are clips on YouTube, and a DVD of the entire match was previously available.

- Tickets ranged from £2.50 to stand, up to £10 for the prime seats.

- Liverpool were the first British team to retain the European Cup.

- Liverpool's fourth European honour in six years (five including the Super Cup).

- Dalglish's goal was his 31st of the season, which would be his best total for Liverpool.

- Ernest Happel would manage Holland to the World Cup final in the summer, and later managed Hamburg SV to the Bundesliga twice and a European Cup in triumph in 1983.

- His next encounter with Liverpool in 1991 as he managed Swarowski Tirol, when Graeme Souness was the Liverpool manager.

- This would be the last time Ian Callaghan's name would be on the Liverpool teamsheet, as he moved to Swansea in the summer, after a record 867 appearances in 19 seasons.

Liverpool 7 Tottenham Hotspur 0

02/09/1978 - First Division - Anfield

The 1978/79 team was as close to perfection as any in Liverpool's history; a watertight defence, a tough, but creative midfield and the peerless Dalglish up front. Alan Kennedy joined as a new left-back, and Souness was established in the superb midfield of Case, McDermott and Ray Kennedy.

A home win, and two convincing away, had already put Liverpool top when the newly promoted Tottenham arrived. Their £750,000 audacious capture of Argentina World Cup winners, Ossie Ardiles and Ricky Villa had captured the imagination, especially added to the talented young Glenn Hoddle and captain Steve Perryman. Ardiles had recovered from an injury inflicted by Swansea's new signing, Tommy Smith. Liverpool were unchanged for the fifth time, as Johnson was on the bench.

Spurs had the first opportunity, as Taylor beat the offside, but could not go past Clemence. A costly miss, as a procession of chances ensued at the Kop end; Dalglish shot over the bar, but then scored twice, both with elements of good fortune. The first after 8 minutes, Case's shot was going wide, but Dalglish, controlled, turned and stabbed it with his left boot. 12 minutes later, Kennedy's shot was blocked on the line, Case shot wide again (or maybe just helping it back into the area), but Dalglish was on hand to flick it in it.

Hughes went off injured, so Johnson's appearance added even more firepower, with Dalglish moving deeper and Neal at centre-back. It only took three minutes for the rejigged Liverpool to score the third and equally scrappy goal; McDermott's deep cross was headed back by Ray Kennedy and surprisingly evaded both keeper and defender.

Tottenham had their chances from an indirect free-kick in the box, but was it well defended with a block from Souness, Clemence save and Ray Kennedy clearing on the line Case hit a bending drive on target this time, but Daines was equal to it, while a Souness shot deflected and Kennedy's shot was blocked. Little had been seen of Ardiles, as he was overpowered by the Liverpool midfield, and Villa had little service.

The second half offered little respite as the cruising home team made it four within 3 minutes of the restart. Souness and Dalglish combined, the latter's shot was blocked, but Johnson followed up to fire home Another powerful Souness drive was saved, before Dalglish freed the running Johnson, who slipped the ball between Daines' legs for the fifth. He was denied a hat-trick when his header was acrobatically cleared off the line by Duncan. Heighway was then brought down, Neal's penalty was initially saved, but Daines had moved too early, so Neal made no mistake with the retake.

The best goal was reserved for last; a glorious sweeping move to crown an incredible performance. Ray Kennedy helped on a clearance from a Spurs corner, finding Dalglish, who played a ball up to Johnson on the halfway line. He immediately fired it into a wide open space for Heighway to gallop in to, and his first time cross was headed in forcibly by McDermott, who had covered a huge distance. Paisley would later describe this as the best goal he ever saw at Anfield.

A stunning result, and Tottenham would not be the last team to suffer from the power of this latest Liverpool team. Early departures in Europe and the League Cup allowed them to concentrate on the league and inflict a series of comprehensive defeats.

- The nine minute highlights from ITV are available on YouTube.

- The first time Liverpool won by seven goals in the top-flight since 1936, and it remains their largest win over Spurs.

- Graeme Souness had been in Tottenham's 1970 Youth Cup winning team, alongside Perryman, but only made one substitute appearance for the first team.

- David Johnson's goal against Everton in April 1978, made him the first player to score in a derby match for both teams (later matched by Peter Beardsley).

- Spurs manager Keith Burkinshaw, spent four years as a player at Anfield, but only made one first team appearance. He would later manage Bahrain, Sporting Lisbon and West Brom.

- Liverpool had previously beaten three World Cup winners in 1967 against West Ham's Bobby Moore, Martin Peters and Geoff Hurst.

Liverpool 2 West Bromwich Albion 1

03/02/1979 - First Division - Anfield

Despite Liverpool's excellent form, West Brom had managed to sneak a point ahead by February, because Liverpool had not played a league game since Boxing Day due to bad weather. West Brom had a thrilling young team with future England captain Bryan Robson, along with the ground-breaking trio of black stars Laurie Cunningham, Cyrille Regis, and Brendan Batson. For Liverpool, Alan Hansen kept his place in defence as Thompson was still recovering from an injury.

Anfield recorded its biggest attendance of the season so far, with gates closed just after two o'clock, as thousands flocked to see the table topping clash. The pitch was very hard due to the freezing weather, so sand was liberally applied, but both teams adapted well.

The home team started quickly, Dalglish forcing Godden into a good save, and Souness hit one effort wide. Dalglish, in excellent form, was the key to Liverpool's best chances and would open the scoring after 21 minutes. Souness found the run of McDermott in the area, and he passed for the unmarked Dalglish to slot in.

The game was being played at a frantic pace, with Liverpool dominant. Dalglish robbed Batson, but Souness could not profit. Fairclough blazed over from close range, as Liverpool's midfield tackling ensured their superiority. West Brom's only real chance came at the end of the half, with a Robson free-kick over the bar.

After the restart, Brown tested Clemence for the first time, but then it was all Liverpool again. The second goal was coming and arrived after 53 minutes. Dalglish picked the ball up deeper, played it forward in to McDermott, his one touch reached Fairclough, who shot in decisively. Liverpool were fully in control, as the excellent Alan Kennedy shot wide and Heighway hit the bar.

Hansen and Alan Kennedy received knocks, as West Brom finally managed a foothold in the match. Cunningham headed just over, and then Brown scored with a powerful header in the 70th minute. An anxious ending proceeded with Cunningham and Regis having late chances.

But Liverpool prevailed, and it was Dalglish, who rightly received the plaudits, as both the Liverpool Echo and Sunday Mirror described this as his finest performance in a red shirt so far. Back on top, they would not relinquish it again this season.

- Although this match was featured on Match of the Day, only the goals are on YouTube.

- Ally Brown's goal was the only one Liverpool conceded in eleven matches from Boxing Day until 13th March.

- Laurie Cunningham transferred to Real Madrid for £950,000 in the summer and played in the 1981 European Cup final.

- West Brom and Manchester United manager Ron Atkinson was born in Old Swan, Liverpool, as although his parents were living in the Midlands, his mother wanted him born with her family on Merseyside.

Liverpool 3 Aston Villa 0

08/05/1979 - First Division - Anfield

Liverpool were relentless after the West Brom match, losing just once in the next seventeen league fixtures. A five point gap provided the opportunity to clinch the title at the start of May, on the 40th anniversary of Bob Paisley's arrival at Anfield.

The opponents were Aston Villa, the team that inflicted that sole loss. Liverpool were unchanged, with Hansen and Thompson now the preferred centre-back partnership, and Johnson up front with Dalglish, at the expense of Heighway. Eighth-placed Aston Villa, included Liverpool-born Dennis Mortimer, Gordon Cowans and John Deehan (who scored twice against Liverpool), but missed the other strikers Andy Gray and Brian Little.

Liverpool only took 48 seconds to make their mark, Alan Kennedy deflecting a McDermott shot in after an excellent team move involving Neal, Dalglish and Souness. A series of chances followed, McDermott shot wide, Hansen ran from the halfway line, but his touch was smothered by Rimmer, Gregory cleared from McDermott, and Johnson missed from Dalglish's creation.

Despite the incessant pressure, they had to wait until 38 minutes for the second, as Dalglish latched on to Neal's header, and angled a shot between defenders and past Rimmer. Villa's only chance was a Mortimer close range shot, blocked by Clemence's chest.

Early in the second half, Dalglish missed a sitter from a McDermott cross, but soon he supplied the third. Chasing a pass to the byline, his cross could only be headed out by Gidman, and McDermott rifled into the roof of the net.

The closing minutes were a party for the Kop as they sang, "Nottingham Forest, You're not champions anymore" and "How's the party going now?" directed at Gerald Stinstadt who had declared "the party's over" after Liverpool European exit to Nottingham Forest.

There would also be a round of "Happy birthday" for Bob Paisley, as he had to be coaxed by the Kop to join the lap of honour at the end of the match. He had even requested the club's presentation marking his 40th year to be held in private.

A modest man, but he had already matched Shankly's three league titles, and was not stopping. This was surely his finest team, as the records toppled.

- There was no televised coverage, but news camera captured the goals and celebrations.

- A record breaking season for the Reds. The total of 68 points eclipsed Leeds' top-flight record. Only 16 goals conceded (and only four at Anfield) was eight less than the previous record, as Clemence kept a record 28 clean sheets.

- Liverpool won 19 and drew two at home.

- The players also claimed a bonus of £50,000 from a national newspaper for the team that hit 84 league goals, as they surpassed the total in their final match.

- Stability was the key with four ever presents in the league (Clemence, Neal, Kennedy Dalglish) and another six playing 30 or more league matches.

- Kenny Dalglish was Player of the Year, contributing 21 league goals, and plenty of assists.

- Emlyn Hughes left for Wolves in the summer, where he completed his medal collection with the missing League Cup.

Liverpool 2 Manchester United 0

26/12/1979 - First Division - Anfield

After knocking Liverpool out in an FA Cup semi-final replay in April 1979, Manchester United, now under Dave Sexton, were hoping they could depose Liverpool in the league at the turn of the new decade.

Liverpool had only added Frank McGarvey and Avi Cohen, but neither had made an impact. Early form was mixed, but after losing in the European Cup to Dynamo Tbilisi, they were unbeaten in the next fifteen matches, winning twelve, and were top of the league again by December. The lead over United was just by goal difference, but having played a game less. So the scene was set for a Boxing Day showdown, a fitting last match of the 1970s at Anfield.

Sexton had kept many of the Docherty players, but improved the foundation with Gary Bailey in goal, Gordon McQueen in defence, midfielder Ray Wilkins and striker Joe Jordan. Liverpool were unchanged as Dalglish and Thompson had shaken off injuries.

It was a wet and windy Boxing Day, but Liverpool wasted no time in putting United under intense pressure. They were boosted by an early lead after 15 minutes from a fine team goal. Clemence threw out, and possession was retained by Neal, Thompson and Souness. The ball reached Hansen on the halfway line, he glided forward, unchallenged, exchanged passes with Ray Kennedy on the edge of the box, and then finished past Bailey.

Bailey kept United in the match with several fine saves, especially from Ray Kennedy, while Nichol had to clear a Johnson header off the line. Despite repeated attacks, the second goal would not come. Even though United had created nothing, there was a mounting concern that they could steal a draw.

It took until five minutes from time before the points were safe. Neal crossed and although Johnson caught it well on the volley, Bailey should have saved, as it went straight at him. The Kop revelled in his misfortune, chanting "There's only one Gary Bailey". In fact, he came closest to scoring for United, as his long kick bounced over Clemence and off the top of the bar.

Just like West Brom the year before, the pretenders to the crown could not cope with Liverpool's midfield power, tackling and passing.

A two point gap already suggested that the new decade would see the league title remain at Anfield again.

- Jock Stein, now Scotland manager, watched the match, and had already given Alan Hansen his debut, but strangely he would only make 26 appearances, as managers often preferred Scotland based defenders. Hansen's older brother, John, also played for Scotland twice, and spent his career at Patrick Thistle.

- Although he had only scored one league goal previously, Hansen scored three in December 1979, and kept two clean sheets too.

- By winning the next two matches, Liverpool had won eight in a row, before drawing with Southampton.

- This season, Liverpool were the first team to wear a sponsored shirt, by Hitachi, but it was still not permitted in televised matches.

1980s

Liverpool 4 Aston Villa 1

03/05/1980 - First Division - Anfield

Liverpool never lost the lead, and the only distraction was a four game FA Cup semi-final marathon against Arsenal, which was finally lost to a solitary goal. Less than 48 hours later, the weary team had the consolation of trying to clinch the league again, with the same opponents as last year, Aston Villa.

The energetic Sammy Lee had replaced the injured Jimmy Case, and the Israeli Avi Cohen was deputising for the injured Alan Kennedy, making only his second league start. Aston Villa's team now had teenage striker Gary Shaw and former Ipswich winger David Geddis.

Like the previous year, Liverpool had the perfect start, a goal after three minutes. Lee crossed for Dalglish, he struggled to shoot as Rimmer was out quickly to smoother, but the ball ran to McDermott who cleverly chipped to the far post for Johnson to tap-in.

This time, Villa would not be overpowered so easily and shocked Anfield by levelling after 26 minutes, as Cohen's attempted clearance spun off his foot into the Kop goal.

Liverpool toiled as the FA Cup exertions took their toll. However, in the second half, an unlikely hero emerged, as Cohen atoned, with a right foot strike that trundled into the same net. The joyous Kop serenaded the new hero with chants of "Avi, Avi, Avi"

The result was no longer in doubt, as Liverpool regained their composure and control. 72 minutes in, Lee's ball forward, was laid off by Souness, inviting Johnson to crash his shot in off the post. Villa's misery was completed by a Blake own goal 6 minutes later, as he deflected Ray Kennedy's effort.

Fairclough and Alan Kennedy brought out the famous trophy for another customary lap of honour. Liverpool may not have been as dominant as the previous season, but they were still far superior to their rivals.

- A two-minute clip of the goals is on YouTube.

- Avi Cohen's only goal for Liverpool.

- Liverpool 12th league title, and Paisley's 4th as manager.

- David Johnson was top scorer with 27 goals (21 in the league), as he established himself in his fourth season at Anfield, while Dalglish had 23 and McDermott 16.

- Terry McDermott's performances were rewarded with both the Writers and PFA Player of the Year awards.

- Six players played 40 or more league matches, and another five played over 36. Legend has it that Paisley used his physio training to assess and purchase players, who were less susceptible to injury.

- The week before Liverpool had signed lower division youngsters, Ian Rush and Richard Money.

- After watching Liverpool twice clinch the title, Aston Villa would win the League themselves in 1981, and the European Cup in 1982.

- A second consecutive season without losing at home, and the record would extend to 85 matches before losing to Leicester City in 1981.

Liverpool 5 CSKA Sofia 1

04/03/1981 - European Cup Quarter-final 1st leg - Anfield

It felt like business as usual in autumn 1980, as just one defeat in a run of 31 games saw Liverpool top the league by Christmas. However, as injuries took hold, there was a run of six games without a win in the New Year, meaning that Cup football would be the best chance of glory. The European Cup resumed with a quarter-final encounter with crack Bulgarian champions, CSKA Sofia (teams from behind the iron curtain seemed to have more mystique in this era). They could not be taken lightly having already knocked out holders, Nottingham Forest, winning both legs too. Liverpool had a strong lineup, but Johnson was injured, so Paisley called on 33-year old Steve Heighway, who had only started two matches all season.

In an open and exciting start, Ionchev surged through, but Clemence dived at his feet. Dalglish had a smart turn and chip caught by Velinov. Hansen came charging forward, and tried a one-two with Dalglish. Although the return was blocked, Dalglish found the eager Souness, who brushed off a defender and McDermott, to shoot in.

CSKA looked vulnerable in the air, and Velinov was fortunate to survive missing a cross and a wayward punch that Dalglish inexplicably missed from six yards. Sofia's luck ran out on the stroke of half-time, as a poor header fell to Lee who rammed home hard and low.

However, Liverpool had defensive concerns too, as Djevizov went around Clemence, but then fired wildly into the Kop, and Markov shot wide too. This was partly due to an early injury to Thompson, but Paisley forcefully made them aware of their responsibilities at half-time.

Within six minutes of the restart, it was 3-0; Heighway beat two men, crossed to Souness, who cracked a splendid rising shot into the Kop net. Before the hour, Ionchev pulled one back, after a through ball split the home defence. CSKA's hopes didn't last long, as Liverpool soon regained their three goal advantage, through a McDermott half volley from the corner of the box.

Even with the excellent strikes, the best was still to come in the 80th minute; Heighway crossed, Ray Kennedy could only head it back, but

Souness raced in, and sent a stunning volley past the keeper. A memorable hat-trick for Souness, but praise was rightly showered on Heighway too, as he tormented the Bulgarian defence, in one of his final appearances.

An accomplished victory, and Liverpool would win the second leg 1-0, to set up a mouth-watering semi-final quartet of Liverpool, Real Madrid, Inter Milan and Bayern Munich, with a collective thirteen European Cups.

- A-nine minute clip of the BBC "Sportsnight" coverage is on YouTube.

- This match was played on Kenny Dalglish's 30th birthday.

- CSKA were the army team of communist Bulgaria, covering 28 sports, and had won five gold medals at the recent Moscow Olympics.

- Liverpool had beaten Alex Ferguson's Aberdeen 5-0 on aggregate in the previous round.

- Graeme Souness' second hat-trick in the European Cup this season. He and McDermott would end up as joint top scorers in this year's competition with Rummenigge on six goals apiece.

- CSKA Sofia would knock Liverpool out of the European Cup the following year.

Liverpool 2 West Ham United 1

01/04/1981 - League Cup Final replay - Villa Park

Initially, the League Cup was considered less prestigious, so Liverpool often did not take part in its early years. However, as its importance grew, they attempted to compete more, but often lost to lower division teams. Alan Kennedy seemed to have won the Wembley final in March 1981 with a 118th-minute goal, but West Ham scored a penalty with the final kick to force a replay.

Although currently in the Second Division, West Ham had experienced players like Phil Parkes in goal, Billy Bonds, and Trevor Brooking. They had even won the FA Cup the previous year, upsetting the favourites Arsenal. For the replay at Villa Park, Souness was injured, so Case came back in, but injuries to Johnson and Heighway meant just a second start for the 19-year old Ian Rush.

The West Ham goal was under severe pressure in the early minutes, with Parkes saving twice from Dalglish and another shot wide. However, West Ham scored after 9 minutes, with their first attack, Neighbour beating Hansen, and crossing for Paul Goddard to head in.

Liverpool renewed their bombardment, with a succession of near misses; Dalglish again, Lee's drive pushed around the post, Kennedy header's bounced on the top of the bar, and Rush smashed against the bar too.

It was only a matter of time, and the equaliser arrived after 25 minutes. A chipped ball from McDermott, dropped over Dalglish's shoulder, he stretched and was able to make contact, hooking it over Parkes, and nestling in the net. Within three minutes, they had turned the game around, as Dalglish's shot was deflected for a corner. Hansen rose highest to meet Case's corner, but the final touch came off Bonds.

Liverpool could not keep up the same pace in the second half, but Parkes was still busy, saving from Neal and Dalglish. West Ham provided some late scares, but Liverpool deserved the triumph for the magnificent first half display. An entertaining and good-spirited match was enjoyed by millions watching on live TV. Dalglish had experienced a difficult season, with injuries and his oppressive workload finally having an impact, but on this evening he was at his masterful best.

- The whole of the match with ITV commentary is available on YouTube.

- Liverpool's first League Cup win.

- Dalglish completed the feat of scoring in every round of this year's League Cup.

- West Ham's centre-back Alvin Martin was born in Liverpool. His son David, a goalkeeper, signed for Liverpool in 2006, making 19 appearances on the bench, but never starting a first team match.

- Ian Rush would not score in any of his seven starts in this season.

- The final was not a full house, as only 36,000 attended, probably due to the TV coverage.

Bayern Munich 1 Liverpool 1

22/04/1981 - European Cup Semi-final 2nd leg - Olympiastadion

Injuries continued to dog the European campaign, as Souness and Johnson missed the first leg of the semi-final against Bayern Munich. A dispiriting 0-0 home draw, with Paul Breitner labelling Liverpool's tactics "unintelligent", a risky move with the return match still to come. Both players returned, but there were new defensive issues with skipper Thompson and Alan Kennedy being replaced by the inexperienced Alan Irwin and Richard Money.

Even at full strength, it would have been a difficult task, visiting the 75,000 Olympic Stadium, where Bayern had won all 20 European Cup matches, apart from 1 draw, and now included the European Footballer of the Year, Karl-Heinz Rummenigge up front.

Unusually Paisley detailed Lee to undertake a man-marking role on the influential Breitner, but only notified him in the dressing room. Things started badly, with Dalglish limping off after a 5th minute foul. Paisley sprung another surprise, bringing on the unknown winger, Howard Gayle, recalling the UEFA official's surprise at his name on the teamsheet.

The visitors did not wilt under the circumstances, and in fact were posing more of a threat. Despite the crowd's racist taunts, Gayle was terrifying the Bayern defence with his pace, and should have been awarded a penalty, after a mistimed lunge by Dremmler. Munich's only real chance of the first half was when Hoeness shot over.

Into the second half, Liverpool still matched Bayern, with Breitner well shackled, and Souness outstanding in midfield. McDermott shot over, after Gayle won a free-kick from another powerful run. Irwin was surprised with a free header and Johnson beat the offside trap, but his shot was deflected over, while Hoeness headed over for Munich.

As the game approached the final quarter, the tie still delicately poised at 0-0, Paisley worried that Gayle had been booked, and might be provoked again. So he substituted the substitute. It was bad timing for the final substitution, as Johnson soon struggled with his hamstring. Paisley realised they could not survive extra time, especially as Bayern were enjoying their best spell of the match. So Kennedy was moved up front, with the hobbling Johnson pushed on the wing. An astute move, as they produced the crucial goal with 7 minutes remaining. A Clemence kick found the Johnson on the wing, he crossed to Kennedy, who chested it down and volleyed home with his right foot in one swift action.

Rummenigge managed to volley an equaliser with 3 minutes left and ensure an anxious finale as Clemence dived at Janzon's feet. Case's breakaway had the Liverpool bench on their feet, and although he didn't score, they could celebrate an incredible result seconds later.

A proud Paisley hailed the evening, as "possibly our best ever European performance" and credited Breitner for the motivation. It was not just the might of the opposition, but also the makeshift defence and losing Dalglish. Surely Liverpool's greatest away performance in Europe so far.

- The whole match is available on YouTube (with German commentary), or BBC highlights.

- Gayle had previously only played 21 minutes of first team football, Money had started only nine games (none of them in Europe), and Irwin just 36 in 2 years.

- Howard Gayle was Liverpool's first black footballer, but only started three more matches, before having a lengthy career with Birmingham City, Sunderland and Blackburn Rovers. Later he declined an MBE for his anti-racism community work.

- Ray Kennedy was born just 20 miles from Bob Paisley's birthplace, one of his key players, and Paisley wrote that he considered him the "most underrated".

- The first time, after four attempts, Liverpool had progressed after not winning a European first leg at Anfield.

- Bayern Munich's Hungarian manager Pál Csernai, would also manage Benfica, Borussia Dortmund and North Korea.

- Ray Clemence and Paul Breitner were the only players who survived from the meeting ten years earlier.

Liverpool 1 Real Madrid 0

27/05/1981 - European Cup Final - Parc des Princes , Paris

The first ever meeting of Liverpool and Real Madrid in Paris would obviously generate a huge scramble for tickets, with a measly 12,000 allocated for each club. The Liverpool fans enjoyed seeking out the stylish European clothing, while the Madrid fans wore white bowler hats accompanied by their omnipresent drummer

Real Madrid still had the most European titles with six, but none since 1966. They gambled on the fitness of Laurie Cunningham, who had not played for six months, and also included several Spanish internationals, such as José Camacho, Carlos Santillana and Juanito, along with the German Uli Stielike who had lost in the 1977 final.

Liverpool were finally at full strength for the first time since November, and Paisley ruthlessly cast aside the young Munich heroes, selecting the established Dalglish, Thompson, and Alan Kennedy, even though they had not played recently.

The first half was scrappy, with conservative tactics and some ferocious tackles flying in, especially from Madrid, as the lenient referee only made two bookings. Souness' mobility was constrained by a early foul by Stielike.

Liverpool had created the better opportunities; Alan Kennedy's shot from distance was pushed around the post, Souness shot well over, another effort was claimed at the second attempt, while Dalglish's shot on the turn lacked any power. Only Camacho's lob for Madrid had Clemence scrambling, but went wide. He would have a glorious chance at the start of the second half, when he beat the offside trap, but his chip over the advancing Clemence was off target again.

McDermott and Lee shot from distance but both were comfortably saved, as the match descended into an uneasy stalemate, and extra time loomed. A goal suddenly came with 9 minutes left. Ray Kennedy took a quick throw-in to his namesake Alan, who charged into the area, avoiding a rash swing and miss by Cortes. As Agustín edged out, expecting a cross to Johnson, Kennedy rifled a shot in at the near post, and ran off to celebrate with the fans behind the goal.

Real desperately pressed, but Liverpool had the best chances on the counter attack; Dalglish shot over and a Souness' shot was well saved. Phil Thompson collected the trophy, and the fans chanted for "Barney Rubble", confusing the foreign press, until they learnt it was Kennedy's nickname, after his resemblance to the Flinstones' character.

Even with an injury hit season, Paisley had still managed to secure another prestigious European honour.

- A DVD is available of the whole match, and highlights are on YouTube.

- Paisley was the first manager to win three European Cups, with only Zinedene Zidane and Carlo Ancelotti matching his feat later.

- Madrid's midfielder Vicente Del Bosque, later managed Real Madrid to two Champions League wins, and Spain to the World Cup and European Championship; the only manager to win all three trophies.

- Manager Vujadin Boškov would leave Madrid in 1982, but manage Sampdoria to a Serie A title and European Cup Winners Cup, but lost in another European Cup final in 1992.

- Ray Kennedy scored in both this year's League Cup and European Cup semi-finals, while Alan Kennedy scored in both finals.

- Ray Clemence's last Liverpool match, as he left for Tottenham in the summer.

- Laurie Cunningham would come on as a substitute in the 1988 FA Cup final win for Wimbledon over Liverpool. Both he and Juanito were killed in road accidents at the ages of 33 and 37 respectively.

- The fourth of six consecutive European Cup finals to finish 1-0.

- 21-year old defender Rafael Benitez left Real Madrid in 1981, after being in their Academy since 1973, but made no first team appearances. He would return as a youth and Under 19 coach, progressing to managing Castilla B (the Real Madrid reserve team).

Liverpool 4 Ipswich Town 0

06/02/1982 - First Division - Anfield

Paris would be the last hurrah for many of Paisley's first great team, as 1981 was a year of transition. Although he conveyed an image of a genial uncle with his cardigans and slippers, he was actually harder and more ruthless than Shankly. Clemence, Case, Heighway, even his beloved Ray Kennedy left, with replacements of Bruce Grobbelaar, Mark Lawrenson and Craig Johnson bought.

It was a painful transformation with the nadir, a Boxing Day reverse at home to Manchester City, saw them rooted in 12th place, eight points behind favourites Ipswich who also had a game in hand. Paisley acted decisively, making Souness captain, and the emerging younger players Ian Rush and Ronnie Whelan would be regulars. The effect was immediate, as Liverpool won eight of the next nine, and were up to fifth just two points behind Ipswich when they came to Anfield (although the visitors had played two less).

They had already inflicted a psychological defeat, winning away at Portman Road in a midweek League Cup semi-final. Could they now damage Ipswich's title hopes? Liverpool were unchanged with their new first choice team. Ipswich were missing Terry Butcher in defence, and striker Alan Brazil was sacrificed for a more defensive formation. They had built an attractive and skilful midfield of Arnold Muhren, Frans Thijssen and John Wark.

The pitch was awful, after a week of heavy rain, consisting of a patchwork of sand and muddy patches that cut up so easily. The Ipswich defensive plan failed early, as the resurgent hosts overwhelmed them. Whelan shot wide, and McDermott's runs were twice offside. Within 17 minutes, they had established a two goal lead. The first, a classy team goal; Hansen to Whelan on to Dalglish, next to Souness, and his incisive pass found for McDermott running through the centre, and finished with aplomb. Soon Whelan made a strong run forward, the return from Dalglish was blocked, but it felt kindly for Rush and his rapid low shot rattled into the far corner.

The shell-shocked Ipswich's only response came as Muhren hit the post, but Liverpool would not let up. Dalglish shot over, McDermott's effort disallowed for offside and a Rush shot deflected wide. A minute before half-time, came the deserved third. Dalglish controlled a long ball from Kennedy, his initial control bounced back off Steggles, and he promptly fired home too.

In the second half, an early Mariner shot was easily saved, before Liverpool renewed their assault. Dalglish and McDermott had shots saved, while Lee hit the post. The fourth came before the hour; Lee whipped a deep cross from the right, and Whelan timed his late run well, headed down and in. Liverpool cruised through the rest of the match. The only scare was Gates being clean through, but Lawrenson made a remarkable recovery tackle.

A comprehensive win and sign that Liverpool were on an unstoppable roll. Now up to third, and above Ipswich, the momentum had definitely changed.

- A ten minute clip from the ITV Big Match is on YouTube.

- During the match, John Wark was hit in a delicate spot, and the Kop immediately responded with "Johnny Wark" in a high pitched chant, that even made Bobby Robson smile.

- A fifth consecutive clean sheet (and just two conceded in nine) for the new goalkeeper Grobbelaar and centre-back pairing of Hansen and Lawrenson.

- The team had also responded by scoring 27 goals in nine matches since Boxing Day.

- Whelan's scored his fourth goal in consecutive matches at Anfield.

Liverpool 3 Tottenham Hotspur 1

13/03/1982 - League Cup Final - Wembley Stadium

The typically entertaining Tottenham team were sixth in the league, but their forte was the cup competitions, winning the FA Cup in 1981, and on their way to retaining it in 1982. Could Liverpool do likewise in the League Cup final?

Spurs had Ray Clemence in goal, and also included Perryman, Ardiles, Villa, and Hoddle from the 1978 mauling, joined by the potent attack of Steve Archibald and Garth Crooks. Alan Hansen had been injured midweek, so Phil Thompson came in; Paisley's first change for fourteen matches.

After an unmarked Whelan headed past the post, Spurs took an early lead; Hoddle passed to Archibald, and he held off Lawrenson to poke in. In reply, Liverpool launched a series of attacks; Clemence saved a Lee header, Rush miskicked in a good position, Souness headed wide and Lawrenson shot over.

After the interval, Grobbelaar had to save well from Hazard, while his predecessor at the other end, Clemence made an even better block from a McDermott half volley. There were also saves from Dalglish and McDermott, while Whelan had two efforts wide. Hoddle's effort could have sealed the win, but Grobbelaar did well again, and Souness cleared Archibald's rebound.

Time was running out and Paisley threw on another striker, Johnson, and urged players forward. With 4 minutes left, Whelan initiated a breakaway, Johnson's cross was half cleared, but he tried again, and this time Whelan connected, sweeping it in the far corner. Rush could have even won it in normal time, as Clemence could only parry his fierce shot up into the air.

During the break before extra time, Paisley noticed the shattered Spurs players laying prostrate, and urged his charges to remain standing. They would be the stronger team in extra time. Dalglish volleyed over and Rush hit the side netting. However, Tottenham were not completely out of it yet, as Villa shot wide, and Grobbelaar saved from Crooks.

The key goal came after 111 minutes, Rush intercepted a short pass, and freed Dalglish down the line. He paused, then picked out the incoming Whelan, who controlled, and smashed it into the roof of the net. Spurs' despairing attempts to rescue the match, left huge spaces for counter attacks. Lee claimed the ball in midfield and sent a long ball to Rush. In a two on one, he set up Johnson, who was delayed by Clemence, but he calmly returned the ball for Rush for a tap-in.

Liverpool's resilience and power had won the day again. Souness went up to collect the League Cup trophy, while Thompson collected the new sponsors' Milk Cup. The celebrations for the new era were marked by Grobbelaar walking on his hands.

- There is a twelve-minute clip on YouTube with Brian Moore's ITV commentary.

- Strangely the Sunday Mirror gave their "Man of the Match" award to Ossie Ardiles.

- Whelan was naturally right-footed, but replaced Ray Kennedy on the left when understudy Kevin Sheedy was injured too.

- Tottenham had not conceded a goal in their seven League Cup matches, until Whelan's late equaliser.

- In his first full season, Ronnie Whelan would score 14 goals.

- Tottenham's first defeat at Wembley in a major cup final.

Liverpool 3 Tottenham Hotspur 1

15/05/1982 - First Division - Anfield

Liverpool were knocked out of the European Cup in the following midweek, but responded by reeling off eleven victories from the next thirteen league fixtures to put them on the verge of an astonishing league triumph. For the second time this season, Tottenham stood in their way of a trophy. Although they may have been more focussed on the FA Cup final the following week, they were still fourth, so would be difficult opponents.

Liverpool were unchanged from a midweek match, with Lawrenson's adaptability seeing him in midfield with Thompson and Hansen paired at the back.

Spurs had to survive an early blitz of five corners in twelve minutes, the closest header over by Rush. Liverpool's finishing was letting them down; Dalglish fell on the ball, Lawrenson mishit, and Whelan shot tamely after a good run. On the 27th minute, against the run of play, Hoddle scored a soaring half volley from halfway in the Liverpool half. Dalglish volleyed over and Clemence saved from Souness to ensure a half-time lead.

The returning goalkeeper received a rapturous reception as he approached the Kop goal at the start of the second half. Soon he was picking the ball out of the net; a Lee corner was met by a looping header from Lawrenson. It seemed fitting, as Paisley had referred to him as the most consistent player of their season. Liverpool turned the game around, within another four minutes. Lawrenson's acrobatic high boot diverted a loose ball into the penalty area, where an unmarked Dalglish controlled with his right foot and stabbed it under Clemence with his left.

Lee had two chances to seal the win and title, but missed both. Whelan also went wide, and Clemence saved from Rush. The final flourish came two minutes from the end; Whelan chesting down a clearance from a long Grobbelaar kick, marched forward and smashed it in.

John Smith, as chairman of Liverpool and the Football League presented the trophy. Souness cavorted happily and casually tossed it back to a startled Whelan, as the Kop celebrated another, if unexpected, title. There was also a tribute chant for Shankly, who had died at the start of the season.

An incredible comeback since Christmas had ensured the triumph, and Bob Paisley would refer to it as the "best of the lot", the impressive feat of winning two trophies whilst in transition. The worrying concern for the rivals was this new team would only get even better.

- A five-minute clip from the LFC channel is on YouTube.

- Tottenham had not won at Anfield since 1912, and would not win there until 1985.

- Liverpool finished with only 23 professionals, as the effects of the recession bit. The average attendance slid from 44,500 to 35,000 in two years. The Anfield Road end was now seated to match the reduced demand.

- Ian Rush in his first full season was top goalscorer with 30 goals, and would be top scorer for five of the next six years. It was also the first of nine seasons when he would score over 20 goals.

- Unusually Liverpool lost more league games at home than away, and scored more away too.

- Phil Thompson became the first man to win six league titles with one club. Despite leaving in January, Ray Kennedy also qualified for his sixth too, but one with Arsenal.

- Arthur Riley retired as head groundsman after 54 years of service, and ended a family tradition, dating back to 1907.

Everton 0 Liverpool 5
06/11/1982 - First Division - Goodison Park

Only David Hodgson was added in the close season, as the clearout was completed with Johnson and McDermott departing. A significant change would be afoot, as Paisley soon announced this would be his final season in charge. Liverpool continued where they left off, and despite successive league defeats in October, they were in top spot again in November ahead of the first Merseyside derby. Everton, in Howard Kendall's second season, were scoring regularly but also conceding too many, so centre-back Glenn Keeley was signed on loan from Blackburn Rovers, making his debut in this match. Liverpool were just missing Whelan, so Johnston kept his place.

Early headers went wide from Johnston and Billy Wright, as it only took 11 minutes for the opener. Hansen intercepted, strode forward, and placed a perfectly weighted ball into the path of Rush, who slotted in. Liverpool swamped Everton, creating a series of excellent chances; Rush hit the post, Dalglish had a header saved, another disallowed for offside and also missed a sitter. Sharp's shot on the turn was Everton's sole response.

After 37 minutes, another excellent through ball from Hansen, put Dalglish clear, so Keeley resorted to pulling him back, and earned a red card. Liverpool could not immediately benefit from the numerical advantage, as Lee hit the bar and Lawrenson's header saved.

It didn't take long after the restart to put the game beyond Everton. After 51 minutes, yet another ball forward from Hansen, and Rush's deflected shot went in. Dalglish nearly scored from a Rush cross, but it was Scotsman who centred for Lawrenson to slide in the third after 55 minutes. Everton must have feared the worst, as Liverpool poured forward, Rush had a goal disallowed and a Dalglish shot was saved.

Rush clinched his hat-trick after 71 minutes; Dalglish had put him through, his first shot hit the post, but reacted first to ram the ball in. He even had time for a fourth, Lee brought the ball out of defence, and fed another ball into his run, he went around Southall to finish, celebrating in front of the delighted Liverpool fans in the Park End.

As John Motson's commentary summarised "Four for Rush, five for Liverpool, and an awful day for Everton". A nightmare on their own ground, but frankly it could have been even worse, with the disallowed goals, woodwork and saves. Everton had no answer to the balls played through midfield, and Rush the lethal recipient.

It was the start of a run of 22 wins in 24 matches, as Liverpool opened an unassailable fifteen point lead, and the league effectively already retained by February.

- A ten-minute clip of the BBC highlights is on YouTube

- The first league derby hat-trick since 1935 by Fred Howe.

- The biggest away win in a derby match for 68 years, and Liverpool's largest ever win at Goodison Park.

- Rush had not scored in his previous seven matches, but would score another hat-trick against Coventry in the following weekend.

- Liverpool now edged ahead with 45 derby wins to Everton's 44.

- Everton contained two former Liverpool players (Johnson and Sheedy) and future Liverpool player, Steve McMahon.

- Four of this Everton team would win League Championship medals three years later, but Keeley would not appear again.

- The week before, Graeme Souness and Sammy Lee had appeared in an episode of "The Boys from the Blackstuff" series written by Alan Bleasdale.

Liverpool 2 Manchester United 1
26/03/1983 - League Cup Final - Wembley Stadium

With the league effectively already in the bag, attention could turn to the cup competitions. There was a surprising FA Cup defeat at home to Brighton, and Widzew Lodz prevailed in the European Cup. However, there was another League Cup final, this time against second placed Manchester United, managed by Ron Atkinson. Their record signing, Bryan Robson was injured, but they possessed plenty of quality, with Ray Wikins, Arnold Muhren, Frank Stapleton and a 17-year old Irish striker, Norman Whiteside. Liverpool were at full strength, with Fairclough on the bench after a series of injuries.

As in the previous year, Liverpool fell behind to an early goal, as Whiteside turned Hansen and squeezed his shot in. Typically they responded with force; Whelan should have scored when Bailey could not gather a cross, but he was off-balance. Souness shot wide from a free-kick, while Bailey made excellent saves from Rush at close range and fingertips to a Kennedy drive. Coppell's shot at Grobbelaar was United's best chance.

Although Liverpool were pressing for most of the second half, they struggled to create any more clear cut chances. Alan Kennedy was always a threat though, shooting over earlier, and it was he who equalised with 17 minutes left; his shot from distance bounced over Bailey's arm.

As early time loomed, Grobbelaar had two let offs. He missed a cross, but Whiteside's header was wide. Then he recklessly rushed out of his goal to crash into McQueen, and was fortunate to escape with a yellow card. In the dying seconds, Liverpool had a three on one break, but Albiston managed to block the pass.

For the third year running, extra time was required. United were tiring and had injuries, as Paisley compared it to the final arrow in a bullfight. A classic Dalglish run and shot was saved low by Bailey. He also tried to blast a shot from distance, but it hit Macari. The ball fell to Kennedy, and he passed to Whelan. His initial attempt at a pass rebounded to him, so he curled a stunning strike with his right foot into the top corner.

In the second period, substitute Fairclough should have wrapped up the win, but shot wildly over, had another shot saved, and then yet another was an even worse miss.

They were not costly, as Liverpool claimed the League Cup again. Captain Souness instructed Paisley to collect the trophy, on his last trip to Wembley. A unique honour for a special manager

- Twelve minutes of highlights are on YouTube.

- Liverpool were the first team to win three consecutive League Cups, winning all three after coming from behind.

- Liverpool's first cup win over Manchester United since 1921.

- Tickets cost £4 to stand, and £16, £13 and £8 for seats, giving receipts of £730,000.

- To round off a successful weekend, at the PFA award on the Sunday, Dalglish won Player of the Year, Rush the Young Player prize, Paisley a special merit award, and six players were in the PFA team.

- In the third round, Liverpool had beaten Rotherham United with player-manager, Emlyn Hughes.

Manchester City 0 Liverpool 4

04/04/1983 - First Division - Maine Road

On Easter Monday, Liverpool were 16 points ahead of nearest rivals, Manchester United, as they closed in on the title. The opponents, Manchester City, were not the same force that beat Liverpool in that significant defeat, less than 18 months ago. They were now in freefall, plummeting down the table since the resignation of John Bond, but still had the experience of Paul Power, Tommy Caton, Asa Hartford and David Cross. Fairclough made a rare start as Rush was injured.

The tone was set early, as Liverpool overpowered City, as Dalglish, Kennedy and Johnston all had good chances, and Fairclough went close twice. City managed to survive until the half-hour, but Baker lost the ball, and Souness cracked a swerving shot from 25 yards, in off the post. It was two just before half-time; Sammy Lee scampered forward, laid the ball to Fairclough for a fierce left foot drive.

Goalkeeper Williams was kept busy again in the second half, with a series of saves, and the woodwork rescued City from a Fairclough shot. Finally City fought with a Hartford shot and Power headed over. It was only a brief diversion, Williams had to save from Souness, while Johnston and Whelan had shots blocked. It took until the 79th minute, before the third goal; Kennedy ran on to a through ball and finished. The one-sided encounter was completed four minutes later when Bond missed a long Grobbelaar kick, allowing Fairclough in for a low shot and his second of the match.

The league was within reach, but not mathematically assured until 30th April. The Paisley era finished with an uncharacteristic run of no wins in the last seven, losing five, but still retained the league by a margin of eleven points.

- Liverpool enjoyed visiting Maine Road at this time, as this was the fifth consecutive win, accumulating twenty goals.

- In a remarkable career, Paisley would win six league titles as manager (then only matched by Aston Villa's George Ramsay), but also he played in one title winning team and coach for another three. As manager, he also won three European Cups, three League Cups, one UEFA Cup, one European Super Cup, and six Manager of the Year awards.

- In another 60-match season, Grobbelaar, Neal and Kennedy were ever presents, and another six played more than 50 matches.

- Liverpool scored 87 league goals, their highest since 1964, with Rush (31 goals) and Dalglish (20) leading the way.

- Manchester City would be relegated at the end of this season, after losing to Luton Town on the final day of the season.

Liverpool 6 Luton Town 0

29/10/1983 - First Division - Anfield

Joe Fagan was promoted internally to the manager role, as the famous backroom and training routines continued. He added central defender Gary Gillespie and striker Michael Robinson, but could still rely on the team that had been so dominant recently. After two successive early league defeats, a Robinson hat-trick at West Ham was a welcome boost, as they had only scored twelve goals from ten league games.

Next up were the Luton Town team managed by David Pleat. After narrowly escaping relegation, they were now more stable, in fourth place and just a point behind Liverpool. They also had England under 21 striker Paul Walsh back from suspension.

Rush was a doubt due to a virus affecting his groin, but was persuaded to play by Roy Evans, despite an unconvincing fitness test. Dalglish was playing a deeper role behind Robinson and Rush, and young Scot Steve Nicol was in for the suspended Johnson in midfield

The champions struck with their first attack after 75 seconds; a Neal shot was inadvertently blocked by Rush, but he smashed it home after Lee set him up. The lead was doubled by the 5 minute mark; Souness headed against the bar, and the predator Rush followed up. Liverpool were irresistible, Rush shot wide, Souness too, while Lee hit the side netting and had a shot saved by Sealey. Rush clinched a first half hat-trick in the 36th minute, heading in a Nicol cross. Dalglish made it four, after an overwhelmed Sealey let the ball bounce over him.

Resuming after the break, there was no let up in the attacking as Nicol had a shot saved. In the 55th minute, Rush seized his fourth and best, a stunning right foot volley from a deep Kennedy cross. Luton managed to hold out for another 30 minutes; Nicol was again denied by Sealey, and Robinson shot wide. But it was Rush who finished the scoring, with his fifth, tapping in again, after Sealey had saved from Souness. Luton's only real chance was when Paul Walsh hit the bar in the last minute.

An outstanding five goal haul, in what would be Rush's most prolific season. The Guardian purred "the most gorgeous display of classy football", and even Pleat described it as "painful to watch, but beautiful". Rush attributed his luck to new boots, and his preparation of softening them with water, a superstition that he would continue.

- Rush was the first Liverpool player to score five in a league match, since John Evans in 1954, and first in the top-flight since Andy McGuigan in 1902. No one has matched since in the league, although Robbie Fowler scored five in a League Cup match.

- On the same day Tony Woodcock also scored five goals, for Arsenal away at Aston Villa.

- Luton's defender, Raddy Antic later managed Real Madrid, Atlético Madrid (three times), Barcelona, and his native Serbia.

- Six goals were shared in the previous Luton fixture at Anfield, as Luton used three players in goal.

- Dalglish's goal was his 99th league goal for Liverpool, and he reached 100 the following month at Ipswich, the first player to score a century for one team in England and Scotland.

- Les Sealey would win the FA Cup with Manchester United, but then would also concede another four in an Anfield visit in 1990, with Donaghy also on the bench.

Athletic Bilbao 0 Liverpool 1

02/11/1983 - European Cup 2nd Round 2nd leg - San Mames

Four days later, Liverpool were in Bilbao for the difficult second leg of their European Cup tie. Under manager Javier Clemente, and a policy of young Basque players, Athletic had overhauled Real Madrid on a dramatic last day to clinch the Spanish league. They had obtained a creditable 0-0 at Anfield, as Liverpool struggled to get past their well organised defence, with goalkeeper Zubizarreta, and defender Andoni Goicoechea.

A trip to the intimidating 47,500 capacity San Names stadium, known as La Catedral, was certainly a daunting proposition, as they had only lost once there in the last year. Fagan kept the same team from the weekend, again preferring Nicol over Johnston or Whelan.

As European veterans, Liverpool knew the first task was to quieten the crowd. Inevitably they would have to absorb a blistering start as Gallego and Sarabia shot over.

However, Bilbao did not make the breakthrough, as Liverpool defended well, and the midfield battled hard, especially the fearless Souness. The first aim achieved, Liverpool started coming forward more, Nicol's shot and Robinson's weak header were saved, and Dalglish went close. Bilbao were still dangerous, but an Argote header was easily saved and Noreiga's shot was deflected over.

Into the second half, the game continued to be absorbing, finely balanced, but Liverpool launched more probing attacks. Robinson put wide after Zubizarreta flapped at Nicol's cross. The all-important away goal came in the 66th minute. Hansen played a ball forward, Kennedy looked to hit the line, but then checked back and surprisingly crossed with his weaker right foot, Rush headed down and the precise header slowly crept in.

Bilbao tried to respond with Noreiga's shot wide, but Liverpool were the bigger threat on the break, Dalglish curled shot was tipped over and Rush missed a sitter.

It had been a professional and model away European performance, as even the Bilbao fans sportingly applauded the visitors off at the end.

After disposing of one of the favourites, Liverpool could concentrate on domestic matters until March. A run of one defeat in 24 fixtures saw them pursuing glory on multiple fronts.

- There are ten minutes of highlights on YouTube.

- Michael Robinson would end his playing career with two years in Spain at Osasuna, and later become the leading football TV pundit there, even voicing an ugly sister in the Spanish version of Shrek !

- Liverpool would only have narrow 1-0 victories in the next two rounds at Anfield, but again were happy with the clean sheet, as they could rely on Rush for an away goal.

- Athletic Bilbao would retain the League this season and add the Spanish Cup.

- Manager Javier Clemente was only 33 at this time (barely a year older than Dalglish or Neal), and would also manage Spain's national team for six years, and later Serbia and Libya.

- Andoni Zubizarreta would win over 100 caps for Spain.

- Nicknamed the "Butcher of Bilbao", Goicoechea could only play in these matches as his 16 match ban for injuring Diego Maradona had been reduced to eight.

Everton 0 Liverpool 1

28/03/1984 - League Cup final replay - Maine Road

The 1980s recession hit the city of Liverpool hard, with mass unemployment as Thatcher's "managed decline" was resisted by the infamous Labour City Council. But at least they had the two best football teams in the country, as Everton started a revival.

Thousands made the journey together south for the first all-Merseyside Wembley final, on a day of heavy rain. Everton had the better first half, but Liverpool improved later. The "friendly final" saw rivals fans sitting next to each other, and were united at the end in singing "Merseyside" together. The midweek replay in Manchester saw another 52,000 fans travelling again.

Kendall's Everton had been transformed with Adrian Heath and Graeme Sharp up front, while Peter Reid, Kevin Ratcliffe and Neville Southall provided a defensive shield, but Sheedy was injured in the first game. Liverpool started unchanged, with Craig Johnston preferred to Nicol, despite his unhappy reaction to substitution at Wembley.

Everton started well again, as Harper shot over and Grobbelaar saved from Reid. But Liverpool soon took control and the lead after 20 minutes. There was sustained possession with Souness, Dalglish and Johnston all involved, before Neal fizzed a ball at Souness. He later admitted he actually miscontrolled it, but the fortuitous touch, let him turn, and as it was sitting up, he glanced a left foot shot that bounced just past Southall for 1-0. The action now quickly switched from end to end, Grobbelaar had to save from Heath and Richardson's volley, while Rush unusually missed a tap in from a Dalglish pass.

Liverpool tried to kill the game off in the second half, but were denied by Southall's agility, saving from Rush and Johnston. Everton valiantly tried to avert their fate as Reid shot wide and Lawrenson superbly tackled Heath. But they were tiring, and Liverpool should have scored at least once on the break through Dalglish, Rush or Souness.

In the end, Souness' solitary goal in the 3½ hours, decided the League Cup, and as captain he collected the trophy again. However, Everton had served notice that they would be the main rivals soon, and

174

there would be more finals to come.

Fagan could briefly celebrate his first trophy as a manager, but there was plenty left to fight for in this busy season.

- The first League Cup final to be showed live and played on a Sunday.

- Liverpool's fourth consecutive League Cup win, and being the third as the Milk Cup they were entitled to keep the trophy.

- Liverpool had already played two replays in the third leg, and replays for 4th and 5th rounds, as well as a two legged 2nd round and semi-finals, meaning they would amass 13 matches in total.

- Thirty minutes of ITV highlights are on YouTube.

- Ian Rush collected the PFA player of the Year award in between the final and replay.

- Everton would win the FA Cup this year, the third successive time that the losing League Cup finalist had won the FA Cup.

- Ian Rush is still the joint top scorer for the League Cup with Geoff Hurst, as both scored 50 times.

- For more about Liverpool in the 1980s, read "There She Goes" by Simon Hughes.

Liverpool 5 Coventry City 0

07/05/1984 - First Division - Anfield

Liverpool had crammed in 23 fixtures since 1st February, losing only two, retaining the League Cup and reaching another European Cup final. The league was still a struggle with Manchester United, and despite only winning once in five, Liverpool still had a two point gap on Easter Monday, with only three games remaining. Coventry City were in 18th place, fighting relegation, but they had won the reverse fixture 4-0 in December with a Terry Gibson hat-trick.

John Wark had been added to the squad, scoring a vital goal on his debut against Watford, replacing Johnston, with Dalglish now partnering Rush, after Robinson's injury.

In a tense first half, Liverpool struggled for rhythm, with too many misplaced passes, creating scant half chances against a well drilled Coventry rearguard. There was a touch of quality 3 minutes before half-time, as Liverpool finally clicked into gear; a quick interchange of passes between Lee, Neal, Dalglish and Souness, allowed Wark to go around the goalkeeper and provide Rush with the simplest of tap-ins to an empty net. The tension relieved and Coventry's resolve broken, the second came in another two minutes, Lee and Wark again providing another close range finish for Rush.

Coventry's best attempt arrived at the start of the second half, but Allardyche's header was cleared off the line by Wark. The game was effectively over before the hour mark, as Rush claimed his hat-trick. A strong run from Lawrenson from the halfway line, set up Rush to go around Suckling, but he was brought down. He promptly got up to send him the wrong way from the penalty spot.

Liverpool were now enjoying themselves, Neal hit the post and Hansen charged forward too, swapped passes with Rush, and released a left foot drive that flew in. The Scottish defender would also start the fifth on 81 minutes, as he supplied a pass to Whelan, his cross shot to far post was diverted in by Rush, adding another to his ever growing tally. A carnival atmosphere prevailed with Grobbelaar even taking a throw-in. The biggest roar came as hundreds of pocket radios relayed the news that Ipswich had just come from behind at Old Trafford.

Manchester United's loss meant Liverpool needed just one more point, which they duly collected at Notts County on the following Saturday. Two trophies down, and still there was a European Cup final to come.

- Alan Hansen's first goal since August 1980.

- Coventry manager Bobby Gould and striker Terry Gibson, would beat Liverpool in the 1988 FA Cup final with Wimbledon.

- Liverpool were the first team to win three successive league titles since the Arsenal in the 1930s.

- Ian Rush would score 32 league goals this season, the highest Liverpool total since Gordon Hodgson in 1930-31, and the first top-flight player to hit 30 goals since 1977. His total of 47 in all competitions is still the best ever by a Liverpool player, winning him the European Golden Boot.

- The average league attendance sunk to a new low of just over 32,000, with less than 10,000 for a League Cup second leg or 12,000 for Dundalk in Europe.

- Despite the multitude of Cup matches, Fagan only used 15 players in the league, with five ever presents (Grobbelaar, Kennedy, Hansen, Lawrenson, Lee), and Neal and Rush missed a single match.

A.S. Roma 1 Liverpool 1   (2 - 4 on penalties)

30/05/1984 - European Cup Final - Stadio Olimpico, Rome

The 67th and final match of the epic season presented a unique challenge as Liverpool would have to overcome Italian champions, Roma, in their own stadium, the same Stadio Olimpico where they had triumphed in 1977. The size of the task was underlined as Roma had not lost at home all season, possessing the Brazilians Falcao and Cerezo with Italian World Cup forwards Bruno Conti and Francesco Graziani, plus top scorer Roberto Pruzzo. In their home European matches, they had scored ten and conceded none, including a bitter semi-final win over Dundee United.

Liverpool received 17,000 tickets, but scarcely sold 10,000 (so the rest were destroyed). The majority of the almost 69,000, went to Roma, fans with riots during the sale as they were desperate to experience their first triumph. The city was adorned with their flags and bunting for the imminent celebration, but the visiting Liverpool fans were not welcome.

With two free weeks, Liverpool prepared with a trip to Israel and a 4-1 victory, relaxing and drinking heavily, which even led to a brawl. A distinct contrast to Roma cloistered in an austere closed mountain training camp. However, they focussed when they returned to Melwood, even practicing penalties, which went very badly, as they lost to the youth team.

Apart from the ineligible Wark, Fagan chose from a fully fit squad, as Johnston returned, and Robinson was fit for the bench. Souness particularly revelled in the large oppressive crowds, like Bilbao and Benfica in the previous rounds. The atmosphere was fierce, as flares and a huge banner were unfurled, but Souness did not blink, leading his players past the Roma home end, and even a communal chorus of a Chris Rea song.

Audaciously, Roma tried to score directly from the kick-off, but Grobbelaar caught it easily. After some initial parrying, Liverpool took the lead inside 15 minutes. Tancredi could not gather a deep Johnson cross, spilling it, Nela panicked, smashed it against the prone keeper, and it fell invitingly for a simple Neal finish.

The early goal resulted in a surprisingly open first half. Roma attacked, but Grobbelaar saved from Grazini at the near post, while the wingers, Conti and Grazini, were troubling the Liverpool full-backs. At the other end, a Rush shot was well saved, and a Johnston effort was disallowed for offside. Pruzzo equalised with a looping header, just before half-time.

The second half would be a more conservative war of attrition. Roma started the stronger with a Falcao shot saved, but Liverpool and Souness worked their way back, retaining the ball better. Dalglish's dipping shot was saved and Nicol almost won it the dying minutes after a great Dalglish ball, but the keeper saved and Whelan could not get the rebound.

Liverpool tired in extra time, so Robinson replaced Dalglish. Roma had two good chances, Conti shot over, and Grobbelaar had to save a dipping shot, but then the game petered out to a penalty shootout; Liverpool's first in a competitive match.

Fagan was not confident, especially as they would be taken at the Roma end, but thanked the players for their efforts. and quietly advised Grobbelaar to try to distract the Roma takers.

The inexperienced Nicol elected to go first, but blasted over. Di Bartholome went straight down the middle to make it 1-0. Neal scored into the top corner, and Conti hit over, after Grobbelaar had made him wait.

Souness powered his penalty into the top corner, and Righetti sent Grobbelaar the wrong way to make it 2-2. Rush with his right foot, put it low and bobbling into the same corner. Grobbelaar was now bending and wobbling on the line, and Graziani grazed the top of the woodwork. Alan Kennedy stepped up, and with a controlled sidefoot, won the European Cup.

An amazing achievement in the home of Roma, that finished an incredible season. The Roma fans rioted, with multiples injuries, and Liverpool fans were targeted. The players celebrated long in the night in the Roman hills, and the next day, 500,000 attended their homecoming parade of three trophies from Joe Fagan's first season.

- The entire match is available on the Champions of Europe DVD, but eight minutes of clips are also available on YouTube.

- Liverpool's fourth European Cup in eight years, and then only Real Madrid had more with six.

- The majority of Liverpool's tickets cost £3.50 for standing, with a one day flight tour costing £193 with Towns Travel or £113 on the train.

- The first European Cup final to be decided on penalties (the only previous draw after extra time had gone to a replay in 1974).

- Graeme Souness' last action as captain was to lift the European Cup, before he departed for Sampdoria in the summer.

- Roma captain Di Bartholome, also moved in the summer, but his career faltered, and he suffered from depression, shooting himself dead on the 10th anniversary of this match.

- Phil Neal was the only player from the 1977 Rome triumph, the only Liverpool player to score in two European Cup finals, and still the only Englishman with four winners' medals.

- Four players featured in all 67 matches (Grobbelaar, Hansen, Kennedy and Lee) with four more playing over 60.

- Read more about this season in "I Don't Know What It is, but I love it" by Tony Evan, which includes several new interviews.

- As a player, Roma manager Nils Liedholm had won four Serie A with AC Milan in the 1950s, and managed them to the Serie A title in 1978-79, and then Roma in 1982-83. He also scored in the 1958 World Cup final, and voted Best Swedish player of all time in a newspaper poll.

Liverpool 7 York City 0

20/02/1985 - FA Cup 5th Round replay - Anfield

It would be impossible for Fagan to repeat the previous season's glories, as Liverpool struggled, missing the influence of Souness, and the goals from Rush (injured for the first fourteen matches). Everton's win at Anfield in October saw Liverpool in 17th and they finally lost hold of the League Cup. However, results soon picked up, and there was still Europe and the FA Cup to contest.

In the earlier rounds, Liverpool had beaten Spurs and Aston Villa, but had been held to a 1-1 draw against York City, due to Sbragia's late equaliser on an icy pitch.

Recent signing Kevin McDonald had replaced Souness, and summer signing Paul Walsh was on the bench, instead of the other new signing Jan Molby. York's leading scorer Keith Houchen was back for York, and had scored against Arsenal in the previous round. They had also kept several recent clean sheets, so their 8,000 fans arrived in high spirits.

Liverpool did not create anything for the first 15 minutes, but then Dalglish released Wark and his cross was finished by Whelan at close range. Before the half-hour, it was two; Neal played into the box, Wark played a one-two with Rush, and fired in. Rush also had a chance cleared off the line after going around the keeper.

In the second half, Liverpool cut loose, as York tired. Whelan made it three after a short corner involving Neal and Nicol. Another 3 minutes and Wark notched his second, a free header from a Dalglish cross. Rush limped off at the hour, but Walsh was equally threatening too, his cross being turned in by Neal on 71 minutes.

Wark completed his hat-trick 6 minutes later, a rebound after Walsh's shot had been blocked. Liverpool were reduced to ten men, as Hansen went off injured too. Walsh still added the seventh near the end, with the best of the night, a cracking volley from a Nicol cross. A hat-trick for Wark, but Dalglish was the star. He had been dropped for the first time in September, but still had so much to offer.

The continued improvement saw Liverpool finish second in the league, but they lost an FA Cup semi-final to Manchester United. The

European Cup final was also 1-0 to Juventus, but overshadowed by a charge from the Liverpool fans, leading to the deaths of 45 people in the dilapidated Heysel stadium. It led to a European ban for English teams, and ruined the previously good reputation of the Liverpool fans.

Fagan had already announced his retirement, so it would be a tragic and heart-breaking end for such a dignified gentleman.

- Dalglish's 750th career game, and he had collected an MBE the previous day.

- Phil Neal's 34th birthday.

- This was the sixth in a run of eight straight home wins in all competitions.

- Liverpool's biggest FA Cup win since 1892.

- Keith Houchen would score and win the 1987 FA Cup with Coventry City.

- John Wark would be top scorer with 27 goals, including hat-tricks in the European Cup, FA Cup and First Division.

Everton 2 Liverpool 3

21/09/1985 - First Division - Goodison Park

New player-manager Kenny Dalglish faced some daunting challenges succeeding Fagan, the first trophy-less season after nine glorious years, a European ban, and the rise of Everton. No one even knew if he could be a manager? Could he combine the role with playing too?

He had the wily counsel of Bob Paisley and Tom Saunders, but was also his own man, and soon asserted his authority. Hansen would be captain, while Beglin and Nicol would be first choice full-backs (dispensing with the European legends Neal and Kennedy). Steve McMahon added more bite in midfield, with Molby given a chance too and the prodigal Craig Johnston returned. Dalglish also pioneered lengthier pre-match warm-ups on the pitch and was keen to experiment with different team formations and tactics.

The first key test would be away to the champions Everton. They had strengthened by adding Gary Lineker, relegating Heath to the bench, but Reid and Mountfield were missing, so Harper and Marshall deputised Liverpool were at full strength, with no place for Walsh, Lee or McDonald, but Dalglish sprung a surprise with Molby playing in a sweeper role.

On a rainy afternoon, Everton kicked off, but their initial probing ball was shepherded back to Grobbelaar, who rolled it out to Nicol. His long ball was controlled by Rush, and laid back to Dalglish, who unleashed an unerring shot from outside the box, that flew past Southall. A stunning opening goal in just 21 seconds. It was only the prelude to a thrilling end to end encounter. Lineker almost replied immediately, but Grobbelaar saved and Southall saved from a Molby free-kick.

On 16 minutes, Whelan intercepted a pass, broke away, and supplied Rush a tap-in for a two goal advantage. A strong run down the wing by Johnston, nearly found Rush, Marshall cannoned the ball against Southall, but Liverpool could not profit from the rebound. Sheedy curled a free-kick around the wall, but Grobbelaar tipped it wide. Just before half-time, it was three; Dalglish held off a strong challenge, to find McMahon, and his low shot from outside the area, crept in.

At half-time Everton swapped defender Marshall for Heath, and a more offensive lineup to rescue the game. Liverpool still had early chances, Dalglish wide after a twisting run, and Rush was offside for another. But Everton's were swarming forward, and Sharp soon pulled one back. Grobbelaar also saved from Heath, while Lineker shot over from close range. Liverpool were keen to exploit any gaps on the break, Southall saved when Rush was clean through, and a McMahon volley was blocked.

The tension was heightened even more as Lineker made it 3-2 with 6 minutes left. Dalglish inexplicably chipped over the bar with Southall on the ground, and then compounded it by missing another simple chance. However, Liverpool held on to win one of the most exciting derby matches ever.

The newspapers were united in heralding a fantastic match, as veteran reporter John Keith described it as the best derby he had covered in over 30 years, and even the watching England manager Bobby Robson stated it was the "best match he had seen in 35 years as a player and manager".

- There was a dispute with the English TV companies at the time, but a ten-minute clip from the European coverage is on YouTube.

- Steve McMahon scored on his Liverpool league debut, against his former team.

- Both teams would be chasing Manchester United, who won their first ten league games this season.

- The Denmark international Jan Molby had been signed from Ajax, where he had played with Marco van Basten, Frank Rijkaard, Ronald Koeman, Jesper Olsen, and the 35-year old Johann Cruyff.

Liverpool 4 Queens Park Rangers 1

08/03/1986 - First Division - Anfield

Questions were being asked by March, as Liverpool lost 2-0 at home to Everton and in midweek Queens Park Rangers had knocked them out of the League Cup. Even Alan Hansen privately informed Dalglish that this was the worst Liverpool team he had played in. A return visit by QPR in the league on Saturday at least provided the opportunity to reduce the five point gap to Everton at the top, as they were in FA Cup action.

Dalglish had seemed reluctant to play himself, but chose this day to return, with Wark coming in too. The QPR team featured the familiar face of Michael Robinson.

The mood was not optimistic, as less than 27,000 turned up, and the atmosphere deepened further after a poor start, as Robinson crossed for Rosenior to score. Liverpool battled hard to reply, with McMahon and Lee going close. They were level after 19 minutes; Molby passed to McMahon, he played a one-two with Whelan, and then finished well. By the half-hour Liverpool were deservedly ahead, as Dalglish split the defence with a trademark through ball that Rush delighted in driving home.

Liverpool were dominating and the previous tensions or bad mood disappeared. Dalglish set up Rush again, but it was disallowed by an offside flag, and Barron stopped a McMahon shot. QPR's sole response was a blocked Robinson effort. Just before half-time, Dalglish created another, his ball into the run of Wark, who made no mistake for 3-1.

The succession of chances continued in the second half; Lawrenson headed over, and Rush, relishing Dalglish's return, was only denied by a flag again. Beglin also had a shot saved at the second attempt, while Wark fired over, and Dalglish released McMahon, but his shot was saved.

Dalglish nearly blotted his excellent return, with a short back pass, but Robinson could not capitalise. The final goal came in the 75th minute, with McMahon meeting a Beglin cross, but it should have been more as Rush, Dalglish, and Whelan all went close too in the final minutes.

Liverpool had found their best form again, primarily due to the vision, creativity and inspiration of the player-manager. He now realised that he had to play in the remaining games to maximise Liverpool's chances. The win moved them into second, above the fading Manchester United, so it would be a Merseyside tussle for the title.

- Dalglish first league start since 1st January. He had celebrated his 35th birthday, four days earlier.

- Liverpool's midweek 2-2 draw with QPR, had seen two own goals from Whelan and Gillespie, and Molby had a penalty saved. QPR would lose the final to Oxford United with John Aldridge scoring.

- Rush was rediscovering his goal touch, after not scoring in December or February.

- For more on this season, read "On the March with Kenny's Army" by Gary Shaw and Mark Platt.

Chelsea 0 Liverpool 1

03/05/1986 - First Division - Stamford Bridge

Dalglish galvanised Liverpool to a storming run of ten out of eleven wins in the league, smashing in 31 goals with just four in reply. Everton had matched Liverpool all the way, but midweek had been pivotal, as Liverpool had won at Leicester, while Everton lost at Oxford. This meant Liverpool could win the league, if they won their last fixture at Chelsea.

Over 10,000 Liverpool fans made the trip to the intimidating venue, where they had such a poor record, but with high hopes after the recent exceptional form. Molby failed a fitness test, so Lawrenson came into a back five again. McDonald held on to his place, even though McMahon was fit again. Chelsea had earlier been in title contention, with their powerful front line of Kerry Dixon, Pat Nevin and David Speedie.

In the early minutes, Liverpool struggled to get out of their own half, as Chelsea asserted pressure, but could not create. Finally, Spackman slipped, letting McDonald shoot, but Godden saved. Liverpool started to take control with a Nicol shot blocked and Johnston effort saved.

The pressure was even more insistent, half way through the first half. After forcing another corner, Gillespie won in the air, and Beglin's fierce shot was cleared off the line by Jones. From the throw-in Whelan's header was flicked on by Beglin, putting through the unmarked Dalglish, and he scored with a cushioned volley. He ran off to celebrate, his arms wide aloft and a broad smile, in front of the travelling Liverpool fans. Chelsea pressed, but could create little again, and Liverpool were closest with Johnston twice.

In the second half, Chelsea tried again, but Liverpool's hard working defence was too well organised. The visitors looked more likely on the counter attack, but Dalglish's chip was too hard and Rush was offside. The tension rose for the final 10 minutes, as Chelsea took off a left-back, and threw on another striker. The action became more frenetic, with each ball contested keenly. They finally created chances, but Speedie and McAllister were both wide, and Grobbelaar relieved the nerves by calmly collecting two crosses.

After the final whistle, intense celebrations ensued, with group photos and thanks to the fans. An incredible run, with Dalglish as a player and manager, had put Liverpool back as champions in his first season. And there was still an FA Cup final to come.

- There are 28 minutes of highlights of the match and celebrations from Match of Day on YouTube.

- The 89 league goals was Liverpool's highest for 22 years.

- The league trophy was presented before the Screen Sport cup semi-final against Norwich on the following Tuesday.

- Liverpool's first league win at Stamford Bridge for twelve years.

- The team coach returning from the match broke down, so the operators sent the empty Everton coach that was nearby.

- Kenny Dalglish is the only person to win the league as a player-manager

- Although Neal had left earlier in the season, he still qualified for an eighth league title medal.

- Craig Johnston's wife gave birth to their second child on the Thursday. The first was named Chelsea, a coincidence, as he was linked to them at that time.

- Nigel Spackman and David Speedie would both later join Liverpool.

Everton 1 Liverpool 3

10/05/1986 - FA Cup Final - Wembley Stadium

A week after the league triumph, came the chance of the double, and again Everton were the rivals. In a busy week, both teams had played, Dalglish had collected the Manager of the Year, Gary Lineker had won the Writers Player of the Year, and Hansen had been left out of the Scottish World Cup squad by Alex Ferguson. Thousands made the journey together from Merseyside again, and with such a huge demand for tickets, some fans resorted to unconventional approaches; one was spotted on the roof and others precariously swung through an opening.

Gary Gillespie missed out due to a virus, so Molby returned in a midfield role. For Everton, Mimms was in goal, as Southall had crucially missed the run-in through injury. This was Liverpool's first FA Cup final in nine years, but Everton's third consecutive.

The opening exchanges were shared, McDonald could not reach a Nicol ball and Grobbelaar cleared a through ball for Lineker. The latter was also superbly tackled by Lawrenson, and Rush headed over. Just before the half-hour, Dalglish misplaced a pass, and Reid sent a long ball for Lineker to chase, Grobbelaar saved his initial effort, but he forced home the rebound.

Everton then looked comfortable and were on top for the next thirty minutes. Steven shot past the near post, and Sheedy too after a defensive mix up, and also had a free-kick tipped wide. Liverpool were out of sorts and unsettled, as Grobbelaar clashed with Beglin. Dalglish shot wildly over after a quickly taken free-kick.

Prospects looked bleak, but changed in an instant. A loose pass by Stevens was intercepted by Whelan, a quick ball to Molby, his precise ball through the legs, allowed Rush to run on to it, round Mimms and put into the empty net. Everton had the next big chance, a looping Sharp header, tipped acrobatically over by Grobbelaar. But the tide had turned, with Molby now dominant in midfield and on 63rd minutes, he created the second goal. Beglin played a long ball, Rush controlled and fed Molby in the box, his rifled cross reached the unmarked Johnson at the far post for a tap-in. Liverpool had turned it around in five minutes, and were suddenly transformed.

Everton switched Heath for Stevens, in a desperate attempt to regain the initiative, but were more vulnerable to a counter attack. Molby waltzed through, but went for power, and Mimms saved with his legs. The third was coming, and it came with a devastating team break on 84 minutes. Whelan regained the ball outside his own box, a flighted ball to Johnston was headed on, Rush controlled, and played to Molby, his quick pass left Whelan in acres of space to power forward. As he approached the area, Dalglish made a run across to the left, but instead, he floated a ball to Rush, who controlled, and shot on the half volley, arrowing into the corner, knocking over a camera.

In the final minutes, Rush had a chance of a hat-trick, with a one on one, but misjudged his chip. The Liverpool fans celebrated as Hansen collected the FA Cup. Not only had they done the double for the first time, but both were at the expense of their local rivals.

- The entire match is available on DVD, and highlights from both BBC and ITV are on YouTube.

- The Liverpool starting eleven only had one player born in England, Mark Lawrenson, and even he played for the Republic of Ireland.

- Liverpool were the third team to win the double in the 20th century, after Tottenham in 1961 and Arsenal in 1971.

- Kenny Dalglish was the first player-manager to win the FA Cup since John Cameron in 1901.

- Ian Rush was the first Welshman to score in the FA Cup final since Noel Kinsey in 1956.

- Gary Lineker scored 40 goals this season, and made a summer transfer to Barcelona. Rush scored 33, was signed by Juventus for £3.2 million. but immediately loaned backed for one further season.

- In addition to Rush, Jan Molby also scored 21 goals (ten penalties), while Walsh, Whelan, McMahon and Johnston, all reached double figures.

- Liverpool never lost when Rush scored in his first 144 matches, but the run came to an end when he scored first, but Arsenal won the 1987 League Cup final.

Newcastle United 1 Liverpool 4

20/09/1987 - First Division - St James Park

Neutrals and writers had respected and even admired Liverpool, but never really loved them. Despite the attractions of Keegan, Heighway, Dalglish, or Rush, they were considered too clinical or pragmatic, or maybe just too successful. This changed in 1987, and the date can be pinned down as accurately as Sunday 20th September, when millions watched the BBC live coverage of a devastating performance.

Dalglish spent the money from the Rush sale wisely, building a thrilling attacking axis of John Barnes, Peter Beardsley, and John Aldridge, that gelled instantly. Like the departure of Keegan, Liverpool had responded to a mortal threat, with something even better.

Their start was stalled by repairs to the Kop, but they won four of the first five, and were already third with two games in hand. Whelan had moved into the centre of midfield to accommodate Barnes, Barry Venison was right-back, so Nicol moved into midfield. Lawrenson started his first match since March.

The BBC had chosen this attractive fixture, as it had Beardsley's return to Newcastle, but also the home debut of Miradinha, the first Brazilian to play in the First Division. He had scored twice at Old Trafford on his debut, so local excitement was at fever pitch.

After initial probing, Liverpool took the lead after 20 minutes; Barnes running from the halfway line, exchanging an effective one-two with Beardsley. His cross was poorly cleared, so Nicol's left boot finished decisively. Nicol nearly had his second with a looping head tipped over. From the resulting corner, Aldridge headed in, but adjudged to have fouled. He only had to wait another minute, as a long cross-field Venison ball was headed down by Barnes, and Aldridge nipped in front of his marker to score. Nicol also scored again with a beautiful chipped shot, but ruled out again, this time for an interfering offside. Little had been seen of Newcastle's attack or Miradinha.

The third came just after the interval; Lawrenson released Beardsley to beat the offside trap, running in, he unselfishly gave Nicol a tap-in for his second. The heralded Miradinha finally appeared, winning a penalty that McDonald converted. Any hopes of a comeback did not last long, Nicol's powerful run was finished by a delicate chip over Kelly for his hat-trick.

A commendable achievement from Nicol, but also a fluent and stunning team performance that was widely praised by the media. A warning message had been issued for the rest of the division, as Liverpool's autumn would be a succession of thrilling one-sided displays.

- Both the entire match and highlights are available on YouTube.

- The transfer of Peter Beardsley at £1.9 million broke the British transfer record, but was only Liverpool's first transfer over £1million, almost ten years after the league's first.

- John Barnes was born in Jamaica, but moved to Britain when he was 12, and played over 200 times for Watford. He was best remembered for scoring a fine solo goal for England at Brazil's Maracanã Stadium.

- By the end of September, Nicol was the top scorer with seven goals in seven games, but would not score again for the rest of the season as he reverted to full-back.

- John Aldridge would score in each of his first eleven league starts for Liverpool.

- A year later Miradinha scored a late winner from the penalty spot, in a 2-1 win at Anfield.

Liverpool 2 Arsenal 0

16/01/1988 - First Division - Anfield

After Christmas, Liverpool had amassed a lead of thirteen points, having been unbeaten in the first 22 league matches. The next challengers were third-placed Arsenal, a young developing team led by George Graham. They had beaten Liverpool in the League Cup final the previous year, and included John Lukic, Nigel Winterburn, Tony Adams, David Rocastle, and Alan Smith, with Michael Thomas on the bench.

For Liverpool, Ray Houghton had signed in October, dislodging Johnston, while Mike Hooper was in for the injured Grobbelaar. A full house was customary now as everyone wanted to see this special team, and were supplemented by a live worldwide TV audience of an estimated 250 million.

Liverpool struggled to break down a stubborn Arsenal defence in the first half, lacking their usual rhythm and incisiveness. There were still several chances though; McMahon's shot was deflected, a Barnes free-kick went over, McMahon miscontrolled in a good position and a Beardsley shot was saved. Arsenal threatened little, as McMahon still controlled the midfield, while Richardson's shot and Adams' volley were both off target.

The defence cracked just before half-time; Barnes got to the byline for a pullback, Aldridge could not connect, and McMahon's shot was blocked. He then scampered after the clearance, keeping it in play, then evaded a challenge. He supplied Beardsley, and his cross shot was put in by Aldridge at full stretch, in front of a delighted Kop.

Within seconds of the second half, Hansen cleared off the line from Rocastle, but then Liverpool reasserted their control. Lukic had to save spectacularly from Beardsley and then Aldridge. Beardsley would not be denied, receiving a flick from Aldridge, he dribbled into the Arsenal area, nutmegged substitute Thomas, and dinked sublimely over the advancing Lukic. Quinn later hit the post, but Liverpool were comfortable winners, extending their lead now to 15 points.

Beardsley may have been initially overshadowed by Barnes, but now was showing his true worth. Afterwards, working as a TV pundit, Michel Platini was effusive, wishing he could play in this team, while a wry Dalglish responded "If I can't get into the side, then nor will he".

- The match was on Match of the Day, so short and longer highlights are on YouTube.

- Mark Lawrenson went off injured, and it would be his last appearance, as he was forced to retire later in the season.

- Peter Beardsley would celebrate his 27th birthday two days later. After scoring four in his first four months, he would score six goals in January.

- This came in the middle of a run of ten consecutive clean sheets, with no goal conceded in 994 minutes.

- Liverpool equalled Leeds' record of 29 unbeaten matches from the start of the season, but then lost at Everton.

Liverpool 5 Nottingham Forest 0
13/04/1988 - First Division - Anfield

April saw a trilogy of matches against Nottingham Forest, still managed by Brian Clough, with England internationals Stuart Pearce and Des Walker in defence, Neil Webb in midfield, and his son Nigel in attack. Forest won the league match at the City Ground, but Liverpool won an FA Cup semi-final at Hillsborough. For the league meeting at Anfield on Wednesday, Ablett was at left-back, and Nigel Spackman had replaced the injured Whelan.

A busy night for Steve Sutton in goal started early, as he had to save low from Barnes and tip over from Nicol. After 18 minutes, Hansen intercepted, forwarding to Beardsley, he released Houghton, who ran at the Forest defence, and after a one-two with Barnes slotted past Sutton. Liverpool were relentless with waves of attacks; McMahon's shot was well saved, Barnes clipped the post with the rebound, Sutton saved from Barnes too, and Beardsley fired over the bar.

It was only a matter of time for the second goal and it came after 37 minutes; Barnes won the ball deep, found Beardsley, his long defence splitting pass was finished by Aldridge coolly lifting the ball over the advancing Sutton. Beardsley tormented the Forest defence all night, and one mazy run ended with a fierce rising shot tipped on to the bar, while Sutton also saved from Houghton after an inventive free-kick, and Pearce had to make a last ditch challenge on Aldridge.

Forest were weakened by the loss of Walker at half-time, but in this mood, the home team showed scant mercy. Beardsley's fierce shot was saved at point blank range. The third came arrived before the hour mark; Gillespie firing into the roof of the net, after a well worked short corner. Hansen should have scored too, but opted to pass when in a good position. Beardsley got his deserved goal after 79 minutes, thanks for the efforts of Barnes, who nutmegged a defender, glided past another, and pulled back for Beardsley to fire low into the corner The fifth came at the end, after Spackman won possession, he raced forward to reach the return ball from Beardsley and provided Aldridge with a tap-in.

A sumptuous dazzling team performance of pace, skill and desire had the writers showering compliments and accolades. On the BBC, the great Tom Finney purred "It was the finest exhibition I've seen the whole time I've played and watched the game". It was definitely one of the finest performances at Anfield and a high watermark for this special team.

The title would be secured two matches later, but Wimbledon denied Dalglish another double with a shock 1-0 win in the FA Cup final. A disappointing end, but still an exceptional and intoxicating season

- The whole match was released on video at the time, and now clips are on YouTube.

- Aldridge had scored five goals in ten days against Nottingham Forest.

- The league defeat to Forest was Liverpool's second and last league loss of the season, a new club top-flight record.

- John Barnes collected his PFA Footballer of the Year award on the Sunday, with McMahon and Hansen completing the top three.

- John Aldridge scored 26 league goals, the highest in the league.

- Liverpool's 17th league title.

- This was the last of seven years, when the First Division trophy stayed on Merseyside, with Liverpool contributing five wins, and Everton two.

Liverpool 5 Sheffield Wednesday 1

8/04/1989 - First Division - Anfield

In the summer, Rush returned, adding even more firepower to Liverpool's frontline. However, injuries, especially at centre-back, Molby's prison sentence and Grobbelaar illness saw Liverpool struggle to fifth place after a New Year's Day reverse to Manchester United. In typical style, they were revived with an unbeaten run of fifteen and nine straight wins before Sheffield Wednesday visited for an 11.30 am kick-off, due to the Grand National in the afternoon.

The Liverpool defence had Ablett and Gillespie at centre-back, with Aldridge still the main striker, as Rush battled a series of injuries. They had also been hindered by an unnecessary distraction of a midweek trip to Dubai to play Celtic. Wednesday, managed by Ron Atkinson since February, were in the bottom half of the table, but could call on the talents of Carlton Palmer and David Hirst.

The visitors had the two earliest opportunities; Dean Barrick passed when he should have shot and Hirst also shot wide. They were costly mistakes, as Liverpool were ahead inside 10 minutes; McMahon with a rasping drive from distance that went in off the post. The score was kept at one, due to a series of fine saves from Chris Turner, while Aldridge missed from very close range, and Beardsley fell over after rounding the keeper. The second finally came just before half-time, as Barnes charged down a defender, beat two men, and executed a magical turn. His shot was blocked, but Beardsley drilled in the rebound.

Beardsley would also assist the third goal after 57 minutes, another strike from distance, this time Houghton firing in. Wednesday could only watch as Liverpool were in full flow. Beardsley grabbed his second with a left foot strike, 8 minutes later, after Aldridge headed down. Dean Barrick pulled one back for Wednesday soon after, another strike from distance, and then Hirst hit the post, as the defence struggled without Gillespie, who had gone off injured. Normal service was resumed, as Turner again denied Aldridge and McMahon twice. Barnes restored the four goal margin in the 80th minute, after Beardsley and Houghton's approach play.

Liverpool were top of the table for the first time this season, albeit briefly until Arsenal beat Everton with the 3 pm kick-off. However, the momentum was definitely with Liverpool and a midweek win at Millwall put them top again. The fans were dreaming of another double as they travelled to Hillsborough for a FA Cup semi-final clash with Nottingham Forest again.

- YouTube has a brief clip of the highlights.

- Peter Beardsley's eighth goal in nine matches, after not scoring in the previous sixteen. He would not score again this season after this match.

- Sheffield Wednesday would be relegated the following season, but bounced straight back and also won the League Cup.

- Despite the return of Rush, Aldridge was still top scorer and actually improved his total to 31 in all competitions.

- Liverpool would win 15 of their last 19 league matches, drawing three and losing just the final one.

Everton 2 Liverpool 3

20/05/1989 - FA Cup Final - Wembley Stadium

The Hillsborough disaster claimed 96 lives, and rocked the club, sport and society. Its impact still resonates today and it will never be forgotten. After the funerals and soul searching, Liverpool took the difficult decision to resume their season. They managed to keep the pressure on Arsenal in the League, and winning an emotional rearranged FA Cup semi-final. It was fitting that the final was against Everton, as the city had been united in grief. For this unique occasion, the FA allowed all the tickets to be shared between the clubs.

Liverpool had Hansen back after missing most of the season, partnering Ablett, and Steve Staunton was now left-back, while Rush only claimed a place on the bench. Everton, now under Colin Harvey, had splashed over £3 million on Tony Cottee, Pat Nevin and Stuart McCall, although the latter was on the bench too.

On an emotional and boiling 99F day, thousands gathered, with local pre-match entertainment from the Spinners and Gerry Marsden. Everton started better, and McMahon needed to clear from Nicol's misheader. But Liverpool scored with their first attack, a long ball from Nicol to McMahon, he drew the central defender out, squared for the unmarked Aldridge to powerfully sidefoot into the top of the net. The early goal helped the Reds settle, and they passed the ball well, creating several good chances. Aldridge should have had a second, but his diving header from a Barnes cross, did not hit the target, and Barnes himself had a header easily saved too. Aldridge also screwed a shot wide and Nicol shot over. Everton were second best, and their only chance of note was when Nevin shot wide.

Early in the second half, Beardsley ran from the halfway line, but Southall blocked with his legs, and soon he hit the side netting too, while Southall also saved low from Barnes. Everton finally mounted late attacks, as Liverpool retreated, keen to play out time. The dramatic equaliser came in the final minute, Grobbelaar could not hold on to Watson's cross-shot, and the substitute McCall bundled the ball over the line.

Into extra time, Grobbelaar soon had to save from Cottee, but

Liverpool's substitute scored too; Rush receiving a Nicol ball in, with his back to goal, swivelled and fired into the top corner. Eight minutes later, McCall repeated his feat, chesting down a Hansen clearance, and volleying in. The goals were coming thick and fast now. Only a minute later, Rush was not to be upstaged, as he stooped to glance a header in from a Barnes cross.

The end to end dramatics continued as the heat had its effect, Steven shot wide, and Southall had to charge out to block a Rush shot, saving from Barnes, and tipping around a Beardsley shot. McDonald shot over from a free-kick, and the final whistle sparked a pitch invasion, but then maybe it was fitting for the fans to be there. Ronnie Whelan collected the trophy.

Again Liverpool were deprived of a double; a dramatic late Michael Thomas winner days later, as Arsenal achieved their required 2-0 victory. But it was a season when many realised that some things are more important than football.

- The whole match is available on DVD, and both clips and the match are on YouTube.

- John Aldridge's goal was Liverpool's first goal in the first half of an FA Cup final, at the ninth attempt. Today only two of Liverpool's 21 FA Cup final goals have come in the first half.

- Stuart McCall was the first substitute ever to score twice in the FA Cup final, matched by Rush, a minute later.

- Steve Nicol was awarded the Football Writers player of the year, but managed to avoid losing the FA Cup final unlike the previous four winners.

- Ian Rush's first goal broke Dixie Dean's record of 19 goals in derby matches, and he would end his career with 25.

- Gary Ablett would win the 1995 FA Cup with Everton; still the only man to win the trophy with both Merseyside teams.

- Five of the participants (Ablett, McMahon, Beardsley, Sheedy & Watson) would play for both teams, although the latter never made a first-team appearance for Liverpool.

Liverpool 9 Crystal Palace 0

12/09/1989 - First Division - Anfield

Dalglish reinforced his defence with Glenn Hysen, but there were no further signings, due to the impact of the European ban. They even needed to sell Aldridge to Real Sociedad, but he would make his final performance on a memorable night.

Hysen played in a defence with Gillespie, and David Burrows on the left, while Aldridge was on the bench. Crystal Palace, under the management of Steve Coppell, were newly promoted with a young team featuring a front pairing of Ian Wright and Mark Bright, with Geoff Thomas and Alan Pardew in midfield.

It only took 7 minutes, for Liverpool to make their mark; Barnes came forward, Whelan's clever side pass to Nicol on the corner of the box, and his shot found the top corner. The second wasn't long behind; Beardsley found Nicol in midfield, his forward pass released McMahon, who chipped over the advancing Suckling. On the stroke of half-time, Beardsley danced through challenges, and when he was stopped, Rush smashed the loose ball in from close range.

Things got much worse for Palace in the second half. Barnes flicked on a corner, and Suckling could not prevent Gillespie's near post header squeezing in. Beardsley slammed the next goal just after the hour, following a one-two with Rush. Five minutes later, Whelan released Barnes from his own half, and then raced forward to get on the end of his return pass. He was brought down for a penalty, and the Kop brayed for a sentimental substitution. Aldridge came on, and he duly converted for his final goal.

Palace then won a penalty too, but Thomas blazed over (he had also hit the post with a free-kick at 1-0). After 79 minutes, Rush was brought down on the edge of the area, and Barnes curled the free-kick into the near post for the seventh. Barnes' corner supplied the next, as Hysen rose unmarked, and headed down. The first scorer, Nicol, ended the scoring in the final minute, meeting a Barnes cross that had evaded Aldridge.

At the end, an emotional Aldridge threw his shirt and boots into the Kop, as they celebrated a substantial win, and also going to the top of the table for the first time this season. Palace responded by immediately purchasing goalkeeper Nigel Martyn, for a club record fee, and would shock Liverpool 4-3 in the FA Cup semi-final in April.

- The entire match was released on video, and now extended and short highlights are on YouTube.

- Liverpool's record top-flight league win. This was also the first league match that had eight different scorers for the same team.

- Aldridge scored 17 times from penalty spot in his Liverpool career, missing just the once, in the 1988 FA Cup final.

- Glenn Hysen only scored two league goals for Liverpool in 72 matches, both against Crystal Palace.

- Liverpool would also win 8-0 this season, in an FA Cup replay against Swansea City.

- Ian Wright would become Arsenal's top scorer, Mark Bright scored 166 goals in his career, Geoff Thomas played for England, and Alan Pardew became an experienced manager.

- In the summer, Steve Heighway had returned to Anfield to take over the Youth Development role, and later was instrumental in pioneering the Academy that produced future stars.

1990s

Charlton Athletic 0 Liverpool 4

11/04/1990 - First Division - Selhurst Park

After the shock of the Palace semi-final defeat, Liverpool had to quickly concentrate on the league, and a midweek away match with Charlton. They had a three point cushion over nearest rivals, Aston Villa and a game in hand, but needed to ensure Palace was just a blip.

Dalglish made wholesale changes by bringing in Venison (unusually in midfield), Ablett, Nicky Tanner (his first start), and Staunton. Most crucially, in place of the injured Rush, the deadline day loan signing, Ronny Rosenthal made his full debut. Charlton were battling against relegation for the third consecutive year.

Liverpool started nervously, Caton's free-kick had to be tipped around, and Minto hit the post after Grobbelaar had missed a cross. Liverpool were struggling to string passes together on the awful shared Selhurst Park pitch, but after 25 minutes, they took the lead. Rosenthal received a header from Barnes, ran at the Charlton defence, with a bobbling ball, and then squeezed a fierce right-foot shot in at the near post.

In the second half, Bolder had to save a Staunton shot, but the latter started the move for the second goal. He played a ball into space for Rosenthal, who outpaced the defender and unleashed another powerful shot, that flew into the net. The new Israeli hero could have scored again, from a Whelan cross, but his touch went wide.

Bolder had to save from a Barnes free-kick after the lively Rosenthal had been cynically chopped down. Rosenthal was just unstoppable. After the hour mark, he laid off a long ball to Barnes, and rushed into the middle to meet the cross with a diving header. A perfect hat-trick of left foot, right foot and header to mark his full debut. He still had another shot wide and Bolder made a fingertip save too. The match ended with a long ball from Molby to Barnes on the wing, he cut inside and hit a low shot into the corner for 4-0.

The perfect response to the upset, set up the final run-in, with two wins and two draws ensuring the 18th First Division title (nine more than anyone else at this time). Rush, Beardsley and especially Barnes had been key, but Rosenthal played a vital part in getting over the line.

- Six minutes of highlights are on YouTube.

- John Barnes had an exceptional season, even eclipsing Rush as top scorer with 22 league goals and 28 in all competitions.

- Bob Bolder spent two years as Grobbelaar's deputy, never making an appearance, but won a European Cup winners medal in 1984.

- This was another season, where Liverpool scored two more goals away from home.

- Alan Hansen's 8th league title, and it would be the last for all of this Liverpool squad.

- Rosenthal would score seven in this loan spell, earning him a permanent transfer.

- In the final home match against Derby County, the trophy was presented and Dalglish made his final appearance, coming on as substitute at the age of 39, Liverpool's oldest ever player.

- Liverpool's tenth league title in fourteen years, but it would be the last for 30 years. Since 1976, Liverpool had also claimed four European Cups, four League Cups, two FA Cups, one UEFA Cup and one European Super Cup, but unbeknownst, it would be the end of an era.

Liverpool 4 Manchester United 0

16/09/1990 - First Division - Anfield

Again it was another quiet summer at Anfield, as Dalglish had forgotten Paisley's trick of strengthening at the top, and the team had grown older. Initially, there were no adverse indications, as they won the first four before the clash with Manchester United. They had just won the FA Cup in Alex Ferguson's fourth season and invested heavily with Gary Pallister, Neil Webb, Paul Ince and the returning Mark Hughes. Hansen was out injured and Dalglish had taken to rotating players more, with Beardsley returning for this Sunday live TV match.

Manchester United had early chances, from Robins and McClair, but it was Liverpool that took the lead after 11 minutes. Barnes and McMahon interchanged passes down the left, Sealey prevented Bruce from deflecting the cross into his own goal, but merely presented an unmissable tap-in for Beardsley. United went close again with Webb hitting the crossbar and Grobbelaar saved well, while Rush shot wide at the other end.

Just after the half-hour, Liverpool doubled their lead; McMahon raced forward and slipped a perfect pass for Beardsley to slot in his second. It got even better just before half-time; Houghton crossed from the right, Nicol's miscued volley went up in the air, and Barnes rose highest to head in.

In the second half, United battled to reduce the lead, as Grobbelaar saved from Webb at close range. But Liverpool were always dangerous on the break; Rush headed over, Houghton shot wide and Barnes' effort was stopped on the line. Beardsley claimed his hat-trick in the final 10 minutes, thanks to Houghton's quick thinking. Liverpool won a free-kick in the United half, Houghton quickly flicked it to the unmarked Beardsley, who lobbed over Sealey, to clinch a memorable achievement. United had not been dominated, but Liverpool and Beardsley were much more clinical.

The winning run would extend to the first ten matches, but defeats to Arsenal and Crystal Palace, and too many draws produced criticisms about team selections, and the pressure increased on Dalglish. The rapid signings of youth players Don Hutchinson, Jamie Redknapp, and the more established Jimmy Carter and David Speedie were either panicked or too late.

- There are short and longer highlights available on YouTube.
- Liverpool biggest win over Manchester United since 1925.
- The first Liverpool hat-trick against Manchester United since Fred Howe in 1936.
- Peter Beardsley had joined Manchester United from Vancouver Whitecaps in 1982, but returned to Canada after a single League Cup appearance.
- Manchester United would knock Liverpool out of the League Cup, a month later.

Derby County 1 Liverpool 7
23/03/1991 - First Division - Baseball Ground

A dramatic 4-4 FA Cup draw with Everton was Dalglish's last match in charge. He had already decided to resign, the increasing pressure since the Hillsborough disaster taking its toll. Ronnie Moran was appointed caretaker manager, but the next three were lost, exiting the FA Cup and losing a crucial match with league rivals Arsenal.

Two wins saw Liverpool regain top spot, and next was a trip to Derby. They were bottom, even though they had England 1990 World Cup stars, Peter Shilton and Mark Wright along with top scorer Dean Saunders Grobbelaar was injured so Hooper filled in again, but the midfield was depleted of Whelan and McMahon, both out for the season, so Nicol was relocated

The exposed Liverpool defence looked shaky early on, as Saunders and McMinn looked to profit. The visitors looked more assured going forward, Molby dropped a long ball for Rush to chase, and Wright had to bring him down for a penalty, that Molby converted. Derby would get a penalty too, after Hooper recklessly brought down McMinn and Saunders equalised.

Liverpool regained the lead inside four minutes, as Rush and Barnes combined, Rush's shot was parried, but Barnes followed up to score. Shilton was becoming overworked, saving from Gillespie, and a double from a Nicol shot and Beardsley header. He could not stop everything, and it was 3-1 in the 39th minute; Barnes released Beardsley, and his low cross was finished by Rush.

Within 2 minutes of the restart, it was four; Beardsley intercepted a short back pass, Shilton saved initially, but Barnes beat him at the near post. Derby were overwhelmed as Liverpool ran riot; Barnes supplied Nicol and his deflected shot went in after 56 minutes. Nicol grabbed another 6 minutes later with a rasping drive after another Barnes and Beardsley combination. He was even denied a quickfire hat-trick as his shot was deflected wide. Into the final minute Houghton made a typical darting run forward, received the ball back from Barnes and finished neatly for the seventh. The forlorn Derby fans chanted "We're so bad, it's unbelievable".

This would be the final time at the top this season, as the next two games were lost, and even the return of former hero, Graeme Souness as manager, could not prevent another Arsenal title triumph. The Deby win was a final flourish from this exciting Liverpool team, but things would be changing.

- Liverpool's biggest away win since 1896.

- Alan Hansen also announced his retirement, a day after Dalglish's resignation.

- The last Peter Shilton appearance against Liverpool. His first was in 1967, and included Leicester City, Stoke City, Nottingham Forest, Southampton and Derby County.

- Derby would be relegated, but Mark Wright and Dean Saunders would sign for Liverpool in the summer.

- Liverpool scored 77 goals in the league with both Rush and Barnes netting 22 each, but the 40 goals conceded was a worrying sign.

Liverpool 3 Auxerre 0

06/11/1991 UEFA Cup 2nd round 2nd leg - Anfield

Souness acted quickly, conscious of the aging squad, the short term signings, and UEFA restrictions on three "foreigners". Beardsley, Gillespie, Staunton, Carter and Speedie were offloaded, and Mark Wright, Dean Saunders, Mark Walters and Rob Jones came in for over £6 million, along with youth players, Steve McManaman and Mike Marsh. From his experiences in Italy, Souness tried to instil more discipline, less drinking, better diet, but found resistance, especially from the older players who remembered his time at Anfield. The results were mixed, as injuries mounted, including Barnes and Wright. The return of European football seemed short-lived with Auxerre winning a UEFA Cup first leg 2-0.

Only 23,000 turned out on a windy evening, due to low expectations or the live BBC coverage. The injuries and foreigner rule meant only four substitutes were listed, as Souness opted for Molby, Houghton, and Rush at the expense of recent record signing Saunders. Auxerre were missing suspended captain, William Prunier.

Liverpool made the ideal start within 4 minutes; McManaman was tripped, and Molby halved the deficit from the penalty spot. Auxerre were struggling against a strong wind, and the noise of the fans relishing a European night under the floodlights.

Grobbelaar had to save from Dutuel, after Liverpool were carved open, but that was their only attempt, as Liverpool increased the pressure. McMahon shot over, before the second came. Houghton received Molby's pass, and scooped a cross to the far post, where Marsh ran in to head home. The Auxerre lead had already been wiped out in 30 minutes. Martini had to save well from a Molby free-kick to ensure no further damage before half-time.

In the second half Rush met a cross with a diving header, but little power, while Roche's volley was straight at Grobbelaar. Houghton missed another opportunity, but was offside anyway. Auxerre suffered another blow, as Darras was sent off after 75 minutes, for a second yellow card, after a foul on Walters. It was Walters that grabbed the winner 8 minutes later; Molby won a ball in midfield, his through ball was flicked on by Rush, and Walters scored with an angled shot into the corner.

Auxerre could offer no response and an unlikely triumph was clinched, with Molby key, after his future had looked uncertain. The fans had made even the half-empty Anfield seem intimidating.

- The whole match and highlights are on YouTube.

- The first time Liverpool had overturned a two goal European defeat (in fairness, this was only the third attempt).

- Despite not playing this match, Saunders still managed nine European goals, including two hat-tricks.

- William Prunier would have a two-match trial at Manchester United at the end of 1995, but was not kept after conceding four goals in his second match at Tottenham.

- Guy Roux was still Auxerre manager in 2003 when the clubs next met, losing 3 - 0 on aggregate with a team featuring Djibril Cisse. In fact, Roux presided over the Auxerre team for 44 years, taking them from the French fourth division, and winning the French title in 1996.

Liverpool 2 Sunderland 0

09/05/1992 - FA Cup Final - Wembley Stadium

The league form continued to be uneven, as injuries and transition pains persisted, limping to sixth place. A shock came after a FA Cup semi-final draw against Portsmouth, as Souness announced he would require a heart operation. Moran stepped up again guiding Liverpool to the final on penalties. Souness was released after 32 days in hospital and permitted to sit on the bench for the final, but Moran was still was in charge and led the team out.

The opponents, Second Division Sunderland also had an unlikely manager, as Malcolm Crosby had been caretaker for four months, and took them to their first FA final since 1973. Their team still contained experienced top-flight players such as Kevin Ball, Paul Bracewell and Peter Davenport.

In another unlikely twist, the Arsenal hero from 1989, Michael Thomas, had joined Liverpool, replacing Steve McMahon. Barnes suffered a new injury, but McManaman could take his place, recovering from his injury in the semi-final.

Another rainy Wembley day produced a heavy pitch. Sunderland were not overawed, with an early Byrne shot, while Grobbelaar pushed a Rogan shot around the post. Liverpool responded as Houghton put Thomas through, but he lifted his shot over the bar, and a Rush shot was saved. In a surprisingly open half, both teams had good opportunities; Byrne missed his kick when unmarked, Grobbelaar palmed a slippy ball away and a Bracewell shot wide deflected too. At the other end, Norman had to save from Saunders, while a Houghton free-kick and McManaman header were both wide. The latter also seemed to be tripped inside the penalty area, just before half-time, but nothing was given.

For the second half, Liverpool switched the lively McManaman to his more natural right wing, and it paid immediate dividends. He beat one defender and flicked the ball in to Thomas, who scored a stunning half volley from an angle. Liverpool now relaxed, as Molby became the fulcrum, controlling the tempo and match. The action was all one way; Molby's shot was tipped over and Saunders headed over. The second goal was inevitable; after 67 minutes, the industrious Houghton let Saunders come forward, he found the run of Thomas, he was stopped, but the ball fell kindly to Rush who finished with an assured sidefoot.

Sunderland could not gain possession as Molby passed and McManaman dribbled them into submission. Norman rushed off his line to deny Rush, but his clearance only went to Houghton, and his dipping effort went close. Norman tipped over a Saunders shot, who also curled one wide. In the end, it was a comfortable victory, and Souness could relax. Mark Wright collected the FA Cup, but a mix-up with winners' medals given to Sunderland players, was quickly resolved on the pitch.

- The whole match is available on DVD, while highlights, and the entire BBC coverage is on YouTube.

- After waiting 73 years for their first FA Cup, Liverpool won five in the next 18 years.

- Ian Rush's fifth goal in an FA Cup final remains a record today.

- The Sunderland team are the last FA Cup final team to be entirely born in the United Kingdom.

- Paul Bracewell lost all four FA Cup finals he played, with three against Liverpool.

- In a season of transition and injuries, there were no ever presents and 28 different players were used.

- Liverpool's sixth place finish in the league, was the worse since 1965, coincidentally, also an FA Cup winning season.

- Although Graeme Souness, won three Scottish League titles managing Rangers, he never won the Scottish Cup.

Liverpool 3 Manchester United 3

04/01/1994 - Premier League - Anfield

By the start of 1994, much had changed. The Premier League had been born with live Sky matches, all-seater stadiums on their way, and Manchester United had ended their long wait for a league title. Liverpool had spent large sums on Nigel Clough, Neil Ruddock and Julian Dicks, but the only bright spots were the young players, Robbie Fowler, Dominic Matteo, Jamie Redknapp, and Steve Harkness. Form was disappointing with not enough wins, as United were already 19 points ahead. They were on course to retain the title, with stars such as Peter Schmeichel, Roy Keane, Paul Ince, Eric Cantona, and Ryan Giggs.

This Tuesday evening clash was televised on Sky, and Fowler blazed over a glorious chance in the first minute Then things went very wrong; Steve Bruce scored from a free header after 8 minutes. Schmeichel saved a weak Fowler shot, and Grobbelaar likewise from Giggs. But then United scored twice in 3 minutes; Giggs chipped Grobbelaar and Irwin scored from a free-kick. Only halfway through the first half, 0 - 3 down at home to their bitter rivals seemed a nightmare scenario.

Fortunately, the three goal advantage didn't last long, as a low Clough shot from outside the box caught Schmeichel by surprise. A revived Liverpool pressed forward; Redknapp shot wide, and then on the 38th minute, Clough latched on to a loose ball that bounced off Keane, and sent it past Schmeichel again. The final minutes were even more hectic; Grobbelaar saved, Giggs missed his kick, and a Barnes cross was blocked.

The second half may have had fewer goals, but still the same end to end excitement, as Liverpool attacked for the leveller, but United had the best chances on the break. A Cantona shot was deflected, Kanchelskis shot over and Grobbelaar saved well from Giggs again. Redknapp had Liverpool's best efforts, but didn't trouble Schmeichel. With time running out, Ruddock laid the ball to substitute Bjornebye, and hurled himself at the inviting cross, injuring himself in the process, but scoring the vital goal. Both teams had late chances to snatch a win, Cantona came closest as he headed wide, but it seemed fair to share the points after such a dramatic and exciting match.

It would be the last classic watched from the standing Kop, as it would soon be seated. Souness would be gone too by the end of the month, after an FA Cup defeat at home to Bristol City. Roy Evans took over, but nine defeats resulted in 8th position, the lowest for 31 years.

- These were the last league goals scored by Nigel Clough for Liverpool.

- A ticket on the standing Kop cost £9 for this match. The Kemlyn Stand had been extended during the previous season, and included the first executive boxes at Anfield.

- Julian Dicks' penalty against Ipswich was the last Liverpool goal in front of the standing Kop. They did not score in the final two games, as Jeremy Goss scored the final goal for Norwich City in a 1-0 win.

- New left-back Stig Inge Bjørnebye had an unfortunate start with a 5-1 defeat on his debut, and only one win in his thirteen appearances in 1992/93.

- Ian Rush had taken 24 games to score his first goal against Manchester United in April 1992. His first at Old Trafford in October 1992 would be memorable as it broke Roger Hunt's record of 287 goals.

- Souness would claim that he had been approached earlier to sign Schmeichel and Cantona, but rejected both.

Liverpool 3 Arsenal 0

28/08/1994 - Premier League - Anfield

Summer 1994 saw a literal rebuilding of the Kop with seats, but also the squad and confidence, with Evans exiling the expensive flops; Wright, Clough, Stewart and Dicks. The remaining old guard of Grobbelaar, Whelan and Nicol would be departing too, as Evans placed his faith in the youth of McManaman, Fowler, Redknapp, Rob Jones, and goalkeeper David James.

A stunning 6-1 opening day victory over newly-promoted Crystal Palace raised some hopes, but Arsenal, still managed by George Graham, with their famed defence, would be a much tougher challenge. They had dominated these encounters recently, keeping seven clean sheets in twelve meetings. The rebuilding meant the Kop was only partially open, and so only 30,000 would see a notable personal performance.

The early exchanges were even; James saved from Jensen, and Seaman from Redknapp. Then something special happened. Liverpool took the lead after 26 minutes; Redknapp's free-kick was headed down by Rush, and Fowler pounced on the loose ball to lift it over Seaman. Three minutes later, Fowler scored again; McManaman received the ball in midfield and ran at the defence. Fowler peeled off to the corner of the box, controlled, and then released an accurate angled shot with his favoured left foot, going in off the post.

Within another 2 minutes, Barnes put Fowler through, Seaman managed to block his shot, but the rebound came back to him, and he lifted it in with his right foot this time. An incredible rapid hat-trick against the best defence in the league. Liverpool were now swarming over the experienced Arsenal team, as the joyous crowd celebrated in the sunshine.

The second half was quieter, as Liverpool consolidated their lead, Molby continued his influence in midfield until he went off injured. On the hour, Seaman tipped over from a McManaman drive. Arsenal had few chances; Dixon's shot went wide, and Smith's header was blocked, while near the end Redknapp shot just wide too for Liverpool.

Fowler's twelve league goals in his debut season had suggested a precocious finisher, but this astonishing hat-trick from the 19-year old had marked him out as a very special talent.

- The hat-trick was timed at 4 minutes 33 seconds, but the Premier League record is now held by Sadio Mané for Southampton with 2 minutes 56 seconds.

- Fowler would score a hat-trick again in the corresponding game the following season, and totalled twelve goals for Liverpool against Arsenal.

- A seat in the Kop now cost £11.

- Rush, Fowler and McManaman had all been boyhood Everton fans.

- In the following week, Roy Evans spent over £7 million on two central defenders, Phil Babb from Coventry City and John Scales from Wimbledon.

- George Graham would be sacked as Arsenal manager in February 1995, for accepting illegal payments, and banned, but later returned as manager of Leeds United and Tottenham.

Bolton Wanderers 1 Liverpool 2

02/04/1995 - League Cup Final - Wembley Stadium

Evans devised a formation to play Babb and Scales with Ruddock as three centre-backs, to allow Jones and Bjornebye to range forward, Barnes and Redknapp to control midfield, allowing a free role of McManaman to supply Rush and Fowler. This idea produced a thrilling team, with plenty of goals and a series of impressive results. The highlight was reaching the final of the League Cup, beating on the way, Blackburn Rovers away, Arsenal and Crystal Palace.

Although Bolton were in the Second Division, they would not be underestimated as manager Bruce Rioch had assembled the young talents like Alan Stubbs, Jason McAteer, and Alan Thompson, with striker John McGinlay. They had already knocked Liverpool out of the FA Cup two years earlier, and inflicted a 4-1 pre-season defeat.

Liverpool started very strongly, as Fowler and Bjornebye had shots saved, while Fowler and Rush were also off target. Bolton came into the match, McAteer shot powerfully, but straight at James. Lee lobbed James as he rushed out, but it hit the top of the net, and James tipped another effort over.

McManaman opened the scoring after 37 minutes with a superb individual goal. There seemed little danger when he picked the ball up in midfield. However, he dribbled around one defender, nutmegged another, and then released a low shot that beat the keeper, Branagan.

In the second half, James was caught out of position again, but Paatelainen shot wide, and Thompson missed another chance. Rush returned a ball to Bjornebye, and his stabbed shot hit the post. The roles were soon reversed, but this time's Rush's flick was saved.

It was McManaman again with another solo effort for the second. He received the ball on the halfway line, jockeyed the defender down the wing, then cut inside the box, and passed a curling shot into the far corner. The advantage only lasted two minutes, as Thompson turned and fired into the top corner, setting up a tense finale. McGinlay, McAteer and Stubbs all tried efforts, but Liverpool were unbowed with the three central defenders playing their part.

As captain, Rush collected the trophy from special guest Sir Stanley Matthews. There was also a new Man of the Match award, named after the legendary winger, that was appropriately given to McManaman, as his goals had made the difference.

Liverpool finished fourth in the league after a dramatic win over Blackburn Rovers on the final day of the season, so hopes were high for the new youthful team and their successful system.

- Liverpool's fifth League Cup would be the only trophy won by Roy Evans.

- Bolton's Mark Seagraves started two cup games for Liverpool, after progressing from the youth team.

- Steve McManaman had only scored one goal in his previous 32 appearances.

- Bolton would be promoted at the end of the season, but Bruce Rioch left to manage Arsenal for one season. McAteer would sign for Liverpool in September.

- John Scales had come on as a substitute for Wimbledon in the 1988 FA Cup final against Liverpool.

- Robbie Fowler was an ever present this season, and top scored, with 25 league goals, and 31 in total, the first of three consecutive years.

Liverpool 4 Newcastle United 3

03/04/1996 - Premier League - Anfield

Evans splashed out £13 million on Stan Collymore and Jason McAteer as hopefully the final touches to the young and improving squad. Initial form was good, but undone by five autumn losses in six matches, exiting both Europe and the League Cup. However, from December, Collymore and Fowler formed a devastating partnership, producing a twenty-match unbeaten run.

They reached the FA Cup final at the end of March, with the league still a slight possibility. They would have to beat Newcastle to stay in contention, but the visitors needed to restart their momentum after their twelve point Christmas lead had evaporated to Manchester United. Newcastle, led by Kevin Keegan with McDermott as assistant, had established a reputation as the fearless entertainers, as returning hero Beardsley partnered Les Ferdinand, mixed with the Gallic flair of David Ginola. In January they had added David Batty for the midfield protection, and Faustino Asprilla as an unpredictable striker. Despite Newcastle's image, it was actually Liverpool who were currently the league's top scorers, and also boasted the best defensive record too.

On a special night, the drama started early, as Liverpool scored in the 2nd minute; a sweeping ball from Redknapp was flicked on by Jones. Collymore tricked the defender, and his deep cross to the far post was headed down and in by Fowler. The lead didn't last long; Ferdinand forced in a shot through James, and Ginola completed the turnaround before 15 minutes with a chip after being freed by Asprilla. The action flowed from end to end, as Liverpool pursued an equaliser, with Redknapp and Fowler shots just off target.

If anything, the second half was even more action packed with a flurry of early chances. A piercing run by Lee was denied by James, while Srnicek saved twice from McManaman and a Scales' free header. Liverpool levelled on 55th minutes; a ball down the line from wing-back McAteer to McManaman, he ran at the defence, squared to Fowler for a clever snap shot finish. Again Newcastle's response was immediate, Asprilla's arched lob descending into the back of the net.

The goals were now flying in, as 10 minutes later, it all square again; a deep cross from McAteer into a dangerous area was finished by Collymore at the far post. A draw was no use to either, so both teams threw caution to the wind, resembling a basketball match of alternating efforts. James saved excellently from Ferdinand, and Srnicek saved from Barnes and Redknapp.

Evans added Rush in place of full-back Jones, sending even more men forward. In injury time, Rush and Barnes slalomed through the defence, exchanging passes. They seemed to have run out of options, but Barnes spotted the unmarked Collymore lurking on the far side. As Martin Tyler memorably shouted "Collymore closing in", he unleashed a fierce left-foot drive into the near post that flew past Srnicek He ran away jubilant, the home fans ecstatic, the visitors stunned, while on the bench Keegan's head slumped. The final few seconds passed for a memorable victory.

The press scrambled for superlatives, with most acclaiming it the best match of the Premiership era, while Evans' described it as "kamikaze". Liverpool had totalled 29 shots and Newcastle 12 in a riveting match.

The main beneficiaries were Manchester United, as Liverpool lost their next league match and Newcastle's challenge wilted. United would also claim the double, after beating Liverpool in the FA Cup final (an occasion mainly remembered for Liverpool's white suits). Liverpool had continued to improve reaching third place, but an even stronger challenge was expected next year.

- The entire match was released as a video, and copies exist on YouTube.

- Collymore's transfer was the last time Liverpool broke the British transfer record, although they currently hold the record for the largest fee received, Philippe Coutinho.

- Ephraim Longworth, is the only outfield player to exceed Rob Jones' 243 Liverpool appearances without scoring. Jones struggled with injuries, and had to retire at the age of 28.

- Ian Rush was given a free transfer at the end of the season, after scoring a record 346 goals for Liverpool.

- Liverpool's best league goal total for five years, and least conceded for seven years. Fowler hit a career best 36 goals in all competitions.

- A week after Liverpool lost the FA Cup final, they won the FA Youth Cup for the first time, with a team that included Jamie Carragher and Michael Owen, against a West Ham team featuring Rio Ferdinand and Frank Lampard.

Liverpool 5 Chelsea 1

21/09/1996 - Premier League - Anfield

Liverpool seemed primed for a serious title challenge; a settled, winning team and formation with the addition of the Patrick Berger, as competition for several positions. The start was encouraging, four wins and two draws, hitting the top the previous week at Leicester City. Collymore had been quiet, so replaced by Berger at half-time, who quickly scored twice.

He would make his full debut against third-placed and unbeaten Chelsea. A new and improving threat in Premier League, they mixed a cosmopolitan flavour of Ruud Gullitt (player-manager), Gianluca Vialli, Roberto Di Matteo, Frank LeBoeouf, but still included experienced and tough British players like Mark Hughes, Dennis Wise and Steve Clarke. Liverpool's Matteo had shook off an injury, to join the revived Wright and Babb in central defence, while Thomas started, as Redknapp was on the bench after another injury.

Di Matteo had an early chance easily saved by James, but then the irrepressible Fowler came to the fore; a header saved, chipped over when clean through, before he finally opened the scoring after 15 minutes, heading powerfully from a peach of a deep cross from Bjornebye. James then had to deny Hughes and Vialli, while McManaman went close for Liverpool.

The second goal was due to Matteo, who was having a fine match against difficult opponents. He claimed the ball in midfield, strode forward and released an ideal pass for Berger to round the keeper and score. Chelsea were desperately wanting half-time to regroup, as Liverpool overran them. Fowler missed from a Berger cutback, but they caused their own downfall when Myers cushioned a header past Hitchcock from another deep Bjornebye cross.

Chelsea made a double switch at half-time, but it made little effect, as Liverpool were four up within another five minutes. McManaman robbed Wise and set up Berger to run in, and slot past the keeper. Soon it was five, a Barnes volley was deflected by LeBeouf past a luckless Hitchcock again.

Chelsea turned angry, with rash challenges earning bookings, and were fortunate to avoid a clear penalty after Hitchcock fouled Fowler. Berger was denied a hat-trick with a left foot drive and a Bjornebye shot deflected. LeBoeuf converted a consolation penalty, as tempers rose again, and Petrescu threw the ball at Thomas.

It didn't matter, as Liverpool had crushed an emerging rival, and the introduction of Berger had provided more options.

- Patrick Berger had scored six goals in a week (two against Leicester and Chelsea and another two in midweek for Czech Republic against Malta). He had previously scored the equaliser for the Czechs in the final of Euro 96.

- Patrick Berger would score a hat-trick in the corresponding game next season, but then not score against Chelsea again.

- Steve Clarke would be a coach for Chelsea (under Jose Mourinho), Liverpool (under Dalglish) and later manager of Scotland and West Brom.

Liverpool 4 Newcastle United 3

10/03/1997 - Premier League - Anfield

A year on from the titanic tussle, things had changed; Newcastle were now managed by a different Liverpool legend, Kenny Dalglish, and it was Liverpool who were Manchester United's main challengers for the title. Bjørn Tore Kvarme had been added to central defence, and Berger preferred to Collymore in attack. Newcastle had injury problems, with Lee and Alan Shearer out, while Ferdinand was only fit for the bench. With Manchester United losing at the weekend, both teams eyed gaining ground in the Monday evening TV clash.

This time the opening was duller and more pragmatic, as Dalglish adopted a defensive formation. It seemed to work as only Redknapp troubled the keeper in the early stages. Suddenly Liverpool exploded into life at the 30-minute mark. McAteer overlapped, Fowler let the cross reach McManaman, and his shot curled into the top corner. Two minutes later, McManaman put Fowler through, his shot cannoned off the post, but Berger followed up to tap into the empty net. There was even a third before half-time, Redknapp released Fowler, and he made no mistake past Hislop this time.

Newcastle seemed so lifeless that a travelling fan threw his shirt at Dalglish. At half -time he brought on Ginola and Ferdinand, but the latter would only last 10 minutes before his injury reoccurred. The changes did little to affect the momentum as the buoyant Reds sought to increase their lead. McAteer went wide, and Hislop saved from Bjornebye and Barnes.

With 19 minutes left, James let a soft Gillespie shot from distance go through his hands. Liverpool were not too ruffled as Berger forced a good save from Hislop. However, when Asprilla's lob nestled in the net with 3 minutes remaining, the tension was palpable. It only took another minute for Newcastle to complete the unlikely comeback, as Barton scrambled in a scrappy goal.

Unbelievably, like the previous year, there was another last-minute twist; Bjornebye flighted a perfect cross, Fowler attacked it strongly, heading down and past Hislop. Another 4-3! Perhaps not as exciting or free flowing as the previous year, but definitely a dramatic climax, and the deserved winners.

Successive home defeats to Coventry City and Manchester United ruined the title dreams, and Liverpool finished a disappointing fourth, with Dalglish and Newcastle claiming the other Champions League spot in second.

- Fowler scored over 30 goals for the third successive season, but would only hit 18 in the future as injuries affected his career.

- David James and Stig Inge Bjørnebye started all 52 matches this season, the last players to be ever present in all competitions, as rotation became more prevalent.

- Bjørn Tore Kvarme was Liverpool's first "Bosman" signing, where players could move without a transfer fee at the end of their contract.

- Bookmakers had given odds of 100-1 for a repeat of the 4-3 scoreline.

- Kenny Dalglish won once and lost four times as a visiting manager at Anfield.

Newcastle United 1 Liverpool 4

30/08/1998 - Premier League - St James Park

Even with the emergence of Michael Owen, a third-place finish seemed far away from the title, with questions of professionalism as the "Spice Boys" tag took hold. The directors sought fresh blood and new ideas, so contracted their first foreign coach, Gerard Houllier from the French Academy. Unfortunately, they foisted on him and Evans, misconceived joint manager roles, doomed to failure, despite an early promise.

The Liverpool team now was a mixture of the Evans regulars, short term "final piece in the jigsaw" signings like Paul Ince, Karl-Heinz Riedle, Steven Staunton, and youth of Jamie Carragher and Owen. Newcastle had Shearer, and new signings Stéphane Guivarc'h, Didi Hamann, and Gary Speed. In midweek they had ousted Dalglish as manager, as Ruud Gullit arrived with promises of "sexy football", so many of the Geordie faithful were wearing Gullit style wigs.

The sexy football all came from Liverpool and the teenager Owen. After 17 minutes, Paul Ince shot from distance, Given blocked, but Owen squeezed in a rebound at the near post. Within a minute, he had his second; running on to McManaman's through ball, and coolly slotting between Given's legs. He might even have had a quick third, but missed from a Berger cross.

Newcastle had a brief hope when Babb was dispossessed and Guivarc'h scored. A brief interlude as they could not cope with Liverpool's pace. Riedle challenged near the halfway line, Owen was on to the loose ball in a flash, sprinting forward, evading one tackle, and then casually dinking over Given. A stunning first hat-trick, as good as Fowler's four years earlier. Berger confirmed the dominance in the final first-half minute with a now typical sweet left foot drive.

Gullit took charge at half-time, changing formation, but Liverpool absorbed any pressure as Brad Freidel saved a Guivarc'h header, Shearer shot wide, while Carragher blocked from Pearce and Ince from Glass. Owen had Liverpool's best chance, but Given saved. The travelling Liverpool fans were delighted, chanting "Dalglish" and "You can stick your sexy football up your arse! as Liverpool saw out another famous win against Newcastle.

Liverpool went top of the league, but it was short-lived. As results deteriorated, it was clear that the joint managers role was not working, so Evans resigned in November, leaving Houllier in sole charge. He finished 7th, 25 points behind the champions, and faced a major challenge ahead.

- Despite being 18, this was Owen's third hat-trick for Liverpool, and he would score over 20 goals in five of the next six seasons. His 1998 World Cup exploits, including a famous goal against Argentina, earned him the 1998 BBC Sports Personality of the Year.

- Michael Owen would score 14 goals for Liverpool against Newcastle. He signed for them in 2005, staying four years until they were relegated.

- The return match at Anfield in December was dramatic too, as ten-man Newcastle went into a 2-0 lead, but Liverpool won 4-2.

- Didi Hamann had unhappy experiences playing against Liverpool as he went off injured after 12 minutes in this match, and was sent off after 30 minutes of the return game.

- Kenny Dalglish's son, Paul, was an unused substitute for Newcastle for this match. He had progressed through the Anfield youth system, and would play eleven times for Newcastle, before moving to Norwich and later successfully managing in the USA.

Liverpool 4 Sheffield Wednesday 1
05/12/1999 - Premier League - Anfield

Similar to Shankly with the 1960s, Houllier literally and psychologically took Liverpool into the 21st century. His French Revolution in the summer of 1999 was the busiest transfer window for Liverpool so far. Didi Haman, Sami Hyypia, Stephane Henchoz, Vladimir Smicer, Titi Camara, Sander Westerveld and Eric Mejier all joined. Some were unknown, some would stay briefly, but some would become legends. Out went James, Ince, McManaman (seeing out his contract for a "Bosman" move to Real Madrid), Dundee, and Leonardson. He also looked at utilising the available young players, Danny Murphy, David Thompson and most importantly, Steven Gerrard. The mentality and culture would need to change, with stricter dietary rules, less drinking (similar to Souness's thinking in 1991), and also an upgrade of the Melwood training facility.

The initial bedding-in period saw some reverses, but four consecutive wins in autumn, although not entertaining, were signs of a more resilient team. A loss at West Ham had been a setback, but the visit of bottom place Sheffield Wednesday was a good opportunity to restart. Five of the recent signings started, with the impressive central defender Hyppia already given the captain role in place of the injured Redknapp.

Things did not go to plan initially, as in the 18th minutes, Alexandersson scored a stunning drive after a free-kick was rolled to him. However, Liverpool quickly replied, Pressman had to save from Camara, and then Hyypia, headed in Thompson's corner for 1-1. Liverpool were now on top as Jonk had to clear from the goal line. Just before half-time, Pressman could only divert Thompson's fierce shot into the air, and Murphy scored with an accomplished volley.

In the second half, Alexandersson had another two shots, one well saved by Westerveld, but Steven Gerrard settled the nerves in the 69th minute. He weaved between two defenders and finished hard and low in the bottom corner. Liverpool relaxed, retained possession, and Thompson curled in the fourth from the edge of the box.

Perhaps the result was hard on battling Wednesday, but the remodelled Houlllier team were progressing, with four well taken goals. The centre-backing parting of Hyppia and Henchoz was much more secure, protected by the diligent Hamann enhanced by the blossoming of Gerrard into the outstanding player of his generation. An unbeaten run of twelve league matches and signing Emile Heskey, pushed Liverpool into second, with designs on finally qualifying for the Champions League.

The dreams were smashed with no goals in the last five matches, but it had been a definite season of improvement and the UEFA Cup place would be significant.

- Steven Gerrard's first goal for Liverpool in his 14th start. Only the second Liverpool goals for Murphy and Hyypia, and Thompson's third.

- Tickets for this Category B game costs ranged from £19 to £21.

- Niclas Alexandersson would sign for Everton, the following summer playing 75 games.

- Michael Owen would be top scorer, but with only twelve in an injury plagued season, as 18 different players scored.

- Gerard Houllier had previously managed Lens, PSG (winning a league title), before managing the French national team. He failed to qualify for the 1994 World Cup, but was more successful as technical director, working with the youth teams.

2000s

Manchester United 0 Liverpool 1

17/12/2000 - Premier League - Old Trafford

The rebuilding continued in 2000, with the addition of veteran Gary McAllister, Christian Ziege, Markus Babbel, and Nick Barmby (who made the short journey from Everton). As Christmas approached Liverpool were still in all three Cup competitions, but four defeats in six league outings saw them slip to sixth, before the ominous away trip to Old Trafford and the recent treble winners loomed.

For the Sunday noon kick-off, the recent signing Igor Biscan started, in preference to McAllister. Carragher was now filling in at left-back, while Owen partnered Heskey up front, so Fowler was on the bench. Ferguson was now onto his second great team, with the likes of Fabian Barthez, and "Class of 1992" alumnus; Gary Neville, David Beckham, Nicky Butt and Paul Scholes. However, a striker injury crisis meant that Dwight Yorke, Andy Cole and Teddy Sheringham were all missing, so Ole Gunnar Solskjær started.

Liverpool edged a cagey first half, as Gerrard and Biscan competed well against a quiet Keane, and Heskey led the line well, typically pressuring defenders and chasing lost causes. The chances came late, with a Heskey header cleared off the line by Scholes. In the 43rd minute, Neville strangely handled with both hands, like a volleyball stroke. For the free-kick, Barmby ran over the ball, and Murphy then stepped up, to curl it around the wall, and in off the post, leaving Barthez flat footed.

Either side of half-time, Owen missed glorious chances, the first he overran, the second bounced off the top of the bar. Solskjær would have United's best chance, but Westerveld turned the shot wide.

The off-key United attempted to respond, and Ferguson tried to use substitutions to change the complexion, but Liverpool were comfortable. Actually, they were more likely to score, breaking with substitute Smicer's pace, only halted by Chadwick hauling him down, and earning a red card. McAllister put the resulting free-kick just around the post. There were still a few nerves, as they had suffered two late goals here the year before. This time was different, as United failed to muster any response, and Houllier recorded a significant and morale-boosting victory.

The mood was heightened the following weekend, as Arsenal were beaten 4-0 at Anfield, and the first inklings that this could be a memorable season.

- Liverpool's first win at Old Trafford for over ten years.

- Manchester United's first home defeat since December 1998, and the first time they had not scored there since November 1998. Chadwick was the first home sending off since April 1998.

- Igor Biscan's first full league start.

- Houllier would win three of four consecutive visits to Manchester United, all 1-0 wins with Danny Murphy the scorer each time, the first Liverpool manager to record three victories there since Bill Shankly.

- Nick Barmby was the first player to move directly from Everton since Dave Hickson in 1959 and scored his first league goal in the October derby match.

- Gary McAllister was the first 35-year to make a post-war Liverpool debut.

A.S. Roma 0 Liverpool 2

15/02/2001 - UEFA Cup 4th round 1st leg - Stadio Olimpico

By February Liverpool had reached the League Cup final, and were still progressing in the FA Cup and Europe. Any remote idea of a cup treble was obscured by another trip to the Stadio Olimpico, and the might of Roma, the current leaders of Serie A. They were again a formidable mixture of Italian internationals and South American stars. Local hero Francesco Totti was in a contract dispute, and Fabio Capello preferred Vincenzo Montellato to Gabriel Batistuta up front.

Liverpool were without Gerrard or Murphy, so McAllister and Hamann played in midfield, and Fowler and Owen were paired in attack, the latter's first start in over a month, as he had struggled with form and injuries. Heskey probably would have played instead, but had pulled out on the day of the match.

Roma retained possession well initially, but soon Houllier's Liverpool were stifling their play and preventing them from finding their rhythm. The defensive axis of Hyppia, Henchoz and midfielder Hamann stopped the creation of any decent chances; the only threat being a Delvecchio header that went past the post.

Liverpool had also lacked any threat, but that changed in the second half. Within a minute, there was a mistake from Rinaldi, as he passed blindly. Owen intercepted, went wide and angled a finish past Antonioli. Roma's only reaction to the away goal, was an Assuncao effort, and soon they were two down Ziege's free-kick was saved, but from the rebound, he played a one-two with McAllister, whipped in a cross with his right foot, and Owen nipped in with a deft header. Roma struggled to raise their game, and substitute Batistuta made little difference, as Barmby went closest near the end.

Like Old Trafford in December, the opposition may have seemed below par, but Liverpool were now hard to break down, fought for every ball and had a clinical finish up front. The Liverpool fans kept behind after the match, were happy chanting "We always win in Rome", marking the best European away performance since in Roma in 1984.

Roma would win the second leg 1-0, often remembered for the referee awarding Roma a penalty, but then changing his mind. Liverpool were slowly starting to re-establish their European reputation, and this year they were the cup tie specialists.

- The entire match is available on YouTube.

- Nick Barmby had already scored four goals in this competition, but injuries would limit his further involvement.

- Michael Owen's first goal since before Christmas.

- The first of three successive European away clean sheets at Roma, Porto and Barcelona.

- Roma's first home loss of the season, and they would go on to win the Serie A title this year.

- Future England manager, Fabio Capello would lose all three ties against Liverpool, including a Champions League Quarter-final with Juventus in 2005.

Everton 2 Liverpool 3

16/04/2001 - Premier League - Goodison Park

By Easter Monday, Liverpool had won the League Cup, booked a place in the FA Cup final, and managed a goalless draw at Barcelona in the UEFA semi-final. Games were coming thick and fast, but there were major doubts that they could also sustain a challenge for a Champions League slot. They were fifth, and had lost a crucial Good Friday match to rivals Leeds.

They could afford no more slip-ups and required all three points from the away derby match. Everton needed the points too, as they still had relegation worries, so had recently signed Kevin Campbell to partner Duncan Ferguson in their attack. Houllier had been regularly shuffling his pack, and in came Heskey, Smicer and McAllister in place of Owen and the suspended Murphy and Gerrard.

The dramatics started early; while Everton were appealing for a penalty, the ball was ushered forward by Hamann to Heskey who ran from the halfway line and hit it hard under Paul Gerrard for 1-0. Fowler nearly reached a Heskey header, and Campbell headed weakly too. Typically tackles were flying in, and bookings were regularly dished out by referee Jeff Winter. Both teams survived scares; Paul Gerrard's weak punch was headed back by Heskey, but Gough cleared, and Gemmill headed wide after Westerveld struggled. Smicer shot wide from a distance, but Everton equalised just before half-time as Ferguson swept the ball in.

The second half was even more dramatic. Everton attacked the Liverpool goal, and Ball fired over from 30 yards. From another failed attack, Hamann sparked another counter attack, Fowler's cross could not be cleared and Babbel followed up to finish cleanly. There was even a chance of daylight two minutes later, but Fowler's penalty kick hit the post.

Things became even more frantic, another handball claim against Carragher was not given, and then Biscan was sent off for a second yellow card with 14 minutes to go. A Nyarko shot was saved by Westerveld, but then a penalty was awarded for a foul on Ferguson, and Unsworth smashed it in.

With minutes ticking away and Liverpool's Champions League dream was fading. Even with ten men, they ventured forward, and Gerrard saved Hyypia's header from a McAllister free-kick. Deep into injury time, the young substitute Gregory Vignal broke forward, and was cynically brought down by Alexandersson, still 44 yards from goal. McAllister pinched a little ground and gestured to the likely target Hyypia at the far post. Instead, he ran up and curled the ball through a disintegrating wall, and it bounced past a startled Gerrard in at the near post. An incredible end to a breathless game, as Liverpool fans and players celebrated another famous derby victory.

The dramatic win seemed to give Liverpool renewed strength and momentum. They beat Barcelona on the Thursday, and the next four league matches, to keep the Champions League place destiny in their own hands.

- Michael Owen was an unused substitute and it would take him eight matches before he scored his first derby goal, and strangely he never scored one at Anfield.

- Liverpool's first win at Goodison since 1990, completed the double over both Everton and Manchester United in the same season.

- Everton had six players booked earning an FA fine, and Liverpool six too with Biscan twice.

- Abel Xavier's fourth derby match for Everton, but in his sixth appearance in February 2002 he would be playing for Liverpool.

Arsenal 1 Liverpool 2

12/05/2001 - FA Cup Final - Millennium Stadium

It was down to the Millennium Stadium in Cardiff for the FA Cup final, as Wembley was being rebuilt. Arsenal still had the experienced defence of Seaman, Dixon, Adams, Keown and Ashley Cole, but Arsene Wenger had added the French flair with Patrick Vieira, Robert Pires and Thierry Henry. For Liverpool, Heskey and Owen were selected as the strikers, and the central midfield of Gerrard and Hamann with Murphy and Smicer on the flanks.

On another boiling hot Cup Final day, there was a controversial start; Ljunberg released Henry, who went around Westerveld, his shot was blocked by Henhoz's hand on the line, but referee Dunn played on. Arsenal were on top with Vieira dominating Gerrard, as Henry's overhead kick went wide, and a Grimandi shot was easily saved. Liverpool's only real chance was Gerrard firing over, after an Owen shot was blocked by Keown.

In the second half, Seaman saved an early Heskey header, but Arsenal were still by far the better team with a series of close misses; a Wiltord volley was deflected, and Pires free-kick went wide. They came even closer, as Westerveld saved well after Henry had been put clear, Cole followed up on the loose ball, but Hyypia cleared on the line. Ten minutes later, he needed to do it again from a Ljunberg shot. Their deserved goal finally came 72 minutes; Pires latched on to a poor Westerveld kick, played it through for Ljunberg to go around the keeper and score. It should have been two soon after, a Henry shot was well saved and Hyypia cleared off the line for the third time.

Houllier gambled by putting on Berger and Fowler, to join McAllister. Owen had been rarely seen, with no service to him. There was one hint now, as Gerrard found him, but the chance went begging. On the 83rd minute, a McAllister free-kick was not cleared, Babbel nodded down, and Owen twisted and fired in on the half volley. Liverpool were suddenly back in the game, and within 5 minutes were ahead. Berger's pinpoint long pass allowed Owen to run into space, he outpaced Dixon, and then shot across Seaman with his left foot. He celebrated in front of the Liverpool fans with a somersault.

Arsenal added Bergkamp, but their only effort was a Keown header which was easily caught. On the breakaway, Fowler hit Seaman's body, when Owen was unmarked. It didn't matter, as soon Fowler, and captain Redknapp, raised the FA Cup. The players' post match celebrations are muted, as there was still another final on Wednesday.

- A DVD of the whole match is available.

- The first FA Cup final where both managers were foreign (and French). It was also the first time in ten years, that a team came from behind to win.

- Liverpool wore a bright yellow change kit, the only time they have won the FA Cup not wearing red.

- Michael Owen had suffered from poor form and injuries earlier in the season, but now was in devastating form with eight goals in four games. It would lead to him winning the European Player of the Year for 2001, the only Liverpool player to win this honour, while at Anfield.

- In the pre-match previews, journalists had noted that Arsenal's previous Cup winning goal scorers over Liverpool, Reg Lews and Charlie George (and Nicholas in the League Cup), had surnames that were also a first name, and this could be continued by Thierry Henry. But they missed that Owen could also be a first name, especially in Cardiff.

Deportivo Alavés 4 Liverpool 5

16/05/2001 - UEFA Cup Final - Westfalenstadion, Dortmund

So to Dortmund for the third final and the treble dream was still alive. The opposition, the Basque fairytale of minnows Alaves, who had finished sixth in the Spanish league, qualifying for their first European campaign. They had shocked Inter Milan, Rayo Vayacon, and Kaiserlauten on the way to the final. Their main striker Javi Moreno had just recovered from an injury, but they also had Jordi, Johan Cruyff's son. Houllier made only one change this time, McAllister in for Smicer. The Liverpool fans dominated Dortmund with their larger numbers, but Alaves fans were enjoyed their day, gleefully pointing to their names embroidered in their specially designed kit.

Liverpool made a devastating start; a McAllister free-kick was headed in by Babbel with only 4 minutes on the clock. Heskey nearly burst through and also had a header saved, as Alaves seemed overawed. Within 15 minutes they were two down; Owen held up the ball and released it for the run of the untracked Gerrard, and he drilled it in hard and low. Liverpool were cruising and made more chances. Was the final already won ?

Alaves quickly changed formation, taking off a third central defender Eggen, and bringing on another striker Ivan Alonso. The impact was almost instantaneous as he headed in Contra's deep cross. Contra was now a growing menace on the wing, as Moreno has a good chance blocked, and Westerveld blocked from Moreno and Tomic. Liverpool regrouped and on the break, Owen was brought down by a reckless charge out of goal from Herrerra. McAllister just squeezed in the penalty, and a 3-1 lead should have been comfortable again.

However, within 5 minutes of the restart Alaves were level. Contra tormented Carragher again, and his cross was headed in from Moreno, who also shot under the Liverpool wall from a free-kick.

Houllier made changes, Henchoz was struggling, so Smicer came on, as the defence was rejigged, and soon Fowler replaced Heskey. Surprisingly Alaves replaced the two-goal Moreno too. Liverpool gradually gained control again, as Owen went close. In the 73rd minute, McAllister found Fowler, he drifted inside, feigned, and then released a right foot shot into the corner for 4-3. A stunned BBC commentator Barry Davies yelled "this isn't supposed to happen in European finals!" Alaves tried to reply again, but Liverpool seemed to have weathered the storm with Westerveld saving from Magno. However, in the 89th minute, Jordi met a corner, Westerveld was stranded, and improbably extra time was required.

A short-lived UEFA initiative, the golden goal, determined the next goal would win the match. Alonso thought he had it after 3 minutes, but was offside. Hamann shot wide, but soon Magno was sent off for a second yellow card. A powerful Berger shot was parried, and Fowler scored, but he is offside too.

In the second period, a Desio free-kick went wide, Fowler could not reach a cross, and Berger fired over. With five minutes left, the pace of Smicer troubled captain Karmona, and he brought the Czech down, earning him a second yellow card too. Down to nine men, there were only a few minutes to take advantage. McAllister took the resulting free-kick, the ball clipped the head of Geli, taking it over the keeper and into the back of the net.

Liverpool celebrated their instant winner, and the 36-year old McAllister soon collected the Man of the Match award from Johan Cruyff. One of the most thrilling European finals ever, and a sobering riposte to critics like Cruyff that had labelled Liverpool boring. Perhaps there was some poor defending, and Liverpool weary as the games caught up with them, but it was still enthralling and unpredictable nonetheless. The Liverpool squad and coaches lined up in front of the famous Dortmund Yellow Wall stand that now housed the travelling Kop, celebrating together a third trophy.

- There are several clips on YouTube including ten minutes of BBC highlights.

- The only European club competition decided by a golden goal, although Germany won the Euro 96.

- Liverpool's third UEFA Cup triumph in their third final.

- This remains the highest scoring UEFA / Europa league one-off final.

- Alaves' Dan Eggen had scored the only goal that gave Brondy a win at Anfield in 1995.

- Liverpool are the only English team to win all of their domestic and European cup ties in one season.

- The treble became five trophies in August, with the Charity Shield against Manchester United and Bayern Munich in the Super Cup. They also claimed the BBC Team of the Year, their third after wins in 1977 and 1986.

- Contra and Moreno would transfer to AC Milan, then Atlético Madrid before lower-division Cordoba.

- Four Liverpool starters and one substitute would appear in the 2005 Champions League final.

Charlton Athletic 0 Liverpool 4

19/05/2001 - Premier League - The Valley

Despite the three trophies, Liverpool had still not achieved their primary goal of Champions League qualification. Three days later they would need to win at Charlton, as rivals Leeds had an easier home match. The Valley was a difficult place to visit, as Charlton had only lost twice there all season and Liverpool would be tired after the strenuous season, and especially from the extra time in midweek.

Houllier made four changes to try to avoid this, bringing in Vignal, Barmby, Berger, and Fowler. It didn't work, as Liverpool looked tired and disjointed in the first half and lucky to survive. Charlton controlled the midfield, and created multiple chances. Kinsella's deflected shot grazed the post after 10 minutes. Svenson also hit the post later, while Westerveld kept out Brown and Svenson. Stuart and Jensen also shot wide, while Carragher survived a penalty appeal.

At half-time, Houllier urged the players for one final effort. Murphy was soon added, as they tried to attack more and Owen's shot was blocked for a corner. It took a moment of inspiration for the vital goal after 55 minutes; a sublime kick over his head from Fowler looped in. Soon it was two; a Murphy drive, from an Owen layback.

Liverpool were now well on top, but Hyypia still had to clear after Westerveld dropped a cross. In the 71st minute, the match was secure, as Owen broke away, and teed up Fowler for a clinical left foot strike. Owen ended the scoring with a deserved goal, after he had robbed Mark Fish.

The end of a remarkable season. Liverpool returned home on Sunday finally celebrating the three trophies in another well attended parade. Houllier had made Liverpool hard to beat, mentally stronger and now used to winning silverware again.

- Liverpool played 63 games and scored 127 goals. No player was ever present, but fourteen played more than 40 matches.

- Michael Owen was top scorer with 24 goals, but also Heskey scored a career best 22 and Fowler 17.

- Liverpool won nine of the last ten matches, with one defeat in the last nineteen. Gary McAllister was key, scoring six goals in nine starts (three penalties and three free-kicks).

- Read more about this season in "Into the Red" by John Williams

- In September 2001, England beat Germany (and Didi Hamann) 5-1, with a hat-trick from Owen, and also goals from Barmby and Heskey.

Leeds United 0 Liverpool 4

03/02/2002 - Premier League - Elland Road

For the next season, Houllier added John Arne Riise as a versatile left footer, two goalkeepers (Jerzy Dudek was first choice), but then lost Babbel and Vignal to serious illness and broken leg respectively. However, the defining event of the season (and the rest of his career) was Houllier being rushed to hospital at half-time during a home match with Leeds, and requiring major heart surgery.

While Houllier convalesced, assistant Phil Thompson took charge, steering Liverpool to the next group stage of the Champions League and the top of the league in December. It was difficult to sustain, as a run of two wins in eight followed, but an upturn began with another win at Old Trafford.

David O'Leary's young team had been a similarly emerging rival in the last three years, but Liverpool now the trophies to show for their progress. Leeds had none, but still spent lavishly on the likes of Rio Ferdinand, Oliver Dacourt, Robbie Keane and the recent transfer of Fowler from Liverpool. His first game against Liverpool was a Sunday noon platform for both teams to renew their title charge.

Gerrard's crunching tackle on Dacourt set Liverpool's tone in the opening minute, as they were stronger, quicker, and sharper. The lead came in the 16th minute as Ferdinand flicked Murphy's curling free-kick into his own net. Martyn had to save well from Owen, while the visitors allowed nothing to pass, with Academy graduate Stephen Wright handling Harry Kewell well.

At the hour mark, Liverpool moved away, the second came from a blistering counter attack. Gerrard's ball with the outside of his boot, freed Heskey, who raced forward, around the keeper and in from a tight angle. Two minutes later, Owen headed down a corner, and Heskey smashed the ball into the roof of the net.

Fowler's sole chance came in the 89th minute, which Dudek saved comfortably. Owen ended a bad day for Leeds, by claiming the fourth; Heskey headed on from a long throw, Owen's initial header hit the bar, but he was quickest to react.

Leeds' form was declining and their financial concerns increasing. For Liverpool, it had been an ideal away trip, with another the following week, a 6-0 mauling of Ipswich (another two for Heskey), which saw a brief return to the top.

- Liverpool biggest ever away win at Elland Road.

- After scoring just one goal in 24 starts, Heskey scored five in three matches.

- As well as ex-reds Dominic Matteo and Fowler, the Leeds teamsheet also contained future Liverpool signings Robbie Keane and Harry Kewell, and Fowler who would return too (via Manchester City).

- Leeds would be relegated two years later, and then again to the third tier in 2007, spending three seasons there.

- Fowler would finish his career with 163 Premiership goals (128 for Liverpool), Owen with 150 (118 for Liverpool) and Heskey 110 (39 for Liverpool).

Liverpool 2 A.S. Roma 0

19/03/2002 - Champions League 2nd Group Stage Matchday 6 - Anfield

In the second Champions League group phase, Liverpool lost the opener to Barcelona, but drew all of the next four matchdays. Unusually, qualification was still a possibility, but they would need to beat Roma by two goals to progress. Roma had a similar team from the previous season, but this time started with Batisituta and Totti up front.

Liverpool's task was made harder by injury to Owen, so Jari Litmanen partnered Heskey up front, and Smicer pushed forward too. The team and fans were galvanised by the surprise return of Gerard Houllier, five months since his last fateful appearance. He emerged into a flurry of flashbulbs, a rapturous reception, and a hug from Capello. The Kop even had a timely "Allez" mosaic in his honour.

Roma were swept away initially by the tide of emotion, and Liverpool's attacking intent. Smicer's fierce shot was touched wide, and from the corner, Murphy was upended. Litmanen coolly converted, sending Antonioli the wrong way. Roma were deluged by a red tide; Gerrard's fierce free-kick hit the keeper, Riise shot wide twice and Heskey headed over. Capello later admitted "I've never seen Liverpool play like this". Roma eventually cleared their heads, so Henchoz cleared one effort and Carragher made a crucial tackle on Batistuta.

Roma made two changes at half-time to change the momentum, with Totti's shot saved by fingertips and another deflected. However, they had little answer to Heskey's power and pace, highlighted by the second goal. Just after the hour, he leaped to meet a Murphy free-kick, and headed in.

Roma were going out, but vainly tried to rally again, with an Emerson shot over, but Liverpool's rearguard was solid, and Riise nearly added a third. It had been a special result and a special night.

Houllier was quoted that "Liverpool could be ten games from greatness", as both the Premiership and Champions seemed possible, but neither materialised. A 4-2 defeat at Bayern Leverkusen ended European dreams, and Arsenal took the title, despite Houllier inspiring an impressive eight victories in the last ten league games. Liverpool had to settle for second, but it was their highest finish for eleven years, so maybe next year.

- Jari Litmanen scored three goals for Liverpool in this year's Champions League, and had previously won the trophy with Ajax.

- Michael Owen had scored Liverpool's first away European hat-trick in the qualifier against Haka and repeated it a year later against Spartak Moscow (Sadio Mané and Diogo Jota are the only players subsequently to score three in a European away fixture).

- Roma had not lost a league or European match since September. Despite losing only two league matches all season, they lost their Serie A title to Juventus by one point.

- The first time Liverpool had finished above Manchester United since 1991, and it would not be repeated until 2014.

Liverpool 2 Manchester United 0

02/03/2003 - League Cup Final - Millennium Stadium

Houllier's fate would be sealed by the 2002 transfers of El Hadji Diouf and Salif Diao, stars of the Cameroon World Cup team, and Bruno Cheyrou ("the new Zidane"). Initially hopes were raised by an unbeaten start of twelve league games, going top again. However, all three signings failed, and the existing players lost form too. A Champions League exit at Basle ensued, and eleven league games without a win during a hard winter. The League Cup provided a welcome distraction, as they reached the final again, and another meeting with Manchester United.

Ferguson's team were on the way to another Premier title, with the expensive signings of Juan Veron, Rio Ferdinand, and the prolific Dutch striker Ruud van Nistelrooy. Dudek had been dropped after a series of mistakes culminated in a calamitous match against United, but regained his place due Chris Kirkland's injury. Houllier selected Heskey and Owen up front, with Diouf on the right wing. Cardiff was the atmospheric again, this time with a closed roof, and pyrotechnics as the teams came out to "Two Tribes".

Manchester United edged a cagey first half, Giggs' shot was easily saved, and van Nistelrooy went wide, before Murphy's dipping shot just went over. The game sprung into life in the 39th minute; Gerrard shot from outside the area, and a deflection from a weak Beckham block helped it loop into the top corner. United tried to retaliate immediately, but Dudek did well to save from a Veron shot and Beckham free-kick, while Henchoz cleared off the line from Scholes.

Liverpool resumed the second half strongly, with Heskey and Owen going close, but soon it was all Manchester United as they pressed for the equaliser. Dudek single-handedly maintained the slender advantage, denying van Nistelrooy on three occasions and Scholes too. Liverpool relied on the break, but Gerrard's great opportunity was blocked by Barthez. However, the counter attack worked with 4 minutes left; Hamann won the ball in midfield and released Owen, he raced forward, drew Barthez and scored from an angle.

Liverpool had another glorious chance when Murphy went to the goal line, but Smicer missed from two yards, and there was more hilarity when Giggs missed his kick in front of goal.

Hyppia collected the trophy, and Dudek the "Man of the Match" award; a redemption after his previous United embarrassment. Liverpool finished fifth in the league, missing out on a Champions League place to Chelsea on the final day. Although Houllier qualified the following year, his time at Anfield was over.

- The entire match is available on YouTube.

- Liverpool have won both League Cup finals against Manchester United, but lost both FA Cup finals.

- Michael Owen scored 28 goals in all competitions, but in the league Diouf and Heskey would only score three and six respectively.

- No Liverpool manager since 1990, has matched Houllier's total of six major trophies.

Liverpool 3 Olympiacos 1

08/12/2004 - Champions League Champions League Group Stage Matchday 6 - Anfield

Raphael Benitez was a popular choice as the new manager, with fresh memories of how his Valencia team had outplayed Liverpool twice. Owen (a cut price move to Real Madrid), Heskey, Diouf and Murphy left, as Djibril Cisse, Luis Garcia and Xavi Alonso joined. Early league form was mixed, due to a plethora of injuries and adapting to the Benitez style. Similarly in Europe, there were struggles, so they needed to beat Olympiacos by two goals, to qualify for the knockout rounds. The stage was set for another famous Anfield night.

Cisse, Smicer, Hamann, Garcia and Biscan were all injured for this match. Chris Kirkland was now preferred in goal, Carragher installed at centre-back, Gerrard partnered Alonso in midfield, and striker Milan Baros returned from injury, with Kewell behind him. The Greek champions, Olympiacos, had a twin Brazilian strike force of Giovanni and the 32 year-old Rivaldo.

With a rousing Kop behind them, Liverpool were straight on the offensive creating a series of chances; Baros had a goal disallowed for a foul, Hyppia headed wide from a corner, Gerrard hit the post with a flick. The goal would not come, meanwhile Rivaldo was a threat, gliding though tackles on a powerful run, before being fouled by Hyppia. He took the free-kick, and shot through a poor wall into the net. Olympiacos were frustrating, wasting time, and going down easily as the half ended on a downbeat mood, as Liverpool now needed three.

Benitez gambled, taking Traore off, and added another striker Florent Sinama-Pongolle, with Kewell moving to the wing. The impact was immediate with a goal in two minutes, Kewell got to the byline, and Sinama-Pongolle put in his cut back. Hope was restored, as the Kop roared on Liverpool's attacks. Gerrard soon scored from distance, but a free-kick was awarded against Baros.

In the 80th minute, the tiring Baros was replaced by reserve striker Neil Mellor; and again a substitute took just two minutes to score. Sinama-Pongolle's cross was headed by Nunez, half saved, but Mellor stabbed in from close range.

Liverpool threw everything forward searching for the vital goal, while Olympiacos battled for their survival, as Kewell went closest. The magical moment arrived after 86 minutes; Carragher put a long ball forward, Mellor cushioned a header back to Gerrard on the edge of the area, he cut across the ball, sending it hurtling into the corner. Gerrard ran to the Kop, his arms pumping, as even the ex-Everton commentator Andy Gray cheered "Oh ya beauty ! What a hit, son".

Liverpool had triumphed, through sheer force of will. Although they had scraped through the group stage, Benitez's tactical skills, his ability to change a difficult situation, a never-say- die spirit, and the passionate backing from the fans, would set them up for a longer run.

- Milan Baros had won the Golden Boot as top scorer in the 2004 Euros with five goals for the Czech Republic.

- Olympiacos had lost all of their previous five trips to England.

- Neil Mellor's only European goal for Liverpool, and Sinama-Pongolle would only score one more.

- Liverpool have met Olympiacos twice (2000, 2004), and on both occasions went on to win the European trophy.

- Steven Gerrard had scored against Olympiacos in 2000 too, and they were selected for his testimonial in August 2013.

- Rafa Benitez had won promotions with Extremadura and Tenerife, and with Valencia won two La Liga titles (the first in 31 years) and the UEFA Cup.

- To read more on this campaign, read "A Season on the Brink" by Guillem Balague.

Liverpool 1 Chelsea 0

03/05/2005 - Champions League Semi-final 2nd leg - Anfield

Benitez first season was bizarre, as they missed out on the top four in the Premiership, often losing abjectly to lowly opposition. But in Europe, they were sensational, impressively seeing off Bayern Leverkusen and Italian champions Juventus, with memorable nights of early frenzied attacks and then resilient defending, with a thunderous crowd backing.

Chelsea would be even tougher, as there was a massive 33 points gap, and at the weekend they claimed their first league title in fifty years. Bankrolled by Roman Abramovich's millions and melded by José Mourinho's genius, they had assembled exceptional talents; Peter Cech, John Terry, Claude Makele, Frank Lampard, Joe Cole, and Didier Drogba. They had already beaten Liverpool twice in the league, and in the League Cup final too.

A 0-0 draw away at Stamford Bridge was a creditable clean sheet, but the lack of away goal might be costly. Dudek was back in goal now, with a consistent defence, and Luis Garcia was a mercurial cult hero with vital goals. Alonso was suspended so the reliable Hamann came in. Arjen Robben was only fit enough for the Chelsea bench.

The Kop was full early, full of hope, as one banner adopted the John Lennon lyric, "You may say I'm a dreamer". Mourinho was not worried about the Anfield effect, claiming they could make a lot of noise, but "cannot play". Approaching the kick-off, the fans were vociferous, as Johnny Cash's "Ring of Fire" had become the anthem for this European campaign.

As on the previous European nights, Liverpool were fast out of the traps, pressing Chelsea, and had their reward in the 4th minute. Riise fizzed in a pass to the edge of the area, a cute flick from Gerrard put Baros through. He reached the ball before Cech, and pushed it past him, but was brought down. Garcia didn't wait for the penalty and clipped the loose ball towards the line. Gallas would desperately attempt to clear, but the goal was given. Mourinho would often bemoan a "ghost goal", but referee Michel later said his linesman confirmed it was over the line. If it had not, then he would have awarded a penalty and dismissed Cech. Anfield erupted into an even more tumultuous cacophony, but Benitez remained passive on the touchline.

Chelsea may have dominated possession, but Liverpool were chasing and challenging for everything, with Hamann, Biscan, and Gerrard immense in the centre, while Baros was always a willing runner. Too often Chelsea resorted to long balls to Drogba, but Hyppia and Carragher were resolute. The only glimmer of an opening was for Cole, but Dudek came out quickly to smoother.

There were more chances in the second half, Riise sliced shot went wide, while also off-target was a Drogba free-kick and a Gudjohnson shot. A Lampard free-kick was on target, but Dudek pushed it around the post. A series of substitutions were made, as both managers tried to influence the final 20 minutes. Substitutes Robben shot went over, and Cisse's header was easily saved, and then his shot just past the post. A Robben cross was missed by Dudek, but cleared by Traore.

Kewell and Nunez kept possession and ran with the ball, while Mourinho desperately opted for central defender Robert Huth as another aerial target. The signal of six minutes of injury time, extended the Liverpool's fans torment, as the action was even more fevered and ragged. Cisse, clean through, tried to chip Cech, but his effort was disappointing. In the dying seconds, Dudek could not clear another Chelsea cross, clashing into Hyppia, the ball fell to Gudjohnson, with the goal at his mercy. His effort went whistling past the far post; a final and glorious chance had gone, and seconds later, the tie was over.

Liverpool had upset the odds and triumphed, reaching their first Champions League final, 20 years after Heysel. The players celebrated in front of the delirious Kop, with yet another rendition of "Ring of Fire". One of the truly great European night at Anfield, and maybe the best.

- YouTube has several clips of highlights, but equally interesting are the clips of the fans.

- A seat in the Kop cost £30.

- Chelsea had scored away in every match since October.

- Liverpool's third successive European clean sheet.

- Luis Garcia had scored against Bayern Leverkusen (three goals), Juventus and Chelsea

- Chelsea's Ricardo Carvalho had won the Champions League with Jose Mourinho and Porto the previous year.

- At this time, Brendan Rodgers was the Chelsea Youth Academy manager.

- Rafa Benitez became Chelsea's interim manager in November 2012, and led them to a Europa Cup triumph and qualified for the Champions League.

AC Milan 3 Liverpool 3   (2 - 3 on penalties)

25/05/2005 - Champions League Final - Ataturk Stadium, Istanbul

A new generation now had their opportunity of witnessing European glory. Although Liverpool were only allocated 20,000 tickets in the 69.000 stadium, it is estimated that over 35,000 descended on Istanbul, congregating in Taksim Square.

Opponents AC Milan were vastly experienced, with a Champions League triumph two years earlier. Their star-studded lineup mixed Italian greats, Paolo Maldini, Alessandro Nesta, Andrea Pirlo with South American imports, Dida, Cafu, Kaka, Herman Crespo, and the talismanic Ukrainian striker Andrily Shevchenko.

The majority of the Liverpool team picked itself, but Benitez opted for Kewell behind the lone striker Baros. Alonso and Gerrard anchored the midfield, at the expense of Hamann.   It was a surprising and courageous move, as Liverpool had been so solid in the previous two rounds. As normal he only named the team in the dressing room, explaining his plan to exploit Milan's age with pace, and keeping possession to stop their counter attacks.

The stadium was far outside the city, in a deserted industrial area, and as the single road became congested, many walked. A concert featuring Liverpool favourites helped lift the spirits.

As the teams came out two Milan players touched the trophy, but the superstitious Liverpool did not. The start was a calamity, as nervous Traore gave away a free-kick. Pirlo flighted in a low ball to an unmarked Maldini, who had held back at the edge of the area, and he hit it into the ground, and up past Dudek. Things could have been even worse, as Carragher had to clear a Seedorf header off the line.

Liverpool tried to reply, as a Hyppia's header forced a save and a Riise shot was blocked. But they were struggling as they could not keep possession in midfield. Even when Kewell went off injured, Benitez still went for a direct replacement with Smicer coming on. Every time Liverpool lost the ball, the axis of Pirlo and Kaka had so much freedom to engineer rapid counter attacks. Twice Liverpool were saved by an offside flag. There would be no reprieve in the 39th minute. Garcia attacked the Milan defence, and the ball hit the prone Nesta's hand, but no penalty was given. While Garcia appealed, Pirlo released Kaka to sweep down the pitch, he chose a precise ball to Shevchenko, who gave Crespo a tap in. Three minutes later, Pirlo passed short again to Kaka, he played a sensational defence-splitting 50 yard pass, that Crespo dinked past Dudek. "Game well and truly over !" shouted Andy Gray in the commentary, and few would have disagreed.

3-0 down at half-time, and the nightmare scenario was it could get even worse. In the changing room, Benitez was calm, with no shouting or finger pointing, just shocked players. Traore was immediately sent to the showers, with a formation rejig of three at the back, like Olympiacos. A physio soon reported that Finnan might not last 90 minutes, so he was swapped instead. Hamann was sent out to warm up, but there was also some chaos as Cisse was also stripped ready, but he was discarded as it was too early for a final substitution.

The new plan was that Hamann would push on to Pirlo, stopping the balls to Kaka, and also allowing Gerrard more freedom offensively. Outside the shell-shocked Liverpool fans launched into a lamented version of "You'll Never Walk Alone".

The impact wasn't immediate, as Dudek had to save well from a free-kick. But Milan were not dominating anymore, slowly they were suffocating, as Pirlo was being overrun. Without access to Pirlo, they had to resort to less accurate longer balls, so Liverpool were winning it back more. They also found more space now, the first sign being Alonso hitting the outside of the post. Growing in confidence, Riise surged down the wing, passes were exchanged between the now influential Gerrard, Alonso, and Hamann, then returned to Riise in an advanced position. His first cross was blocked, but his second attempt found Gerrard, who met it with a directed looping header that beat Dida. 3-1, Liverpool had some hope again, "hello, hello" gulped a startled Clive Tyldesley on the television commentary, as Gerrard ran back, his arms desperately encouraging the fans.

Milan soon lost the ball from the restart, and Baros was played through, but was blocked. The linesman flagged for offside, but play continued and went out for a throw. Kaka took the opportunity to fix his shin pad, but the throw was taken quickly, Alonso, square to Hamann, on to Smicer. The Czech suddenly released a shot, that Baros did well to avoid, and caught Dida by surprise, as it arrowed into the bottom corner. 3-2 ! Smicer's face was contorted in delight, and the mood had changed very quickly.

Milan were rocking, the believing Liverpool fans raucous, as Ancelotti passively chewed his gum on the bench. Again Milan could not keep possession from the restart, as Liverpool swarmed over them. Carragher came forward into space, found Baros, his smart layoff was for the run of Gerrard, but he was cynically tripped by Gatusso for a penalty. The Italian complained, while Carragher was insistent that Nesta should be sent off. Garcia collected the ball, but was soon overruled, as Alonso had been designated the penalty taker. After the delay, he stepped up; his right foot shot was in the corner, but Dida stretched to block it with one hand. The ball rolled back slightly, and Alonso reacted first, firing it over Dida with his left foot into the roof of the net. 3-3! His celebration run was curtailed by Baros' arm around the neck, bringing down to the turf. An incredible six minutes had seen Liverpool wipe out a seemingly invincible lead.

In the euphoria, they even chased a winner; Riise's fierce shot was blocked by Dida. Slowly Milan restored their composure and came forward again. Dudek fumbled a cross, but Traore cleared Shevchenko's shot from the goal line, while Carragher made an important tackle on Crespo. At the other end, Garcia was nearly put through.

In extra time, Liverpool were exhausted, as the titanic efforts took their toll. The Milan substitutions had their desired effect, especially the pacy winger Serginho, so Gerrard was drafted in to the right-back position (his third of the match). Carragher was suffering from severe cramp, but still made important blocks, as they desperately hung on. Two minutes remained when a deep cross was met by a textbook header down by Shevchenko. Dudek pulled off a stunning save, but the ball rolled back, and Shevchenko seemed certain to score from such close range. However, his stabbed shot cannoned off Dudek's chest and flew over the bar. An incredible double save, and reinforced the growing belief that Liverpool were destined for glory. The final act was a blocked Riise shot from a free-kick, so the tie went to penalties.

Preparations were more advanced by 2005, as Dudek and goalkeeping coach Manuel Ochotorena had meticulously researched the Milan takers. However, it still left to his instincts at the time, while Carragher reminded him of Grobbelaar's Roma distractions.

For the first Milan penalty, Dudek carefully handed the ball to Serginho, staring him in the eye, and then retreated to his line, but still moved around as Serginho blazed over. Hamann, who had sustained a broken toe, sent a firm shot into the right corner to give Liverpool an early advantage. For Pirlo, Dudek moved around again on the line, then raced off his line to save his shot. Cisse coolly side-footed to the right, sending the Dida the wrong way. 2-0 and the trophy seemed within grasp. But there was another swing of the pendulum, as Tomasson and Kaka both scored, and Dida tipped Riise's placed kick to the left, around the post. 2-2. With a penalty in hand, the pressure was on Smicer; he calmly side-footed to the right like Cisse. Milan needed to score the next, but Shevchenko's weak penalty, was straight down the middle, and Dudek threw up an arm to bat it away.

All the exhaustion disappeared, as the Liverpool players sprinted from the halfway line to mob Dudek and then celebrate with the delirious fans. An astonishing comeback had been completed by a remarkable win. The greats such as Diego Maradona and Johann Cruyff lined up to pay tribute, as most people hailed it as the greatest comeback and the best European final ever. Gerrard collected the trophy and commenced a night of celebrations for the players and fans. The home coming, the following day, even topped previous parades, with an estimate of 750,000 ecstatic Liverpool fans.

- A DVD double -pack contains the complete match, and highlights of the previous rounds.

- The 50th European Cup / Champions League final.

- Paolo Maldini's goal, timed at 52 seconds, is still the quickest in a Champions League Final.

- Liverpool's fifth triumph meant they were entitled to keep the trophy, and it was the same trophy Manchester United had won in 1999.

- The match actually spanned two days, as it started at 9.45 pm local time and was not completed until just before 12.30 am.

- Gerrard's header was Liverpool's only headed goal in this year's European campaign of fifteen matches.

- Smicer scored in his last match for Liverpool, his only goal of the season. It was also his first European goal since 2002, when he scored the second goal as Liverpool came from 0-3 down to draw 3-3 with Basle.

- Xavi Alonso's first penalty in his professional career, he was selected as Baros and Gerrard had already missed this season.

- The Liverpool starting XI consisted of two Englishmen, two Spanish and seven other nationalities, bought for a total of just over £40 million.

- Superstitious fans pinned their hopes on the omens of the date being the same date as the first European Cup win, or coincidences of a Pope John Paul dying (he was a Polish goalkeeper too), and Prince Charles' wedding (or Ken and Deidre Barlow if you prefer). Benitez also followed his tradition with his lucky underwear and pen.

- The final inspired a stage show and movie "One Night in Istanbul" and a short film "Six Minutes that Shocked the World" that starred Gerrard and Carragher.

- Carlo Ancelotti would win subsequent matches against Liverpool as manager of AC Milan, Chelsea, Real Madrid, Napoli, and Everton.

- Herman Crespo was on loan from Chelsea, and returned to score against Liverpool the following season, while Andriy Shevchenko would join in 2006 and score too.

- Liverpool had used three different goalkeepers during this European campaign as Chris Kirkland and Scott Carson also featured.

Birmingham City 0 Liverpool 7

21/03/2006 - FA Cup 6th Round - St Andrews

Benitez used the Champions League money and success to rebuild the squad with goalkeeper Pepe Reina, the energetic Momo Sissoko, Bolo Zenden, and Peter Crouch joining in the summer while Robbie Fowler and Daniel Agger were added in January. They were needed in another hectic season, that started on 13th July with a Champions League qualifier first round, and took in the World Club Championship in Japan before Christmas.

Goals became a difficulty in the New Year, as an eleven game spell saw no more than one scored in any match. However, a 5-1 win over Fulham and 3-1 at Newcastle saw the goals start to flow. The FA Cup match at Birmingham, was just two days after the Newcastle trip. Although Steve Bruce's Birmingham were struggling, it could still be a tricky tie, as they had done the double over Liverpool the previous season and drawn both encounters this season.

Bruce was limited by Heskey failing a fitness test, so Mikael Forssell was the main striker with Jermaine Pennant supporting. Benitez made six changes, including a surprise return for Sissoko, initially wearing goggles, after a serious eye injury.

Any worries were cast aside, as Liverpool raced into a two goal lead in the first five minutes. The first came after 55 seconds, Hyppia heading in a Gerrard free-kick after Sissoko had flicked it on. Crouch added a second, with a stooping header from a perfect curling Gerrard pass.

Gerrard nearly provided another for Crouch, but it was intercepted. The match was effectively over before half-time, as Crouch got his second, from a Garcia through ball. He was twice denied a hat-trick, from a shot and header. The only City threat was came from crosses by the busy Pennant.

There was no let-up in the one way traffic in the second half, as Taylor had to tip over from Alonso. Before the hour, a good team move, allowed substitute Morientes a simple finish. Riise made it five with a powerful left foot drive, and then Tebilly sliced a Kewell cross into his own net. Cisse rounded off the scoring in the last minute, with a shot that went through the beleaguered Taylor.

Benitez had been accused of disrespecting the FA Cup the previous year, but another semi-final win over Chelsea saw Liverpool head to Cardiff again.

- A YouTube clip has all the goals.
- Liverpool's biggest away win in the FA Cup, and Birmingham's largest FA Cup defeat.
- Peter Crouch's 11th and 12th Liverpool goals, after not scoring in his first eighteen appearances until 3rd December.
- Birmingham City's midfielder, Stephen Clemence is the son of Ray Clemence
- Liverpool's 30th clean sheet for the season already (with 27 for Reina) including eleven in a row from 20th October until 15th December.
- Birmingham City would be relegated at the end of this season, and Jermaine Pennant would join Liverpool.

Liverpool 3 Everton 1

25/03/2006 - Premier League - Anfield

The next Saturday lunchtime, Everton were visitors, as the Reds aimed to maintain a Champions League position. Everton, were now managed by David Moyes, and had pipped Liverpool to fourth place the previous season. Their summer recruitment had not worked out, as they slumped to 17th at Christmas, but a strong recovery saw them now in 9th place. They had the defensive pair of Alan Stubbs and David Weir, with Phil Neville and Tim Cahill in midfield and James Beattie up front. Liverpool were at full strength, with Benitez making just one change with Kewell now starting.

Everton started well as Cahill missed a chance, and Beattie's effort was disallowed. Gerrard was booked for kicking the ball away, and soon red-carded for a mistimed tackle on Kilbane, leaving Liverpool to play over 70 minutes with ten men.

The whole team rose to the challenge; Alonso and Sissoko tenacious in the centre, and Kewell and Garcia industrious in helping back, while Crouch was holding up the ball well. Conversely, the dismissal seemed to improve Liverpool, as they seemed more likely to score, as Garcia went close with a chip. They went ahead just before the interval, as an inswinging Alonso corner skimmed off Phil Neville's head into his own net.

The start of the second half was even more one-sided as Liverpool penned Everton back. Crouch headed on a long ball, and Garcia lobbed over the advancing Howard, to make it 2-0 to the ten men. They celebrated in front of the Kop with Reina running the length of the pitch to join in. Everton could not get out of their own half, as Garcia had a shot blocked and a Kewell's shot was tipped away.

It took to the hour for Everton to make their mark, Cahill scored from a corner. They could not build on this, as Wright saved from Kewell, and Hyppia's header was disallowed for offside. Everton brought on Ferguson and Andy van der Meyde, but the latter only lasted five minutes, as he was also sent off, for swinging an elbow at Alonso.

With the numbers now balanced, Liverpool were comfortable. Crouch missed an easy header, before Kewell scored an arrowed drive with 6 minutes remaining. It could have been even more, as Crouch and Garcia missed late chances.

A typical derby with two red cards, and nine bookings, but Liverpool, against the odds, had triumphed. It also demonstrated this was not a one-man team, and the foreign contingent understood the importance of the local pride.

- Steven Gerrard holds the Liverpool record for red cards in the Premier League, with seven (two against Everton and Manchester United each).

- Liverpool would also beat Everton 1-0 in February 2010, after Sotirios Kyrgiakos was sent off before half-time.

- Gerrard and Beattie wore a special number 08 shirt to publicise Liverpool being the European City of Culture in 2008.

- Pepe Reina would win the Golden Glove for most clean sheets for all of his first three seasons.

- Rafa Benitez was appointed the Everton manager in June 2021, the first person to manage both clubs since William Barclay in the 1890s.

Liverpool 3 West Ham United 3   (3 - 1 on penalties)

13/05/2006 - FA Cup Final   - Millennium Stadium

The Everton win was part of an eleven-match winning run, as Liverpool finished third with 82 points, and reached the FA Cup final. It would be Liverpool's 62nd and final match of this arduous season that had started ten months ago. They were strong favourites against West Ham, who had finished 9th in their first season back in the Premier League, under the manager Alan Pardew. Garcia and Hayden Mullins were both suspended after being sent off in their league meeting two weeks earlier. Dean Ashton and Alonso both played after injury concerns.

Liverpool started another final badly again. Carragher turned a Scaloni shot into his own net after 21 minutes. Soon Reina fumbled an Etherington shot, and Ashton pounced on the rebound for 2-0. There was a swift response, with a Crouch volley being disallowed for a tight offside, and then another long lofted ball from Gerrard was volleyed in by Cisse. The dangerous Ashton shot just wide again as the Hammers deserved their half-time lead.

Into the second half, there another Istanbul echo, as Kewell went off injured. Reina needed to make a fine double save to deny Harewood and Benayoun, but then Gerrard equalised; an unstoppable shot into the top corner after a nod down from Crouch.

Now level, it seemed likely that Liverpool would go on to win. But the game took another twist after 64 minutes, as a Konchesky cross or shot, deceived Reina and sailed into the back of the net. Liverpool threw men forward to rescue the game, as Morientes headed over and Gerrard shot wide. Just as they were announcing injury time, the ball fell to Gerrard well outside the box. He didn't hesitate and hit a bullet of a shot that flew into the corner from 30 yards, one of the best FA Cup final goals ever.

Extra time was a war of attrition and injuries, as multiple players went down with cramp on the hot day, with Cisse and Harewood virtual passengers. The best chance fell to the latter as his flicked header hit the post, and he could only swing a leg, directing the rebound wide. Sissoko kept Liverpool on the move, as Riise and

Hyppia shot wide.

Another 3-3 final draw, and on to penalties. This time it was Reina to be the hero, as he incredibly saved three from Zamora, Konchesky, and Ferdinand, while Hamann, Gerrard, and Riise all scored to record Liverpool's 7th FA Cup.

Like the previous year's Champions League final, sportswriters bandied superlatives, with some coining the term "the Gerrard Final". Two sensational final wins in two years had marked Benitez as an expert tactician who built resilient teams.

- The entire match is available on DVD, and clips are on YouTube.

- Liverpool's penultimate appearance at the Millennium Stadium, where they had won six, and lost two matches.

- Carragher scored eight own goals in his career, including two in the same match against Manchester United in 1999.

- Yossi Benayoun and Paul Konchesky would both sign for Liverpool. The latter is the only player to score in an FA Cup final against Liverpool, and later play for them.

- Steven Gerrard would score 22 goals this season, his best total yet, often playing on the right of midfield, and would win the PFA Player of the Year award.

- Gerrard became the only player to score in the finals of the FA Cup, League Cup, Champions League, and UEFA Cup.

- Alan Pardew was famous for scoring the winning goal against Liverpool in the FA Cup semi-final in 1990. He would also manage Crystal Palace to an FA Cup final in 2016, but lose to Manchester United.

- Liverpool's 82 points was their best total for 17 seasons, but still 9 points behind Chelsea, reflecting the increased competition for the Premier League.

Barcelona 1 Liverpool 2

21/02/2007 - Champions League Round of 16 1st leg - Camp Nou

Benitez was always active in the transfer market, often moving on recently signed players that could not meet his requirements. Summer 2006 saw a remodelling of his offensive options, with striker Dirk Kuyt, the tempestuous Craig Bellamy, and Jermaine Pennant, while January improved defensive protection with Alvaro Arbeloa and Javier Mascherano (on loan). Although comfortable in third place, Liverpool were never really in the title race, so had to look to Europe again. They won their group, but were unlucky to be drawn with defending champions, Barcelona. Managed by Frank Rijkaard, they were missing Samuel Eto'o but still fielded stars such as Xavi, Ronaldinho, Deco and the 19-year old prodigy, Lionel Messi.

With a free weekend, the squad prepared with a bonding trip to the Algarve. but it went awry as Bellamy attacked Riise with a golf club after a karaoke dispute ! However, both were still selected, as Benitez devised a plan of using the right-footed Arbeloa, at left-back, to stop Messi cutting inside.

Inevitably they had to endure a torrid start; Reina saved from an offside Saviola, Beletti shot over, and Ronaldinho tumbled, but no penalty was forthcoming. There was no surprise when Deco's header opened the scoring after 15 minutes, and it could have been extended as Saviola shot wide, and Deco's shot was blocked by Reina's legs.

Gradually Liverpool weathered the storm with Alonso, Sissoko and Gerrard scrapping in midfield, and made a chance with Bellamy heading into the side netting. Just before half-time, the Welshman equalised with another header. Finnan crossed from the right, Bellamy's connection was firm, but Valdes made a mess of the save, taking the ball over the line. Kuyt made sure afterwards, as Bellamy wheeled away celebrating with a mock golf swing.

The second half was much more balanced. Valdes saved twice from Gerrard, and Kuyt should have put a header on target. At the other end, a Ronaldinho free-kick went over, and Reina saved from his weaving run, and Arbeloa blocked Messi from the rebound.

The decisive goal came on 74 minutes; Kuyt miscontrolled a fine through ball by Gerrard, but a poor clearance allowed Bellamy to set up Riise, to finish with his weaker right foot, high into the net. Barcelona obviously renewed their attacks; Reina had to rush off his line to deny Saviola, but was fortunate that a misjudged Deco free-kick came back off the post. Benitez utilised the substitutions wisely so they could claim another famous victory in the Camp Nou, courtesy of goals from the two Algarve combatants.

Liverpool battered Barcelona in the opening stages in the second leg (Benitez was to claim it as their best 30 minutes), with only the woodwork and Valdes denying them. The former Chelsea player Guðjohnsen came on to give Barcelona the lead, but Liverpool held on to go through on away goals.

- Alvaro Arbeloa's first start for Liverpool.

- Liverpool remained unbeaten in their fourth trip to the Camp Nou, but did concede their first goal. Rafa Benitez had not lost there on his three trips with Valencia.

- The first time Liverpool had knocked out the reigning European Champions.

- Craig Bellamy holds the record for scoring for eight different Premiership teams.

- Pepe Reina had been in goal for Barcelona against Liverpool in the 2001 UEFA semi-final.

Liverpool 1 Chelsea 0   (4 - 1 on penalties)

01/05/2007 - Champions League Semi-final 2nd leg - Anfield

After easily overcoming PSV Eindhoven, Liverpool would meet Chelsea in the semi-final again, but this time the task was different, as Chelsea had won the first leg 1-0. They had added Michael Essien and John Obi Mikel to strengthen their midfield, with Salomon Kalou as a winger. Benitez chose Crouch and Kuyt as the strikers, with Pennant and Zenden on the wings (instead of Alonso), and the tigerish Mascherano was now the midfield ball winner.

Liverpool chased an early leveller, with Pennant the key threat, having a shot blocked, and Gerrard shot wide. After 22 minutes Liverpool scored with a training ground set piece that Benitez had not used since his Valencia days. Several players rushed in, as Gerrard approached a free-kick near the touchline. Agger stayed on the edge of the area, meeting Gerrard's rolled pass sweetly, low past Cech to make it 1-1. Searching for a decisive away goal, Drogba was put through, but Reina blocked well, and Essien also headed wide, as Agger was also defending well.

Liverpool edged the second half, with the dynamic Mascherano winning the midfield battle. A Crouch header was saved by Cech's feet, Kuyt hit the crossbar with a header and a Zenden shot was saved too. Chelsea's best effort was a wayward Lampard free-kick. However, Liverpool had needed to defend well, as Carragher cleared a Cole cross from close range, and Reina came out quickly for a through ball.

In extra time, again the best chances fell to the home team. Alonso shot over, Kuyt's shot was saved, but he was offside anyway. He then had the ball in the back of the net from an Alonso rebound, but was offside again. Chelsea's were half chances, with a weak Drogba header, and a Wright-Phillips' cross that went across the area.

There was a flurry of substitutions (with an eye on penalties), and substitute Fowler set up Kuyt late, but his glorious opportunity was well saved by Cech. For the third consecutive Benitez year, a crucial tie would be decided by penalties.

Benitez sat calmly, cross-legged on the edge of the pitch. Zenden, Gerrard and Alonso all scored to Cech's right, while Reina repeated his

Cardiff heroics, saving from Robben and Geremi. Kuyt stepped up to score, with a low shot into the corner, taking Liverpool to Athens for another final with AC Milan.

The irony was that although Liverpool had a better team, and played more consistently, they lost 2-1 this time. However, Benitez was rapidly building a inimitable reputation for the special European nights, and the mood was optimistic with increased investment imminent.

- Daniel Agger's first European goal for Liverpool.

- The referee, Manuel Mejuto González, had also been in charge of the 2004 Olympiacos match and 2005 AC Milan final.

- Liverpool's seventh successive European Cup semi-final win

- Chelsea had not lost in their previous 23 matches, since a 2-0 defeat against Liverpool in January.

- In three years, Benitez and Mourinho would meet in three semi-finals, (two Champions League and one FA Cup) with Liverpool winning all three. In total they would meet fifteen times in these three seasons.

- Liverpool were only the second team in ten years, to successfully overturn a Champions League semi-final first leg defeat.

- Liverpool had now won ten out of eleven penalty shootouts, the only exception away at Wimbledon in the League Cup.

- Pepe Reina emulated his father Miguel, who played in goal in the 1974 European Cup final for Atlético Madrid.

- As Benitez practiced rotation there were no league ever presents. Peter Crouch top scored with 18 goals in all competitions.

Liverpool 6 Derby County 0

01/09/2007 - Premier League - Anfield

The Americans George Gillett and Tom Hicks had bought Liverpool earlier in the year, and seemed to finance a record spending spree with Lucas Leiva, the promising Ryan Babel, Andrily Voronin, Yossi Benayoun arriving and Mascherano's loan would become permanent. However, the most exciting transfer was the club-record fee of in excess of £20 million for the 23-year old Fernando Torres from Atlético Madrid; a strong, quick and deadly centre forward.

He had looked promising, but only scored once in his first four appearances. Surely there would be opportunities to improve this, against the recently promoted Derby, who were already bottom of the league. The preparations for the match were rocked by the announcement that Benitez had parted from his long-time assistant Pako Ayerstan with accusations of "betrayal". Carragher and Gerrard were injured, so Hyppia was captain, as Alonso and Mascherano formed the centre of midfield.

Liverpool could not break through initially, with Babel and Pennant probing down the wings, and a Torres header was well saved. The resistance was broken after 26 minutes, a deep Alonso free-kick, curled over everyone and into the net. Kuyt missed twice from Pennant crosses, but Babel made it two just before half-time. An intricate passing move resulted in Arbeloa finding Babel on the edge of the penalty area, he feigned to shot, stranding two Derby defenders on the ground, then cut inside and fired into the top corner.

It got much worse for Derby in the second half. In the 56th minute, Mascherano's sliding tackle freed Torres, he dashed towards goal and finished with his left foot. For the fourth, Babel teed up Benayoun, he was swiftly tackled, but the ball ran to Alonso, who finished precisely for his second. In the 76th minute, Kuyt shot from an acute angle, Bywater could only parry, and Voronin tapped in. A minute later, Voronin's forward pass, was miscontrolled by Todd, and Torres pounced, going around the Bywater for another cool finish. Kuyt nearly scored too just at the end, but Bywater saved.

A welcome sign that the enhanced Liverpool could score goals, and that Fernando Torres would be the real deal. The 67 league goals scored this season was the highest for Benitez so far, and they totalled 117 in all competitions.

- The first time Liverpool were top during the Benitez era, and it would be the biggest Premier League win during his tenure.

- Ryan Babel's first Liverpool goal and Voronin's first at Anfield.

- Torres was nicknamed "El Nino" (the kid) and had captained his beloved Atlético Madrid at the age of 19.

- Pako Ayerstan would later manage Maccabi Tel Aviv, Valencia, Las Palmas and in Mexico.

- Ryan Babel would be the first Premiership player fined for a tweet, after he posted a mocked up photo of referee Howard Webb in a Manchester United kit !

- Derby County would be relegated at the end of the season with a record low of 12 points.

- Voronin had played for Bayer Leverkusen with Dmitar Berbatov in a 2005 Champions League tie at Anfield (but neither scored).

Liverpool 8 Besiktas 0

06/11/2007 - Champions League Group Stage Matchday 4 - Anfield

By November, Liverpool had slipped to seventh place, and Benitez had seemed to have lost his Champions League's touch, with just one draw in the first three, only scoring twice. They would now need to win all three remaining matchdays to ensure progress. First up were Besiktas, who had won the reverse fixture two weeks earlier. Torres was not fully fit, so only warranted a place on the bench, with Voronin and Crouch entrusted with striking roles.

The mood was edgy in the early minutes. as Sedef put a cross wide, but soon Liverpool threatened, as Voronin and Crouch went close while Benayoun hit the outside of the post. It took 20 minutes for Liverpool to break through; Crouch regained possession, his first shot was saved, but he netted from the rebound.

The nerves settled, a Riise header was cleared off the line and Crouch fired wide. The second came after 32 minutes, Voronin crossed for Benayoun, who had time to control and fire in.

Benayoun had a hat-trick before the hour mark; with two quick-fire tap-ins after Hakan could not hold Riise's shot or Gerrard's free-kick. Hakan did better to stop efforts from Babel and Gerrard, as his goal was under siege.

In the 69th minute, Gerrard played a one-two with Voronin, and his shot was deflected in. Substitute Babel then claimed a double in three minutes; the first a deft back flick from a Benayoun cross, and the second more fortuitous, as a defender's clearance cannoned off him and looped in. He too should have secured a hat-trick, but hit the bar with an unmarked header.

Reina was finally called into action to save low to deny a Bobo header, but the final goal came in the 88th minute. Mascherano sprayed the ball out to Benayoun, and his cross was glanced in by Crouch.

Liverpool would ensure their progress by beating Porto 4-1 and Marseille 4-0 away. No one would relish meeting Liverpool and Benitez in the Champions League knockout phase now.

- Rafa Benitez's 50th European match as Liverpool manager.

- Still the record victory in the Champions League Group stage.

- Liverpool biggest win since beating Swansea 8-0 win in 1990.

- Babel and Benayoun's first European goals for Liverpool. The latter would also score an Anfield hat-trick this season in the FA Cup against non-league Havant & Waterlooville.

- Peter Crouch had lost his place to Torres, starting only started one league game, but five Cup matches so far.

Liverpool 4 Arsenal 2

08/04/2008 - Champions League Quarter-final 2nd leg - Anfield

After the early European troubles, Liverpool impressively won home and away against Inter Milan (who had not lost all season), part of seven straight wins that saw Liverpool and Torres hit top form. Arsenal awaited in the quarter-finals, and it set up a trilogy of games in six days. The Champions League first leg and Premier League were both drawn 1-1 at the Emirates stadium.

Crouch had played well in the second match, so he would partner Torres in place of Babel, with Kuyt now utilising his non-stop energy on the right wing, while Martin Skrtel had strengthened the defence. Alonso and Mascherano was the central pairing, so Gerrard unusually found himself on the left. Arsenal league hopes were dying, but they were still eight points ahead of the Reds, with a team that featured Williams Gallas, Kolo Toure, Cesc Fabregas and Emmanuel Adebayor. Even though the opposition were domestic, the atmosphere and dramatics were typical of Anfield on a European night.

Arsenal started much the better and deservedly took the lead after 13 minutes. Reina had been quick to block Adebayor, but they worked the ball to Diaby who fired in. The Spanish keeper was busier and did well to punch away a dangerous cross. Liverpool finally came to life after half an hour, as Hyppia equalised with a free header from a corner that went in off the post. All square. Gerrard went close soon after.

Attacking the Kop in the second half, Liverpool were much improved, with Crouch and Aurelio's shots saved, and another Crouch effort wide. Benitez's selection seemed to pay off after 69 minutes; Crouch headed on a long goal kick to Torres, with his back to goal, he shielded the ball, turned quickly and fired into the top corner.

Arsenal immediately reacted, sending on Robin van Persie and the 19-year old Theo Walcott. Adebayor missed a sitter, but then Walcott fended off all challenges in a quick break from the edge of his own area. He crossed for Adebayor, who could not miss and danced merrily in front of the Arsenal fans.

Benitez had already brought on the pace of Babel for Crouch, and from the restart he made a difference, as ran at the defence and drew a clumsy foul by Toure. Gerrard swept the crucial penalty past Almunia's dive.

Arsenal threw everything forward, but the Liverpool defence were resilient now. In stoppage time, Kuyt hacked away a clearance, Babel gave chase, outsprinted the last man Fabregas, and then slotted in. Anfield erupted, and Babel was mobbed, with Reina running the length of the pitch again.

Another glorious night that Benitez had specialised in. Another semi-final with Chelsea beckoned, but this time their new manager Avram Grant would triumph. The season had ended without silverware again, but Liverpool looked set for a serious title challenge, especially with Torres such a threat.

- Sami Hyppia scored in three Champions League quarter-finals.

- Torres scored 33 goals for Liverpool in this debut season, with 24 in the league. His three hat-tricks included two in successive home matches and he also beat Ruud van Nistelrooy's record for a debut season.

- Ryan Babel would score twelve times for Liverpool as substitute, more than he did when starting.

- Rafa Benitez recounts his memories and tactical analysis of all Liverpool's European matches in this era in his book "Champions League Dreams".

Manchester City 2 Liverpool 3

5/10/2008 - Premier League - City of Manchester Stadium

There had already been several signs of discontent between the American owners and Benitez, but he was still allowed to spend well over £30 million on Robbie Keane, Andrea Dossena, and the winger Albert Reira. After his four years of building, Benitez was ready for a title challenge. The early indications were very positive as Liverpool won eight, and drew three. Keane had scored his first goal in midweek, but was on the bench, with the team having a settled look.

Manchester City had been down to the third tier, but were now flush with new money after the September takeover by the Abu Dhabi Group. The team managed by Mark Hughes, was a mixture of old Manchester City players like Richard Dunne and Stephen Ireland, but now enhanced by signings such as Joe Hart, Vincent Kompany, Pablo Zabaleta. The new wealth was reflected up front, with the Brazilians Jo (£19 million) and Robinho (£32 million).

The early exchanges were shared, one Riera cross was blocked by Hart and another skied by Kuyt. A Robinho shot was saved by Reina, but on 18th minutes, Ireland smashed in a goal. Then Garrido scored from a free-kick to leave Liverpool trailing 2-0 at half-time.

Liverpool were more positive and improved in the second half; Kuyt was denied a penalty after being clipped by Dunne and Mascherano shot wide. Within 10 minutes, Gerrard released Arbeloa, and his low cross was scrambled in by Torres. Although City were now second best, Robinho missed a simple chance to restore the two goal margin from close range.

Zabaleta was sent off for a dangerous foul on Alonso, and this only made the game even more one-sided, as Keane was brought on in place of Mascherano. The equaliser came two minutes later, with Torres' glancing header from a Gerrard corner. The Spaniard missed a chance for his hat-trick, stretching to shoot over. Benayoun came on too, as Benitez went for the win. This last change seemed to have backfired, as Skrtel had to go off with a serious injury. Even with ten men apiece, Liverpool still looked most likely to score. Two minutes into injury time, Benayoun darted to the line, pulled back a cross, a Torres shot was blocked, but it fell for Kuyt to sweep it home.

A stunning recovery that showed a maturity and resilience that would help sustain a title tilt. The unbeaten start would last sixteen matches, with a win at Chelsea later in the month putting Liverpool top.

- Dirk Kuyt's first league goal in 26 matches, since Newcastle United in November 2007, although he had contributed six important Champions League goals in the meantime.

- Robbie Keane's dream Anfield career would only last until the next transfer window, as he returned to Tottenham.

- Benitez had tried to sell Alonso to finance a move for Gareth Barry in the summer, but could not find any suitable buyers. Alonso responded with his best season for Liverpool.

- Liverpool would come from behind to win five times in eleven matches in this period.

- Albert Riera had played with Pablo Zabaleta in Spain, and also made 15 appearances for Manchester City in a loan spell.

- One of Liverpool's only two wins in their first nine visits to Manchester City's new stadium.

- Four of this Manchester City team would win the Premier League in 2011/12.

Liverpool 4 Real Madrid 0

10/03/2009 - Champions League Round of 16 2nd leg - Anfield

Liverpool had finished 2008 top of the League, but the New Year saw too many draws, and an FA Cup defeat to Everton. However, European glory was eyed again with a win on their first visit to the Bernabeu Stadium. Reigning Spanish champions Real Madrid may not have been at their peak, managed by Juande Ramos, but they still had an array of expensively acquired stars Iker Casillas, Pepe, Sergio Ramos, Fabio Cannavaro, Wesley Sneijder, Raul, Arjen Robben, and Gonzalo Higuain. Despite their deficit, the Spanish press were still bullish, as the Real supporting newspaper Marca headlined "This is Anfield.... so what ?"

After the sale of Keane, Benitez had settled on a system of Gerrard playing off Torres. Babel played instead of the injured Reira and Benayoun, with Kuyt on the right again. Alonso and Mascherano anchored the midfield.

Liverpool tore into Madrid from the first whistle. A great turn by Torres presented a good chance, but Casillas saved with his legs. From the corner, Casillas tipped a Mascherano shot on to the bar, which had even the Argentinean ruefully shaking his head in disbelief. The pressure told after 16 minutes, as Torres and Kuyt overpowered Pepe, and Torres stabbed in; celebrating in front of the travelling fans, a happy moment for the ex- Atlético man. Casillas was keeping Madrid in the tie, as he saved from Gerrard's stretch to meet a Torres cross.

Before the half-hour, Liverpool were awarded a penalty after Heinze's handball, and Gerrard slammed it in. 3- 0 on aggregate now, and there was little chance of a Madrid recovery as Liverpool swarmed over them. With the notable exception of Casillas, their defence was struggling to match Liverpool's mobility and ferocity. As Henry Winter opined in The Times "Pepe was hopeless. Popeye could have done better. So could Olive Oyl !" Benitez later revealed his intention had been to press high, but let the centre-backs come forward, so it would leave space behind. Finally Reina had to save twice from Sneider, one at full stretch from a free-kick.

In the 2nd minute of the second half, Babel beat Ramos, pulled the ball back, and Gerrard met it on the half volley with a rising controlled shot into the Kop net. Gerrard was denied a hat-trick by another save after a sweeping move. Madrid fought for pride as Gago shot wide and Raul headed over. Casillas again had to save well from a Torres curler. Liverpool could now afford to rest players, but substitute Dossena scored in the final minute, after Babel broke and the tireless Mascherano crossed.

A stunning victory, and would have been even more without the superlative Casillas. Marca recanted with the admission that "Liverpool humiliated Real from 1 to 93 minutes". Madrid legend Zinedine Zidane stated that Gerrard should be considered as one of the very best in the world. This would be the European highlight of the season, as Chelsea would win a quarter-final meeting.

- This is still Real Madrid's heaviest aggregate defeat in the Champions League era.

- Jerzy Dudek was on the Real Madrid bench, as he was their backup keeper for four years.

- Rafa Benitez would manage Real Madrid between June 2015 and January 2016.

- Torres' second goal against Real Madrid, as he had only scored once in nine matches for Atlético Madrid.

- Andrea Dossena's first goal for Liverpool.

- Steven Gerrard's 100th European appearance for Liverpool.

- Casillas would return to Anfield with Porto in 2018 and 2019, keeping an acclaimed clean sheet in the first visit.

- In his time as Liverpool manager Benitez supervised European wins over Real Madrid (home & away), Barcelona (away), Inter Milan (home & away), Juventus and Chelsea (twice).

- Arbeloa and Alonso would both move to Real Madrid at the end of the season, winning the League title in their first season. They were both involved in their successful Champions League campaign in 2014, but did not play in the final.

Manchester United 1 Liverpool 4

14/03/2009 - Premier League - Old Trafford

Benitez had substituted Torres and Gerrard early, as there was a critical Saturday lunchtime visit to the league leaders at Old Trafford. The Manchester United fans had taunted that Benitez was "cracking up" as they built up a seven-point lead. They had an excellent team with a fearsome attack of Cristiano Ronaldo, Wayne Rooney and Carlos Tevez, with a bench of Berbatov, Scholes and Giggs. Benitez lost Alonso to injury, and then Arbeloa in the warm-up, so in came Hyppia and Lucas.

Ronaldo gave United the lead after 23 minutes from the penalty spot after Park had been brought down. Benitez adopted the same tactics as against Madrid, allowing Vidic to come out with the ball, creating space for Torres. Vidic erred in letting a long ball from Skrtel bounce. Torres pounced, running in the space, drawing the keeper, and clipping in.

The teams traded chances. Ronaldo's free-kick was saved by Reina at the second attempt and Carrick shot over. At the other end, Torres and Gerrard's pace was troubling United, and this produced a penalty in the 44th minute. From Reina's long kick, Torres freed Gerrard, and he was brought down by Evra. He got up to fire the spot kick in, and celebrated by kissing the TV camera, the start of an Old Trafford ritual for him.

United battled to equalise in the second half, Reina saved Ronaldo's free-kick from distance, but a cross hit the post and Rooney's shot was deflected. However, Liverpool were still a threat, as a Lucas shot was saved, and Aurélio's effort blocked. Another rapid break paid dividends; a long ball from Lucas, Kuyt laid it off, and Gerrard steamed past Vidic, who pulled him back, earning a red card. From the free-kick Aurélio, curled it over the wall and into the net with van der Sar flat footed.

Against ten men, Liverpool were comfortable now, and should have added more. Torres tried to shoot from the halfway line, and Gerrard missed a sitter after being set up by Babel. In stoppage time, substitute Dossena latched on to a long kick from Reina, and coolly lobbed over the stranded goalkeeper.

Benitez's tactics, and targeted long passing had punished United. An incredible week with eight goals against such famous opponents, and the high watermark for the later Benitez era. He briefed the assembled press on how to beat United, in the hopes of inspiring their next opponents. United faltered in the next match, but scrambled a win against Aston Villa. Despite winning ten of their last eleven games, losing only twice all season, Liverpool just fell short again.

- Dossena's second and last goal for Liverpool.

- Benitez 100th Premier League win as Liverpool manager.

- The first time Liverpool had scored more than three at Old Trafford since 1936.

- Manchester United had won eleven straight league games before this match.

- The total of 86 points was Liverpool's highest in the Premier League so far, and they became the first team to lose only twice, but not win the league title.

- Vidic would be sent off in three successive encounters with Liverpool and four times in total.

- Steven Gerrard would score five times at Old Trafford, four of them penalties.

- Phil Thompson revealed that Liverpool had been offered Cristiano Ronaldo for £4 million when he was playing for Sporting Lisbon, but passed, because they were already committed to signing the French teenagers, Anthony Le Tallec and Florent Sinama-Pongolle.

2010s

Liverpool 2 Chelsea 0

07/11/2010 - Premier League - Anfield

Liverpool and Benitez parted company amid the swirling financial calamity of the owners' financial collapse. Roy Hodgson was entrusted with an unenviable challenge, on the back of his European experience, and having just taken Fulham to the Europa League final.

Mascherano and other Benitez signings left, but their replacements; Raul Meireles, Christian Poulson, Paul Konchesky, and Joe Cole all struggled. Gerrard was blighted by a recurring injury and Torres, injured after the World Cup, appeared disinterested. Hodgson was always destined to fail in such circumstances, but it was shocking how quickly. Losing to Everton was regrettable, but at home to Blackpool and Northampton was much worse, as Liverpool flirted with the lower reaches of the table.

There was one brief moment, a chink of light, as they scraped together three wins in a row, and the visit of Chelsea was sure to raise the team. Gerrard was back and Torres was retained, despite widespread criticism of his poor performance the previous week. Liverpool were still in the bottom half of the table, and defending champions Chelsea were top with a five-point gap, under Ancelotti's leadership. Nicholas Anelka was up front alone, as Drogba was on the bench after a fever overnight.

A reengaged Torres opened the scoring after 11 minutes, controlling a flighted pass from Kuyt, and firing past Cech. The Spaniard was the focus of attention, as he shot low past the post, and flicked on to Maxi Rodriguez, who shot over. Chelsea were missing Lampard and Essien in midfield and struggled to handle the renewed vigour from Gerrard, Meireles and Lucas. Torres second, just before half-time was even better; Meireles led a breakaway, and found Torres on the corner of the area, he cut inside and fired a curling shot into the far corner.

In the second half, Chelsea added Drogba, and put Liverpool under pressure, Ramires went close, and Reina saved well from Zhirhov and Malouda. However, Hodgson's team survived, with stout defending, and Kuyt even forced a save from Cech. There was just a final late scare when an Anelka shot went under Reina, but hit the bar.

Liverpool and Hodgson had claimed a significant victory, and something to build on. But it was a false dawn and new horrors awaited.

- Fernando Torres scored seven goals in eight matches against Chelsea, including his first Liverpool goal.

- Torres was the first current Liverpool player to win a World Cup final since Roger Hunt.

- After leaving Liverpool Torres would win the Champions League, and two Europa Leagues, but two of these were substitute appearances.

- Roy Hodgson has the shortest reign of any permanent Liverpool manager, just 31 matches.

- Hodgson only won one of seven games as Blackburn or Fulham manager against Liverpool, but he won two out of three in his next job at West Brom. He is the only man to manage both Liverpool and England.

- Daniel Sturridge made his first of three substitute and one starting appearances against Liverpool for Chelsea.

Liverpool 3 Manchester United 1

06/03/2011 - Premier League - Anfield

Hodgson would be gone by January with Liverpool in 12th place, and a disillusioned Torres would soon follow. However, optimism was generated by the new owners FSG, (then known as NESV), the return of beloved Kenny Dalglish as interim manager and the Torres' money going on strikers Andy Carroll (a club record fee of £35 million) and Luis Suarez from Ajax.

Results improved almost instantly, and an eight game unbeaten run lifted Liverpool to sixth. The revival would be tested by the league leaders, Manchester United. Noticeably, Dalglish had dispensed with all the Hodgson signings, apart from Meireles, as Suarez and Kuyt would start up front. Andy Carroll had been injured when he signed, but was now fit for a place on the bench.

It would be Suarez who caught the eye that day. Early on, he nearly diverted a Meireles shot in. Berbatov replied by hitting the outside of the post with a bending shot. The Liverpool midfield started to take control, winning the ball and frequently supplying Suarez. He created the first after 34th minutes, beating three United defenders in the area, with quick feet and tight control. He put the ball through the legs of van der Sar, and Kuyt was on hand to ensure the ball went over the line.

Five minutes later, he also had a hand in the second, as his cross was inexplicably headed back into the area by Nani, and Kuyt headed in from close range. Tempers became frayed after an x-rated Carragher tackle on Nani, and then Raphael on Lucas; both causing mass confrontations.

United were determined to get back in the game in the early stages of the second half, but substitute Javier Hernández shot wide, Giggs shot over and Meireles cleared off the line. Liverpool withstood the pressure, and sealed the win, just after the hour. Van der Sar could not hold a Suarez curler around the wall, and Kuyt followed up to score. A hat-trick for Kuyt, all from close range, and all with the assistance of the irresistible Suarez.

Carroll came on for his debut after 74 minutes, and immediately got his head to a long free-kick, but van der Sar saved easily. Hernandez scored a consolation with a header in the last minute, but the result was not in doubt.

Liverpool would finish sixth, but happier after a traumatic season. They had also discovered a tireless, but also controversial talent in Luis Suarez.

- Kuyt's first and only Liverpool hat-trick.

- Liverpool's last Premiership win over Alex Ferguson.

- Dalglish's last home match as manager against United had seen the Beardsley hat-trick.

- Dalglish had turned 60 two days earlier, so the Kop sang "Happy Birthday, King Kenny".

- Dimitar Berbatov had scored a hat-trick in the reverse fixture in September.

- Dalglish's appointment saw a goalscoring spike for two players. Maxi Rodriguez had only scored four times after 48 matches, but would end the season with two hat-tricks. Meireles had not scored in his first twenty matches under Hodgson, but scored in six of Dalglish's first seven matches.

- Michael Owen had signed for Manchester United in 2009, and although never a regular, he did win a Premier League winners medal this season.

Cardiff City 1 Liverpool 1   (2 - 3 on penalties)

26/02/2012 - League Cup Final - Wembley Stadium

Dalglish's appointment was made permanent, and the new owners invested heavily, following a "Moneyball" concept of football analytics with Damien Comoli, as the first director of football strategy. Signings included Jordan Henderson, Charlie Adam, Stewart Downing, Jose Enrique, and Sebastian Coates, while Craig Bellamy returned on loan. Like 1999, some were successful, others less so.

League form was disappointing, but in the domestic cups, Liverpool were invincible. In the League Cup they had recorded impressive victories away at Stoke City, Chelsea and Manchester City as they reached the final. There would be lower division opposition again, but again Cardiff City would provide a tricky encounter. Managed by Malky MacKay, they had won two ties on penalties, and mostly consisted of lower league players. The Liverpool teamsheet featured most of their new signings.

Liverpool were on top early and nearly made an ideal start after two minutes, as Johnson hit the bar and Gerrard put the rebound over. Soon Heaton had to save a Carroll header. Against the run of play on 19 minutes, Mason scored through Reina's legs. Liverpool tried to reply, but Adam shot wide, Gerrard over, while Heaton also saved from Suarez and Agger.

In the second half, Henderson shot wide, but Cardiff had chances on the break from Gestede and Miller. Bellamy came on, and Liverpool equalised on the hour. Adam's shot was deflected for a corner. Downing's kick was met by Carroll, Suarez hit the post, but Skrtel forced in the rebound. Liverpool looked like the only winners now, a Skrtel snapshot wide wide, while Downing and Adam were both denied by Heaton. Miller had a Cardiff best chance in the last minutes, but hit over.

Into extra time Liverpool were much stronger again, as Cardiff valiantly defended. Suarez's low shot was tipped around the post, and then his header was cleared off the line. Carroll, Bellamy and Johnson all had efforts off target. Kuyt came on, and scored within five minutes; coming forward, his initial shot was cleared, but he followed up and drove home the rebound. In the dying minutes Cardiff exerted pressure to rescue the final, and Kuyt had to clear off the line from Kiss. From the corner, Gunnarson headed on, and Turner poked home.

Another penalty shootout was required in a Liverpool final. The first three were missed (Adam blazed well over). Cowie and Kuyt both scored, but Gestede hit the post. Downing and Whittingham, made it 2-2, effectively taking it to sudden death. Johnson converted, but Anthony Gerrard shot wide, so Liverpool had won the League Cup again. The football writers praised Cardiff's spirit, but most acknowledged that Liverpool deserved it.

- Liverpool's first trip to the rebuilt Wembley, and the first of three visits in ten weeks.

- Liverpool's first major trophy since 2006, and last until 2019, extended their League Cup wins record to eight.

- Dalglish completed the feat of winning all three domestic trophies as a player and manager (the only Liverpool manager to win all three). He had also won the league as a manager with two different teams (matching Tom Watson and Herbert Chapman).

- Anthony Gerrard is a cousin of Steven, also born in Huyton, and had been released by Everton as a youth.

- Cardiff reached the league playoffs, losing to West Ham, but were promoted to the Premier League the following season.

- Craig Bellamy would later play and coach his hometown club, Cardiff City.

- Standard tickets cost from £40 to £90 at the new Wembley.

Liverpool 3 Everton 0

13/03/2012 - Premier League - Anfield

Despite the cup success, FSG's aim was Champions League football, and Liverpool were never in contention. By the time of the derby match in March, they were seventh, having lost three successive league fixtures, with just one league win in eight in 2012. Injuries had played their part, so this was the first time that Gerrard, Suarez, Carroll started together. Everton made six changes, but kept the trusted Moyes defence of Phil Jagielka and Sylvain Distin, with Marouane Fellaini an effective foil in the air.

Liverpool struggled to break down the well-organised defence, as Suarez and Gerrard probed. Howard saved from Gerrard after Suarez released him, and Henderson's rebound was blocked. Carroll's looping header went wide, and Suarez's shot saved. Everton's best chance ended with Pienaar firing over

The defence was breached after 34 minutes; Kelly's low shot was blocked by Howard, but the ball spun to Gerrard, and he delightfully placed it into the top corner, past a group of bodies and a defender on the line. Kelly nearly scored too, while Reina had to save a Stracqualursi header.

In the second half, Everton initially attempted to attack more, but Suarez was dangerous on the break, once denied by a tackle and another by offside. In the 51st minute, he wriggled his way in from the touchline, the ball fell into Gerrard's path, and he smashed it in. Moyes made a triple substitution, but with little impact; Carroll's shot whizzed past the post and Suarez missed too. In injury time, Gerrard lead another breakaway, passed to Suarez, who checked, and returned to Gerrard, for the simplest opportunity to sweep into the Kop goal for his hat-trick, and anther special memory.

A month later, Liverpool also beat Everton again in the FA Cup semi-final, but would lose to Chelsea in the final. The two finals could not save Dalglish, as he was judged by his eighth place league finish, and dismissed in the summer.

- David Moyes had recently celebrated his 10th anniversary as Everton manager. He would not win at Anfield in all 12 appearances as Everton manager (or 5 visits with subsequent clubs), so the Kop chanted "10 more years!"

- The first derby hat-trick since Rush in 1982, and first at Anfield since 1935. It was Gerrard 400th league game for Liverpool, only the fifth Premiership player to reach this landmark for just one club.

- Steven Gerrard would score ten times against Everton in his career.

- Liverpool hit the woodwork 33 times in the season and missed seven penalties.

- Marouane Fellaini had played against Liverpool for Standard Liege in a Champions League qualifier in 2008, and would never score against Liverpool for Everton or Manchester United.

Newcastle United 0 Liverpool 6

27/04/2013 - Premier League - St James Park

In Dalglish's place, the owner selected a young and exciting manager, Brendan Rodgers. His first months were troubled by a chaotic transfer window and poor results, leaving Liverpool in the bottom half of the table by December. However, the performances improved, Suarez was always a threat, aided by the much more successful January window signings of Daniel Sturridge and 20-year old Brazilian Philippe Coutinho

They had moved up to 7th by April, but the lengthy suspension of Suarez for biting was expected to restrict their progression. Newcastle, now under Alan Pardew, had finished fifth the previous year, but were struggling this term and needed the points from early Saturday evening kick-off. The Liverpool team had a mixture of Benitez, Dalglish, and Rodgers' signings, as Carragher was making one of his final appearances, after he announced his imminent retirement.

Liverpool only had to wait 3 minutes for the first goal; Downing's third cross, was headed in by an unmarked Agger, as he beat an ineffective offside trap. By 17 minutes, it was two; a long ball was laid off by Sturridge to Coutinho, his return pass split the defence, and Sturridge unselfishly set up Henderson to tap into an empty net. Newcastle offered little, but Perch should have scored from a free header.

Pardew made two substitutions at half-time, but one of them, Ben Arfa was soon dispossessed by Coutinho, who came forward, threaded through another killer pass, and Sturridge finished with aplomb. On the hour it was four, Henderson won the ball in midfield, and the through ball from Gerrard, allowed Henderson to return the favour to Sturridge, giving him a tap in. Fabio Borini came off the bench and scored within two minutes, poking in a shot from a Downing pass.

Newcastle could not cope with Liverpool's movement and passing, but especially the vision of Coutinho. Debuchy was sent off for a second yellow card, and from the free-kick, Henderson's cross evaded all as it sailed into the net. Coutinho was later denied his warranted goal, as Elliot touched the drive on to the bar.

He may not have scored, but Coutinho was sensational, and the fans looked forward to a full season with him creating chances for Suarez and Sturridge. Rodgers had endured a difficult baptism, but was building the team he wanted.

- Liverpool's joint biggest away in the Premier League so far, and matched the biggest ever win against Newcastle (1967 when Hateley scored a hat-trick).

- Newcastle's biggest home league defeat since September 1925.

- Fabio Borini's first goal for Liverpool.

- Philippe Coutinho arrived from Inter Milan, where he had initially been managed by Rafa Benitez, but fell out of favour with the next manager, and had been loaned to Espanyol.

- Brendan Rodgers had to retire from playing professional football at the age of 20. He managed Swansea City to promotion and then 11th place in the Premier League.

- Daniel Sturridge scored ten goals in his fourteen Liverpool league appearances this season, including a hat-trick against Fulham two weeks later. Suarez was still top scorer with 23 league goals, up from 11 the previous season.

- Carragher retired after 737 appearances, the second-highest ever for Liverpool, and always wearing the number 23 shirt.

- Everton finished above Liverpool for the second consecutive season, the first time this happened since Liverpool's promotion in 1962.

- Jordan Henderson had established himself as a regular in the Liverpool midfield, despite Rodgers initially trying to sell him.

Liverpool 5 Norwich City 1

4/12/2013 - Premier League - Anfield

Despite another busy transfer window, only goalkeeper Simon Mignolet and Mamadou Sakho really established themselves as regulars, but Kolo Toure occasionally provided some experience in defence. Without the distraction of European football, allied to the fact that both Manchester clubs and Chelsea had changed their managers in the summer; could this produce a "perfect storm" of a surprise title challenge?

Suarez's return from suspension had helped Liverpool to the top in October, but a poor defeat at Hull City saw them fourth at the start of December. There was a quick chance to respond with a midweek game at home to Norwich City. Coutinho's return from injury typically coincided with a Sturridge absence. Rodgers struggled to play the three offensive threats together, but the emerging youth Raheem Sterling often stepped up.

After the Hull shock, the home team started nervously, and Hoolhahan might have scored early, but then they slowly started probing. Coutinho beat three defenders, but his shot was blocked, and Henderson also dragged a shot wide. Suarez settled the nerves after 15 minutes, launching a ball, that sat up nicely, from over 35 yards dipping into the Kop net.

On the half-hour, he made it two, hooking in a Coutinho corner, that Gerrard had ducked (or missed). He then completed an incredible first half hat-trick in 35 minutes. Receiving a pass from Sterling, he flicked the ball over one defender, paused, before hitting an unstoppable rising shot into the far corner. In his celebrations, he seemed even more surprised at his own brilliance than the fans.

The attacking intent continued in the second half, a diving Gerrard header was cleared off the line, and Ruddy saved well from Allen and Suarez. The Uruguayan had to wait until the 74th minute for his fourth, bending a free-kick around the wall. He even created the fifth for Sterling at the end, with a cutback. Gerrard was also unlucky with a sublime flick that came off the post. Annoyingly Liverpool lost their clean sheet to a Johnson goal. Their attack was peerless, but the defensive lapses would provide costly.

Suarez was taken off in the last minute, to earn his rapturous round of applause for an astonishing individual performance, in what would be an incredible season for him and the team.

- Suarez scored his third hat-trick against Norwich in four games, the only Premiership player to complete this feat. All ten goals were past John Ruddy.

- Suarez would score six hat-tricks for Liverpool in his 3½ years. This was the start of a fertile spell, where he scored ten goals in four December matches, a Premiership record for a calendar month.

- Ten days later, a 5-0 win at Tottenham would be the sixth time that Rodgers' team had scored five or more in the League, matching the entire six years of Benitez, but the downside was just two clean sheets in 16 matches.

Liverpool 5 Arsenal 1

08/02/2014 - Premier League - Anfield

Suarez's purple patch took Liverpool to the top at Christmas, but successive away losses to league rivals, saw them slip to fourth, and eight points behind leaders Arsenal. Wenger's team appeared a tough proposition, especially the midfield power and creativity of Mikel Arteta, Jack Wilshere, Santi Cazorla and the recent £42 million signing, Mesuit Ozil. But Rodgers didn't blink, choosing both Coutinho and Sterling, as well as the two strikers. As the offensive options improved, he now had defensive injury concerns, which meant Toure and Ally Cissoko came in for rare starts, with Flanagan switching to right-back.

The start was fast, furious and never to be forgotten. In the first minute, Suarez was pulled back. Gerrard curled in an inviting deep free-kick, and Skrtel connected with his knee to make it 1-0. He was also required in his defensive role, to block Giroud, and clear off the line, after Mignolet had spilled a cross.

The action was non-stop in this open start, Sturridge forced Szczesny down to save, and Flanagan's shot was pushed wide at the near post. From the Gerrard corner, Skrtel's looping header from distance passed both the goalkeeper and defender on the line. Two up in 10 minutes, the Reds were now rampant, and Arsenal's impressive midfield overwhelmed. Wilshire had to clear a ball across the face of the goal, and Suarez put Sturridge through, but he dinked a one-on-one past the post. Another corner was sent to Suarez outside the area, he unleashed a thunderous shot, which smashed against the post, and came back so quickly that Toure's attempted rebound went wide.

After 16 minutes, it was three, with a devastating break; Henderson dispossessed a startled Ozil, released Suarez, and his cross was easily converted by Sterling running in, just beating Sturridge. The clock had barely hit 20 minutes, when Coutinho robbed Arteta on the halfway line, and his precise long ball played in Sturridge, who wouldn't miss a second one on one. An incredible start, 4-0 up after 20 minutes and fully merited, as Liverpool were hungrier and more ruthless.

It would be impossible the continue to play with that pace and intensity, so Liverpool retained possession and their lead, with just one shot from Suarez, as a stunned Arsenal offered little. The awed Liverpool fans even broke into spontaneous applause before half-time, to salute the performance.

In the second half, Arsenal tried to build some momentum, but Liverpool were lethal on the counter attack. Sterling was put through, his initial shot was blocked by Szczesny, but he netted the rebound. He should have had a hat-trick, but missed stabbing home, after a Suarez flick.

Arsenal mustered a token resistance, Mignolet saved from Oxlade-Chamberlain and Wilshere, but Szczesny still had to tip over Suarez's free-kick that was going into the top corner, and a Henderson chip went awry. Arsenal scored from the penalty spot with Arteta. In the final minutes, a Coutinho shot was straight at Szczesny, and he also blocked a shot from Sterling,

The best Anfield opening ever had renewed Liverpool's title aspirations, and a late midweek win at Fulham convinced that something special was happening.

- Arsenal were unbeaten on their previous five trips to Anfield, and Liverpool had only won one of the last twelve encounters .

- Martin Skrtel's header was Liverpool 23rd from set-pieces already this season.

- Skrtel would score seven league goals this season, including another double away at Cardiff, but also conceded four own goals this year.

- The first time Liverpool had scored five against Arsenal since 1964.

- Kolo Toure had already won the Premier League with Arsenal in 2004 and Manchester City in 2012. The following season he would play for Liverpool against his brother Yaya in a competitive match for the first time.

- Alex Oxlade-Chamberlain would sign for Liverpool three years later

- Arsenal beat Liverpool 2-1 in the FA Cup the following weekend

- Luis Suarez had requested a move to Arsenal in the summer, but their bid of £40 million and £1 had been rejected.

Liverpool 3 Manchester City 2

13/04/2014 - Premier League - Anfield

The Arsenal game was the start of a nine match winning run that put Liverpool on top of the table. But it was very tight as rivals Chelsea and Manchester City (who were four points behind with two games in hand), both had to come to Anfield in the final weeks. Liverpool fans were at fever pitch, and greeted the team coach as it arrived 90 minutes before kickoff.

Rodgers was brave again, going with the four attacking players that had destroyed Arsenal. With Johnson back at right-back, Flanagan continued his excellent spell at left-backBig spending City had still had Hart, Kompany and Zabaleta in defence, but had also invested heavily in the quality of Yaya Toure, David Silva and Sami Nasri. Edin Dzeko was up front, as Sergio Aguero was only considered fit for the bench.

The match was scheduled for a 1.37 pm start on the Sunday, as the players and fans marked the imminent 25th anniversary of the Hillsborough disaster.

Liverpool typically started on the front foot, with a Coutinho shot deflected wide. In the 6th minute, Suarez held off a defender, put Sterling thorough, he stopped, feinted to go one way, but then quickly stroked the ball through the gap for 1-0. Yaya Toure shot over for City, and Sturridge missed a good opportunity from a Sterling pass. Liverpool were working hard, especially the strikers, denying Manchester City time to build.

In the 25th minute, Gerrard had a free header from a corner, but Hart tipped it over. Gerrard took this corner, and Skrtel flicked an inswinging cross past Hart. City tried to respond, a Dzeko shot was blocked by Gerrard, while Sterling and Johnson together cleared a header from a corner, and Mignolet made a fine save from Fernando. Liverpool's best chance fell to Coutinho, but he dragged his shot wide.

James Milner came on just after half-time and quickly made a goal for Silva. Sturridge made the wrong choice in a promising position, his attempted shot was blocked and he was injured in the process. Silva shot across the face of the goal, and another of his shots was deflected off Johnson to make it 2-2 after 68 minutes. Midfielder Allen replaced Sturridge, as Rodgers tried to maintain more possession in midfield.

Substitute Aguero broke away, but Silva's stretch put the ball past the post. Nasri shot wide, Mignolet saved from Dzeko while Liverpool were repeatedly caught offside. In the 78th minute, against the run of play, Kompany miskicked clearing a throw-in, and the ball came to Coutinho, who rifled in decisively for 3-2.

The final minutes were frantic, with Demichels' header easily saved, while another Liverpool breakaway was offside. Henderson was sent off for a wild lung after miscontrolling, and Skrtel got away with punching a clearance. The final whistle brought great relief and celebrations, as an emotional Gerrard gathered the players, reminding them that this was just one win, and urging "Don't let it slip".

Sadly, Gerrard famously slipped two weeks later, allowing Demba Ba to score in Chelsea win, which swung the title to Manchester City, but it had been a very close and thrilling race.

- James Milner would win Premier League medals with both Liverpool and Manchester City (twice).

- Liverpool scored 101 league goals, a top-flight record for them. Eleven times they scored four goals or more. Manchester City also scored over 100 too, a remarkable achievement as only one team had done this previously in the Premier League era.

- Luis Suarez was the joint European Golden Boot top scorer with 31 league goals (no penalties) and 17 assists. Sturridge was second for Liverpool with 21. This was the first time two Liverpool players had scored over 20 league goals since 1963/4.

- 84 points was a new Premiership record for Liverpool and would have been enough to win the Premier League on eight previous occasions.

- Liverpool scored a new Premiership record of 48 away goals.

- For more about this year, read "We Go Again" by David E Usher.

Liverpool 3 Tottenham Hotspur 2

10/02/2015 - Premier League - Anfield

Suarez left in the summer for Barcelona (he was already suspended for another biting incident), and the money was used to fund Adam Lallana, Lazar Markovic, Dejan Lovren, Alberto Moreno, Emre Can, Mario Balotelli, and Ricky Lambert, but with varying fortunes.

The goals dried up, as Sturridge was often injured, and the replacements rarely scored, so the pressure was on Sterling. Liverpool went out of the Champions League at the group stage and were only mid-table by November. However, one defeat in fifteen, saw some hopes of a revival in February, when Tottenham visited with their new manager, Mauricio Pochettino. They already had some of his key players in place, with Hugo Lloris, Kyle Walker, Eric Dier, Jan Verthongen, Eric Lamela, Harry Kane and Christian Eriksen all playing.

Spurs were four points ahead and had only lost once in ten, so a win was essential in the race for Champions League qualification. Rodgers had flirted with playing three centre-backs and wing-backs. Sturridge was back as the lone striker, his first start since August, a timely boost as Sterling was now injured.

The confident Liverpool began impressively; Gerrard curled a free-kick just over the bar, Markovic volleyed over too, and Lloris had to save well from a Sturridge shot. The deserved goal came after 15 minutes, as Sturridge controlled a Mignolet kick, the ball came to Markovic, and his bobbling shot from the edge of the box sneaked past Lloris. Kane equalised after 25 minutes, from a Lamela pass. Lloris did better to get his body behind a Jordan Ibe shot, while Sturridge's cheeky backheel hit the post.

Five minutes into the second half, Sturridge won a penalty after a clumsy tackle from Rose, and Gerrard converted Again the lead did not last long, as Mignolet could not hold Erikson's free-kick, and Dembele pounced. Liverpool brought on Lallana and Balotelli, and they made a vital impact. Ibe and Lallana combined on the right wing, and Balotelli stabbed in the cross. Can was excellent in seeing out the win from an entertaining and fast paced match.

It was a final stand from Rodgers as Liverpool only won one of the final seven, losing an FA Cup semi-final to Aston Villa, and ending with an embarrassing 6-1 reverse at Stoke. Although he survived the summer, he would be dismissed in September after one win in nine (although six were draws).

- Steven Gerrard retired at the end of this season. He made over 700 appearances and scored 186 goals. He would end as Liverpool's top league goalscorer for this season with just nine goals, as the total slumped from the previous year's high to 58.

- Liverpool fifth consecutive win over Spurs, scoring 18 goals in total.

- Balotelli's first and only league goal of the season in his 13th appearances after 48 shots. It was also Markovic's second and final league goal of the season.

- Harry Kane's first appearance at Anfield, and the first of his four Anfield goals so far.

- After Christmas, Liverpool went six away league games without conceding.

- Rodgers, Benitez and Houllier all failed to finish in the top four, in the season after finishing second.

Manchester City 1 Liverpool 4

21/11/2015 - Premier League - Etihad Stadium

Although Ancelotti was on the shortlist, Jurgen Klopp was identified as the outstanding candidate to replace Rodgers; enthusiastic, charismatic, and renowned for his successful "Gegenpressing" Dortmund team.

He inherited a confused squad of inconsistent recruitment, with the sale of Sterling helping to finance the signings of Christian Benteke, Roberto Firmino, Divock Origi, James Milner, Danny Ings and Joe Gomez. He was immediately beset with injuries, as Ings and Gomez were ruled out for the season. Home form was patchy, but early away performances were encouraging, including a victory at champions Chelsea. Liverpool were in tenth place when they travelled to league leaders Manchester City, who in addition to Sterling had also spent over £50 million on Kevin de Bruyne.

For the first time, Klopp fielded Firmino, Coutinho and Lallana together, to form a mobile and flexible strike force, with Milner as captain on his first return to the Eithad Stadium.

The formation paid off within 7 minutes; Coutinho robbed Sagna, sent Firmino away, and his return cross was put into his own net by Mangala. De Bruyne was City's main threat, with a series of dangerous crosses, but they were defended well. Milner shot over the bar, before the second on 23 minutes. Firmino picked the ball up in midfield, and cut across the defenders in an angled run, then laid a reverse ball for Coutinho to put between Hart's legs. The forwards' pressing and movement were troubling the City defence, ably supported by a competitive midfield.

Hart had to save from Coutinho, but could not prevent the third just before the half-hour, as Can's backheel put Coutinho through, and his square ball was tapped in by Firmino. Firmino had another two chances soon after, one Hart saved with his legs, and another just past the post. Aguero scored his customary goal to give City some hope after a half that Liverpool had dominated.

Pellegrino made a double substitution at half-time, but it barely affected the momentum. Coutinho's shot was deflected and Firmino had another shot saved by Hart's legs. Liverpool defended stubbornly, allowing City few chances, apart from Mignolet saving from Aguero. Substitute Benteke had a one on one, but Hart blocked again. From the corner, the ball dropped invitingly for Skrtel to smash it in.

A convincing 4-1 away victory, with a pattern for the future, at the home of the team that would be Klopp's main rivals.

- Roberto Firmino's first goal for Liverpool on his 14th appearance (eight starts) and would end the season as top scorer with ten league goals.

- Jurgen Klopp had won promotion with Mainz, consecutive Bundesliga titles with Borussia Dortmund and also reached a Champions League final.

- Liverpool's first win in seven matches at the Eithad in the league, since the 3-2 win in 2008.

- The first time Manchester City had conceded four at home in the Premier League since 2003.

- Aguero has scored seven goals in nine matches for Manchester City at home to Liverpool.

- In February, Liverpool would lose the League Cup final on penalties to Manchester City, but win 3-0 in the league three days later.

Liverpool 4 Borussia Dortmund 3

14/04/2016 - Europa League Quarter-final 2nd leg - Anfield

Another marathon campaign of 63 games ensued, as Klopp experienced the rigours of an English season. In Europe, Liverpool had recorded an impressive win over Manchester United, but fate decreed a quarter-final tie against his former team, Borussia Dortmund. A decent 1-1 draw in Germany, seemed to give Klopp the advantage for the second leg.

Most of his players were still at Dortmund, under new manager Thomas Tuchel, notably striker Pierre Aubameyang, who had already scored 36 this season. For Liverpool, the in-form Origi was preferred to Sturridge, with Milner captain again as Henderson was injured.

Dortmund shocked the Kop in the first 10 minutes with a series of penetrating attacks. Aubameyang curled wide and had another shot saved, but Mkhitaryan scored from the rebound. The Gabon striker added the second from a devastating break. Liverpool would need at least three now, and battled bravely; Origi had one shot saved, another wide, Firminio's diving header went wide as did a Coutinho shot. They always had to be wary of the rapid Dortmund counter attack, as an Aubameyang shot went past the post, and Mignolet fingertips deflected a cross away from him.

Boosted by Klopp's half-time talk, Liverpool soon cut the deficit; Can drove forward, and released Origi, who slotted past Weidenfeller. The experienced Dortmund seemed to weather the storm, and a rapier counter attack saw Reus restore the three goal requirement.

Klopp brought on Allen and Sturridge, and in the 66th minute Coutinho pulled one back with a low drive into the corner. Origi shot over, but after 78 minutes, Sakho stooped to head a low Milner corner in. Dortmund made two defensive substitutions, reducing their counter attacking threat, as Liverpool pressed them back.

Into injury time, Liverpool won a free-kick. Instead of hitting long into the box, Milner played it down the line for Sturridge. He then raced forward to receive the return, and hung up a cross to the far post, that Lovren met with power. The Kop erupted in delight, but it wasn't over yet though, as Gundogan curled a late free-kick past the post.

Another famous European night, and Klopp had inspired Liverpool to an unlikely comeback. They would beat Villareal in the semi-final, but lose 3-1 to Seville in the final. Two finals in a year, no trophies, but Klopp had impressed with the initial squad at his disposal.

- Borussia Dortmund scored more in the first ten minutes, than the previous thirteen German teams at Anfield.

- Two more assists for James Milner, and he would end the season with seven goals and fourteen assists.

- Just the second Liverpool goal for both Lovren and Sakho.

- Mkhitaryan, Aubameyang and Sokratis would all play for Arsenal against Liverpool in the Premier League in August 2019, suffering a 3-1 defeat.

- Thomas Tuchel had succeeded Klopp as manager of both Mainz and Dortmund and would later beat Liverpool as manager of Paris SG and Chelsea.

- 39 different players were used this season with a club-record 22 different goalscorers.

Liverpool 4 Leicester City 1

10/09/2016 - Premier League - Anfield

Klopp's first full season, would not have European football, so there were less transfers, but Sadio Mané, Georginio Wijnaldum, and Joel Matip would all play major roles in the future. Their purchases were offset by the sales of Benteke, Allen, and Ibe. There would be no home bow until September, so the rebuilding of the Main Stand could be completed. The first visitors were the 5,000-1 shock Premier League champions, Leicester City. They had lost Kante, but managed to keep hold of Jamie Vardy and Riyad Mahrez. For Liverpool, Coutinho was on the bench after a tiring Brazil trip, so the front three consisted of Sturridge, Firmino, and Lallana, as Lucas filled in at centre defence because Lovren was injured.

The live TV teatime kickoff was preceded by a parade of former stars. Liverpool pressed from the front with Klopp's style now firmly embedded, and it took just 13 minutes to mark the occasion. Lucas passed to Milner, he passed up to Firmino, who cut across a defender to fire in an angled shot. Soon after Mané and Lallana combined, but Sturridge's shot was saved at the near post. Lucas would also start the second after 31 minutes. He found Henderson, who released Sturridge, his cheeky flick, left Mané to beat Schmeichel.

Liverpool were cruising, but in the 38th minute, Lucas gifted Vardy a goal. Suddenly the new team looked nervous, as Mignolet could not reach a throw-in, and Huth's header bounced off the top of the bar.

Klopp regrouped the players at half-time, and they resumed their pressure, as Sturridge's shot was blocked by Schmeichel. Within 10 minutes, Winjanldum set up Lallana, to fire a curving shot into the Kop net. Vardy had a great chance, but Mignolet saved with his legs, while Henderson blazed over after good approach work, and Mané combined with Firmino, but his shot was smothered by the keeper.

In the last minute, as Leicester attacked, Henderson released a long ball for Mané to chase, he avoided a rash charge out from Schmeichel, entered the box, and provided a tap in for Firmino.

The new-look team and Anfield were off and running, and they would be top for the first time under Klopp by November.

- The new Main Stand allowed the attendance to exceed 53,000, the highest since 1977. The average league attendance of 53,000 would be a new high.

- Standard tickets in the new Main Stand cost £59, but 7,000 seats in the stadium were now reserved for the more expensive hospitality packages.

- Lallana's goal was Liverpool 100th under Klopp in just 57 games.

- Sadio Mané had eventful games against Liverpool the previous season. He scored a late equaliser, but was then sent off at Anfield, scored in a 6-1 home League Cup defeat, and then scored two goals (and missed a penalty) as a second-half substitute, as Southampton overturned a 2-0 deficit.

- Jamie Vardy scored seven goals in a five-game spell against Liverpool.

- Despite winning the title for Leicester, Claudio Ranieri would be sacked in February, as Leicester were one point above the relegation places. He had previously managed Chelsea, Juventus, Valencia, Atlético Madrid, Parma, Roma, Inter Milan and Monaco, but Leicester City was his only league title.

Liverpool 3 Middlesbrough 0

21/05/2017 - Premier League - Anfield

One win in ten at the start of 2017, saw Liverpool depart both cups, and damage the chances of Champions League qualification. Doubts were raised about the intensity of Klopp's style, amid a series of injuries and loss of form. However, they recovered in the spring, losing only one in eleven (to Crystal Palace with Benteke scoring twice), so were fourth on the last day of the season, aiming to prevent Arsenal's normal late qualification surge.

The opponents, Middlesbrough, already relegated, contained ex-Liverpool player Downing and Arsenal loanee Calum Chambers. Liverpool were missing captain Henderson and Mané, but Sturridge had come back in.

The first half was tense and frustrating, as Boro defended stubbornly with men behind the ball. A series of chances were created though; Clyne should have hit the target with an early chance, Coutinho had one saved and another wide, while Firmino, Can, and Sturridge all went close. Despite all the pressure, there was also a lucky escape, as Lovren survived a tangle with Bamford that could have resulted in a penalty and red card.

Klopp acted as a cheerleader to encourage the crowd for more noise, while the news came through that Arsenal were already beating Everton 2-0, even with 10 men. The breakthrough came in stoppage time; Clyne played a ball forward, Firmino astutely flicked it on to the running Wijnanldum, and he smashed it high into the net at the near post.

The goal relaxed Liverpool in the second half, and there were two more quick goals. Coutinho first curled a free-kick in, and then Lallana swept in after a lightning break seemed to have broken down. There were no more goals, but plenty of chances; a Coutinho shot tipped wide, a misjudged Winjanldum volley and a Sturridge shot just over.

Liverpool celebrated their fourth place with the traditional end-of-season lap of appreciation. It had been close, but they had deserved it. This was the sliding door moment for Klopp, as the Champions League qualification allowed him to attract further high-quality recruits.

- Coutinho's goal was his 15th from outside the area, the most by any player in the Premier League since his signing.

- The final appearance for Lucas, as he soon moved to Italy.

- Coutinho, Mané, and Firmino all scored over ten league goals.

- Wijnanldum's first nineteen goals in the Premiership (eleven with Newcastle) were all in home fixtures.

- Only Liverpool's second Champions League qualification and top-four finish in the last eight years.

- Middlesbrough's previous visit to Anfield was a 2014 League Cup tie that needed a shootout of 30 penalty kicks before Liverpool triumphed 14-13.

NK Maribor 0 Liverpool 7

17/10/2017 - Champions League Group Stage Matchday 3 - Stadion Ljudski vrt

Two draws in the first two Champions League matchdays meant a win was essential away at the Slovenian champions, Maribor. Liverpool had bought Alex Oxlade-Chamberlain and Andy Robertson. Some eyebrows were raised at £38 million spent on Mohammed Salah, but many now trusted the judgement of the Sporting Director, Michael Edwards, with his growing reputation for astute deals.

However, a failure to sign a centre-half resulted in porous defending, but an explosive "fab four" of Salah, Firmino, Coutinho, Mané, with any result possible. Mané would miss this tie, as would Lallana, who rarely appeared now due to a series of injuries. Karius was again preferred in goal, and Milner was captain in place of the rested Henderson.

Liverpool's start was as bright as their luminous orange kit, with a goal after 5 minutes; Salah tore inside, and provided Firmino a simple tap in. Before 15 minutes it was two, as Coutinho met Milner's cross on the volley. Another Milner cross was just put wide by Firmino, but there was little delay, as they were three up inside 20 minutes; a Firmino through ball fed Salah and he scored from the right.

Salah and Coutinho both had shots saved, and the fourth duly arrived before half-time, as Coutinho released Moreno, and his cross was tapped in by Salah, beating Firmino to the ball. The onslaught continued in the second half, as a Coutinho free-kick was pushed away, before Firmino scored again after 54 minutes,

Klopp made substitutions, one of them, Oxlade-Chamberlain would be straight in the action. His shot was blocked by the keeper's legs, but soon Sturridge put him through to slot in. In the final minute, Alexander-Arnold's shot was deflected in to make it seven.

A stunning away rout, but typically in the next match Liverpool suffered a crushing 4-1 reverse to Tottenham. If only they could improve the defence.

- Liverpool's biggest ever away win in Europe, and also the joint record for any club in the Champions League era.

- Liverpool would also score seven against Spartak Moscow in matchday six, as they amassed 23 goals in the group stages.

- Maribor's manager, Darko Milanic, had lasted 32 days as Leeds manager in 2014.

- Alex Oxlade-Chamberlain's first goal for Liverpool. He is the son of Mark Chamberlain, also an England international.

- Mohammed Salah had signed for Chelsea in 2014 for £11 million, but only played thirteen league games, scoring twice, before he was loaned to Fiorentina and later sold to Roma. He was more successful in Italy, scoring nineteen goals in his final season at Roma.

- Salah and Philippe Coutinho were born three days apart in June 1992.

- Trent Alexander-Arnold, born in West Derby, had been with the Liverpool Academy since the age of six, initially as a winger, but converted to a right-back, as it was seen as an easier route into the first team.

- Coutinho scored for a fourth consecutive away game.

Liverpool 4 Manchester City 3

14/01/2018 - Premier League - Anfield

After the Spurs debacle, Liverpool went seventeen games unbeaten, as the front four flourished, especially the surprising Salah. However, Coutinho still desired a move to Barcelona, so a huge fee of £145 million was arranged (including performance payments). £75 million of it was immediately given to Southampton for the long-term target, Dutch centre-back, Virgil van Dyke. He made an immediate impact knocking Everton out of the FA Cup, but a tight hamstring kept him out of the visit from Manchester City.

Pep Guardiola, now in his second year at Manchester City, had assembled an expensive squad including Ederson in goal, Kyle Walker, John Stones, and Leroy Sane. The money was well invested, as they were undefeated in the first 22 league matches, building an unassailable 15 point lead at the top. For Liverpool, Robertson was securing the left-back position after Moreno's injury, and Oxlade-Chamberlain had effectively replaced Coutinho.

Oxlade-Chamberlain justified his inclusion in the 10th minute, with a powerful run from midfield, and a low hard shot from just outside the area that arrowed into the corner. Liverpool were in fine form, as Salah stabbed wide, Firmino headed wide, and a Salah curler saved. They were also defending well, especially Robertson marking Sterling. Manchester City had just two chances with a Sane shot deflected and de Bruyne shot saved, but against the run of play, Sane's powerful shot beat Karius at the near post.

The second half started more evenly, as Otamendi hit the bar, and a Salah shot was saved, but at the hour mark, Liverpool exploded; A through ball was played by Oxlade-Chamberlain, Firmino shrugged off Stones, and smartly chipped over Ederson. A minute later, Mané hit the outside of the post. City were rocking, unable to cope with the incessant pressure. Another minute later, Salah won the ball from Otamendi, passed to Mané on the edge of the area, and this time his right-foot shot flew into the top of the net. Before the 70th minute, Ederson came out thwart an attack, but his clearance only went to Salah, and he lobbed the ball back from over 30 yards. The new invincible were 4-1 down, and Liverpool were running riot!

They were determined to maintain the lead, with constant pressing, as Robertson set the standard, chasing the ball between three City players. Liverpool came closest as Wijnanldum had a shot past the post. However, they would tire, as City scored after 84 minutes, when a deflection ran kindly for substitute Bernardo Silva, and Gundogan made it 4-3 in injury time. There was even time for a nervous free-kick, that an offside Aguero headed past the post.

City may have rallied, but Liverpool thoroughly deserved the victory, and set a marker that they would be a threat to City's dominance. The explosive multiple goals in a short period had quickly become a trademark of this Klopp team.

- Mo Salah would score 32 league goals this season, breaking the Premier League record for a 38 match season.

- Emre Can made the most tackles in this match, but had not signed a new contract and would leave for Juventus on a free transfer at the end of the season.

- On eight occasions in this season, Mané, Firmino and Salah all scored in the same match.

- Before joining Manchester City, Pep Guardiola and won three league titles with both Bayern Munch and Barcelona, and two Champions League trophies.

Liverpool 3 Manchester City 0

04/04/2018 - Champions League Quarter-final 1st leg - Anfield

Selling Coutinho had been risky, but the goals still flowed, and now they more secure at the back, especially with van Dyke, and the midfield stronger. There was an upturn in results, with seven wins out of ten, and six clean sheets. The Champions League quarter-final draw had shades of 2005, with Liverpool's special European pedigree against the big spending runaway League leaders. Lovren partnered van Dyke in the defence with Milner included in midfield for experience, creativity and tackling. City were able to add Kompany, Silva and Jesus Gabriel, but conscious of their previous beating, Guardiola was cautious, so added Gundogan as an extra man in midfield, instead of Sterling

His plan worked for 12 minutes, but then Liverpool scored with their real attack. Milner set Salah away from the halfway line, and he created a good chance for Firmino. The shot was blocked, but he managed to flick it on to Salah, who had kept running, and he smashed it into the Kop goal. Sane tried to reply, but he shot wide. The Anfield atmosphere was electric now as the fans responded to a series of crunching tackles. Typical was the 20th minute, when Milner won a ferocious 50-50 block tackle, so the ball came to Oxlade-Chamberlain, and like January, he fired past Ederson from outside the area, this time a rising shot that was even more spectacular.

Manchester City were struggling to contain Liverpool, even with an extra midfield player, as the home team were faster and more determined, inspired by the fans again. Just after the half-hour, it was three. Salah broke forward again to the corner of the box, his initial shot was blocked by Kompany, but he curled the rebound to the far post, where Mané leapt to head down and in. The Kop were ecstatic with the new "Allez Allez Allez" chant resounding around the stadium.

The only problem now was that there was still an hour of football left. City came forward, but could not get past van Dyke and Lovren, who were also well protected by the hard-working midfield. City had to be careful, as Liverpool looked to counter attack; a Robertson shot was blocked, Firmino shot over the bar, and van Dyke over too from a set piece.

In the second half City typically dominated possession, but again Liverpool were now solid. Chances were less frequent as Otamendi headed over and Sane shot wide. Liverpool always had enough bodies behind the ball and made important tackles. The Kop was a little quieter, still willing the team on, but keenly observing the strategic battle, as an away goal could swing the tie.

Liverpool's threat was reduced by an injury to Salah, and Sterling came on too, so they retreated more, with Dominic Solanke's main role to retain the ball. In the end, Karius only had to save a deflected shot. The clean sheet of no away goals in the second half, was as important as the three first half goals, as City had been outthought and outfought.

The away trip would still be daunting, with the expected City bombardment, as Henderson would be suspended and Salah an injury doubt. For 45 minutes, Manchester City pummelled Liverpool, but only had one goal to show. In the second half, Liverpool came out more, Salah scored the crucial away goal after 56 minutes, and Firmino the winner, giving Liverpool a handsome 5-1 aggregate triumph.

- During the Champions League run, three players would play against their previous team; Firmino (Hoffenheim), Milner (Manchester City), and Salah (Roma).

- Liverpool added Manchester City to their list of domestic rivals that they had knocked out Europe; Manchester United, Chelsea, Arsenal, and Tottenham.

- Klopp now had won more matches against Pep Guardiola, than any other manager.

- Milner would end with nine assists, the best ever for a Champions League season.

- Loris Karius had played for Manchester City youth teams and Under 21 team, but never made a senior appearance before he was transferred to Mainz.

- Only the fourth occasion Guardiola had lost a Champions League match by three goals or more, in 133 fixtures.

Liverpool 5 A.S. Roma 2
24/04/2018 - Champions League Semi-final 1st leg - Anfield

Another Champions League semi-final and the opponents were old rivals, and Salah's former club, Roma. They had recorded a remarkable 3-0 victory in Rome over Barcelona, and their team contained 2014 Manchester City title winners Kolarov and Dzeko. Apart from Gomez and Can, Liverpool were at full strength, with Milner preferred to Wijnanldum.

Anfield was as vociferous as normal for this European spectacle, with Allez Allez Allez again to the fore. The early goal did not materialise, but not because of a lack of trying. Mané was the chief culprit, putting one over the bar when clean through, miskicked from a good cutback, and another denied for offside. Alisson Becker was busy in goal, saving well from Salah (twice) and Firmino. Roma had few chances, but Karius was lucky when a Kolarov shot went through his hands onto the bar.

Finally Roma cracked after 35 minutes, Salah unleashed a curling shot into the top corner. They were now suffering, as Lovren bounced a header off the bar, and Alisson had to save from substitute Wijnanldum. The overdue second came in injury time, as Firmino broke forward, released Salah, who coolly clipped over Alisson, but again he did not celebrate.

The second half started in the same pattern, as the third came after 10 minutes, with Salah breaking forward, and provided Mané an easy finish. The rampaging full-backs both had efforts, Alexander-Arnold shot over and Robertson's blocked. Just after the hour, Salah broke away, teased a defender, and gave Firmino a tap in. The Brazilian soon had a second heading in a Milner corner to give Liverpool an incredible 5-0 lead after 70 minutes. Roma could not cope with Salah's pace and trickery.

Liverpool tired and Roma battled for the lifeline of away goals, with attacking substitutions. Schick's header was saved by Karius, but Dzeko scored after 80 minutes, and then Perotti from the penalty spot. After such a tremendous evening, Liverpool were hanging on now, as Dzeko and Nainggolan were both off target.

The final score of 5-2 was still enough, as Roma could only win the return leg 4-2, with two late goals. Liverpool lost the final, 3-1 to Real Madrid in Kiev, due to two Karius mistakes and an acrobatic Bale goal. Salah had gone off injured in the first half; a poignant end to a thrilling season for him and the team.

- Only the second team to score five goals in a Champions League semi-final.

- Alec Oxlade-Chamberlain's serious injury in this match would sideline him for a year.

- Before the second leg, Klopp's long-term assistant, Željko Buvač, left on a "leave of absence". He would not return, being replaced by Pep Lijnders.

- Alisson Becker would sign for Liverpool in the summer, the £65 million fee was a world-record for a goalkeeper, but it only lasted for one week.

- Salah would end with an incredible 44 goals, Firmino 27 and Mané 20. All three would score ten in the Champions League, a new feat for one team.

- Klopp had now lost six finals in a row (three for Liverpool and three for Borussia Dortmund).

- Liverpool had also lost their last three European finals, after only losing just one of the previous nine.

- Liverpool scored a Champions League record of 47 goals in this year's campaign.

Liverpool 1 Everton 0

02/12/2018 - Premier League - Anfield

In addition to a new goalkeeper and previously agreed Naby Keita, Klopp also signed Fabinho and Xherdan Shaqiri, as the squad depth was improved again. After a slow start, Fabinho became a key player, adding more protection for the solid combination of Gomez and van Dyke, with Alisson impressive in goal, as more clean sheets ensued.

Despite being unbeaten in the league by December, Liverpool were only second, as Guardiola's Manchester City were even more relentless. With City winning again on Saturday, Liverpool needed a win in the Sunday derby match to keep in touch. Everton were now managed by Marco Silva, and had invested heavily over the recent years in Richarlison, Gylfi Sigurdsson, Andre Gomes, Yerry Mina, and Jordan Pickford.

Everton had the best of the early chances; Mina headed wide, Alisson saved at point blank range from Gomes' header, and Gomez cleared the rebound from the line, and then Alisson saved at Walcott's feet. Liverpool's best chances came when Salah put Mané through, but he shot over, and Pickford had to save well from Shaqiri and Salah.

Liverpool were more on top in the second half, as Salah and Mané (twice) shot wide. Klopp threw on Sturridge and, then surprisingly, the out of favour Origi. The latter had more impact, he sprinted down the wing, but his cross was just ahead of Mané, and from a corner, he hit the post at close range.

Into four minutes of injury time, a blue flare landed on the pitch as the Everton fans thought they were safe. Gueye went down injured, adding a little more time. Just time for one more opportunity, with a free-kick deep in their own half. Alisson rushed forward to tap the ball, allowing Alexander-Arnold a better angle with a moving ball. His long ball was headed away to van Dyke on the edge of the box, but an attempted volley was skied, so he turned away in disgust, as the LFC TV commentator lamented "Oh Virgil!". But the ball arched up and came down, bouncing on the top of the crossbar, as Pickford desperately flailed to reach it with his fingertips. Incredibly it bounced again on the bar, and then back into play for a simple header for Origi, who had followed up. Anfield erupted into hysteria, and Klopp could not contain himself, running on the pitch to hug Alisson.

Another derby had been decided with a very late freakish Liverpool winner. Also, like 2001, it provided a spurt, as Liverpool won all eight matches in December, finally displacing Manchester City at the top of the league. The resurrection of Origi would also have repercussions for later in the season.

- Liverpool's website has clips of the goal from multiple different angles.

- Divock Origi's first Liverpool goal since May 2017. He was an unlikely hero, as it was only his second substitute appearance of the season, often not even making the squad. He had been out on loan for the entire previous season at Wolfsburg, so seemed likely to leave, with even Everton mentioned as a destination.

- Origi's third goal in derby matches at Anfield, and he would score two more in the same fixture next year.

- In the seventh home league game, Liverpool had still only conceded one goal.

- Liverpool have scored four late winners against Everton in the Premier League era; Rosenthal (1993), McAllister (2001), Mané (2016) and Origi (2018).

- This was part of a record unbeaten run of 23 derby matches between October 2010 and February 2021.

- In the next home match, Liverpool would beat Manchester United 3-1 with two goals off the bench from Shaqiri, and Jose Mourinho would be sacked the next day.

Liverpool 5 Watford 0

27/02/2019 - Premier League - Anfield

At the end of February, Liverpool's title charge was spluttering, drawing three of the last four as Manchester City just kept winning. A midweek encounter with Watford provided a chance to return to winning ways, but it would not be easy as they were in 7th place, due to their competitive midfield, with Troy Deeney and Gerard Deulofeu up front. Henderson was on the bench, as Klopp opted for Milner, while Matip and Origi replaced the injured duo of Gomez and Firmino.

Since the departure of Coutinho, and injury to Oxlade-Chamberlain, Liverpool had adopted a narrower midfield, allowing the full-backs to come forward more, and create numerous chances. This would be amply demonstrated in this match, as after 9 minutes, Alexander-Arnold whipped in a perfect cross and Mané in the centre forward position headed in powerfully from close range.

After 20 minutes, the same combination produced the second; Mané's control of a cross fell behind him, but he quickly improvised, to score an impudent backheel past Foster.

Liverpool struggled to get a decisive third, with Salah hitting the post from another Alexander-Arnold ball, and Robertson's cross just evaded Mané for a tap in. Watford offered little, as the imperious Fabinho dominated the midfield.

In the second half, Salah was stopped by Foster, and Mané's effort was deflected wide. The goal finally came after 66 minutes, as Origi received a ball from Robertson, cut inside, and beat Foster at his near post. Alisson then made his only save of the night, blocking a Gray shot with his body.

Alexander-Arnold supplied his third assist, with a free-kick that van Dyke headed in on 79 minutes The big Dutchman would make it two in three minutes, with another header, this time from a Robertson cross.

A resounding 5-0 win was just what was required, as Liverpool kept a slender one-point lead. However, a draw at Everton, gave City the edge, and the run-in saw both teams winning all of their last nine matches in the most competitive Premier League title race ever.

- Alexander-Arnold would finish the season with 12 Premier League assists, and Robertson 11; unprecedented totals for full-backs.

- Liverpool had now scored 16 goals in the last three home games against Watford; the first time they had scored five or more against opposition in the three successive seasons.

- Liverpool would accrue a club record of 97 points (enough to win all but two of the previous Premier Leagues) and a new club top-flight record of only one defeat. They became the first team to get over 90 points or lose just once, and not win the league.

- Salah and Mané shared the Golden Boat with 22 Premier League goals each, with Pierre Aubameyang while Alisson won the Golden Gloves for most clean sheets.

- This was the second in a record sequence of 24 consecutive home wins.

Liverpool 4 Barcelona 0

07/05/2019 - Champions League Semi-final 2nd leg - Anfield

In between the desperate and tiring Premier League chase, there was still the Champions League; Bayern Munich and Porto had been impressively dispatched, but Spanish Champions Barcelona would be an even more formidable challenge, as their famed attacked contained Messi, and former Reds, Suarez and Coutinho, both making their first returns. Despite playing so well in the Camp Nou, Liverpool lost 3-0, with Suarez and a Messi double. Both teams could regret late opportunities, Salah hitting the post, and Demeble missing a sitter with the final kick.

The task to overturn the three goals was made even harder, as both Salah and Firmino were out with injuries. Klopp brought in Shaqiri (his first start since January) and Origi, while preferring Milner to Wijnanldum in midfield. The Kop, were in full voice again, perhaps more in hope than expectation, but then magic had happened so often at Anfield on a European night. Even Klopp in his pre-match teamtalk, said "Normally it is impossible," adding "but as it is you, you have a chance!" Salah was present too, with a shirt bearing the inspiration "Never give up". Barcelona, already crowned Spanish champions, had rested their players at the weekend. With their firepower, they were supremely confident, as their official Twitter feed read "We score, Liverpool need FIVE - and we're going to get at least one... agreed?", while Suarez gracefully announced, he would not celebrate, if he scored.

Liverpool made a typically fast start, rushing straight at Barcelona, not letting them acclimatise, with multiple repossessions and winning 50/50s. Shaqiri shot wide first, but the desired early goal came in 7 minutes; an Alba misheader fell to Mané, he fed the onrushing Henderson, his left foot shot was saved, but an unmarked Origi netted the rebound. Tempers were raised, as Robertson clipped Messi's head, and Fabinho was harshly booked for a strong challenge on Suarez. The latter was not exactly being welcomed back by the Kop. Barcelona settled, passing the ball well, keeping possession, and carving out some decent chances, with Messi inevitably the key. He dragged one shot wide, had another tipped over by Alisson, and the keeper also pushed away a Coutinho effort. Liverpool efforts fell to Robertson, one wide and another saved. In stoppage time, Alisson made an important block as Alba was through from a Messi pass.

At half-time, both teams could be encouraged. Liverpool had a goal and hope, but Barcelona seemed to be comfortable now. However, the Reds had injury issues; Henderson was playing through the pain, cycling on an ergometer to keep his knee mobile. Robertson was more serious, from a Suarez kick, so Milner went to left-back and Wijnanldum came into midfield; another fateful European half-time switch.

Liverpool were straight on the offensive again, Roberto just denied Mané, when he was through. From the corner, van Dyke made a connection with his foot, but it was palmed away. Barcelona were still a threat on the break, as Suarez was clear, but this scuffed shot was easily saved by Alisson.

Then came another legendary European sequence. After 53 minutes, Alexander-Arnold gave the ball away cheaply, but won it back, came forward and hit a low cross into the area. Wijnanldum arrived with a late run, met it with his side foot, and ter Stegen could not prevent it going in. From the restart, Liverpool immediately attacked the Kop again. Origi was pushed too wide for a shot, so attempted a switch to the other wing. Milner played a subtle reverse pass to Shaqiri, his sweet left footed cross was met by a towering leap and header from Wijnanldum. The players celebrated in front of the euphoric Kop, with the substitutes joining, while Barcelona looked stunned; their lead had vanished.

Just like Istanbul, Liverpool had levelled a major deficit, but there was still over 30 minutes left, would there be another twist? It was difficult to sustain the same level of attacking intensity, as Barcelona tried to mount a response, and Liverpool pragmatically retreated. Fabinho was excellent in winning the ball, especially as he was on a tightrope after the early booking, while Alisson made another timely save from Messi at the near post.

After 78 minutes, patient and probing passing led Alexander-Arnold to win a corner. He placed the ball on the spot, but walked away as Shaqiri trotted over to take it. Suddenly, Alexander-Arnold turned back and pumped the ball into the middle. Origi reacted first, cushioning his strike as it bounced up to him, past the surprised Barcelona rearguard. The quick-thinking was undoubtedly an impish stroke of genius from the precocious talent. But maybe he had remembered that the team's analysts had advised that Barcelona were slow to reorganise at set-pieces. The ballboys had also been briefed to ensure a quick return of any balls.

For the first time in the tie, Liverpool were ahead, and Barcelona desperately sought an equaliser. The nearest they came was a cross that went across the penalty area, but was unmet. Liverpool had glorious chances on the break; Wijnanldum headed over and Sturridge shot over too. In the last seconds, Fabinho intercepted in midfield, and won a free-kick from Messi. It was laid off to Milner who saw out the remaining seconds.

Anfield erupted again, as several of the victors fell to their knees with tiredness and emotion. The entire squad and backroom assembled in front of the Kop, joining in another special communal "You'll Never Walk Alone". Even after the heights of Inter Milan, St Etienne, Chelsea, this was an exceptional night, probably the greatest. Despite the challenges, every player had given their all and recorded a famous result. This was not the fury of the Dortmund comeback, but a controlled, passionate, and mature performance.

Four days later, Liverpool beat Wolves, but Manchester City won too, claiming the league title. A huge disappointment, so close again, but at least now, there was still another chance of silverware.

- The entire match is included on the "Liverpool Champions of Europe" DVD. A highlights clip on the BT YouTube channel has over 13 million views. There is also a plethora of behind-the-scenes footage on the LFCTV Go service, including "Inside Anfield" and a "Watchalong " with Jurgen Klopp and Pep Lijnders.

- The Barcelona viewpoint is provided by episode seven of Rakuten TV's "Matchday" documentary series.

- This was the first time a three-goal deficit had been overturned in a Champions League semi-final, and only the fourth time in the knockout phase. The last European Cup semi-final to see such a swing was in 1986.

- Wijnanldum was the first Liverpool substitute to score twice in Europe since Babel against Besiktas.

- Referee Cüneyt Cakir had also been in charge of the dramatic 4-3 win against Borussia Dortmund.

- Alisson Becker had been in goal for Roma the previous year, when they overturned a 4-1 deficit in Barcelona, with a 3-0 win in Roma.

- Barcelona's record defeat to English opposition.

- Liverpool had now beaten the retaining Spanish, German, Portuguese and French champions.

Liverpool 2 Tottenham Hotspur 0

01/06/2019 - Champions League Final - Wanda Metropolitano Stadium, Madrid

In the second all-English Champions League final, Liverpool would face Tottenham, who also had an incredible semi-final triumph, scoring three times in the second half, away at Ajax. There were similarities in the team's playing styles, and both managers were still waiting for their first trophies after building these impressive squads. With three weeks to wait, Klopp gave the players a week off, and then they spent a week in a Marbella training camp, including a secret match against a Benfica B team, who were instructed to set up and play like Spurs.

Both teams had injury concerns to key strikers, as Harry Kane and Firmino had missed the end of the league season, but both were passed fit. Kane replaced semi-final hat-trick hero Lucas Moura, and for Liverpool, their hero Wijnanldum started instead of Milner.

Like 2005, there was a dramatic start; Mané made an early break, his ball hit Sissoko on the arm and the referee awarded a penalty after just 47 seconds. Salah had to wait for VAR to concur, and then smashed it down the centre. His first kick of the final, and redemption after last year's injury heartbreak. Liverpool's subsequent chances fell to their full-backs; Alexander-Arnold just shot wide and a Robertson shot was tipped over a fine run. Tottenham came closest in injury time, but Eriksen shot over. It had been a poor half, as the teams seemed rusty after the extended break or just nervous, as both struggled to keep possession, but Liverpool had the all-important lead.

There were few early chances in the second half, as Salah had a shot blocked and Lloris cut out a Robertson cross. Around the hour mark, Milner and Origi came on. A strong run from Mané, led to an early chance for Milner, but his shot went just wide.

Spurs tried to increase their tempo and exert more pressure as Moura came on. Dele Ali tried a curling chip, but Alisson saved easily, van Dyke stopped a Son run and Ali headed over. After 79 minutes, Alisson made a vital double save, beating away a Son shot from distance and then Moura's weak shot from closer, and then he tipped around an Erikson free-kick.

Despite being more defensive, Liverpool still mustered some attacks, and on the 86th minute, Rose carelessly gave away a corner. Milner took it, the ball was not cleared, Matip flicked on to Origi, and he shot from an angle with his left foot across Lloris for 2-0. Although Tottenham forlornly threw everything forward in the dying minutes, Alisson was equal to anything on target

It was Liverpool's European triumph again, as Henderson shuffled and lifted the trophy, the first success of the Klopp era. Like Real Madrid in 1981, it may have been a disappointing spectacle, but no one in Liverpool was complaining.

- The entire match is available on the "Champions of Europe" DVD, but there are also highlights on YouTube, including a wonderful two-minute clip following Klopp after the final whistle.

- Tickets cost €600, €450, €160 and €70, with 17,000 allocated to each club.

- Joel Matip's first assist for Liverpool.

- The Liverpool starting XI consisted of three Brazilians, two Englishmen, two Dutch and four other nationalities, bought for an estimated total of £335 million.

- Jurgen Klopp's first European trophy, after three final defeats.

- Liverpool's sixth European Cup win, then surpassed Bayern Munich and Ajax, putting them third with the most wins behind Real Madrid and AC Milan.

- All of Liverpool's European Cup wins have been when wearing red shirts, beating opposition in white.

- Mauricio Pochettino was sacked by Tottenham in November after a poor start to the following season.

- After Klopp's first trophy, Liverpool would win the European Super Cup in August and the World Club Cup in December.

Liverpool 3 Manchester City 1

10/11/2019 - Premier League - Anfield

Despite media eservations that Liverpool may have missed their best title chance, Klopp was content with the squad with no major signings. His faith was rewarded with a blistering start of ten wins out of the first eleven league games, opening up a six-point lead over Manchester City. Their impending meeting would be crucial to both, as the gap could be down to three or up to nine

Liverpool were at full strength apart from Matip, so Lovren started. City had more issues as Kompany had not been replaced, while Aymeric Laporte and Ederson were injured, but they had new signing Rodri in midfield, and the front axis of De Bruyne, Sterling and Aguero. Guardiola had seemed to have learnt from their previous Anfield defeats, as on their last visit, they had earned a 0-0 draw by slowing the game.

The match exploded into controversy in the 6th minute. In the Liverpool area, the ball brushed the hand of Silva and then Alexander-Arnold. City appealed for a penalty, but Liverpool swept forward with Mané, his cross was cleared, but only to Fabinho, he controlled it, and fired in a stunning drive. Guardiola and the City players were incensed, but the new VAR system detected no obvious error.

City tried to reply; Sterling beat the offside from a free-kick, but his header went wide, and another free-kick just missed Stones and Aguero, both from De Bruyne's excellent delivery. In the 13th minute, Liverpool extended their lead. Alexander-Arnold started another move with a sumptuous dipping cross-field pass to Robertson, he took one touch, swung in a deep cross that Salah stooped to head in after its bounce. A stunning lightning counter attacking goal with typically full-backs key.

Both teams had further chances as the game flowed from end to end. Aguero shot, but Alisson pushed away, and Angelino hit the outside of the post. Bravo saved from Firmino after a run by Alexander-Arnold and also Salah's curling shot. Fabinho was superb in the midfield, ably supported by the industrious Wijnanldum and Henderson.

Early in the second half, Henderson powered to the byline and put over a deep cross that Mané headed in at the far post. Another three goal lead over City at Anfield, and justly deserved. Inevitably City fought back, but could not create any major chances, as Liverpool defended well. With 12 minutes left Silva squeezed in a goal, and Sterling spurned a good opportunity, as Liverpool started to tire. However, they managed to prevent any more chances, and recorded a definitive moment in what would be a historic season.

- Only Fabinho's second goal for Liverpool, hence his "about time" celebrations.

- Klopp's eighth win over Guardiola (a record), and the first time he had lost four times at the same venue.

- Manchester City had only won once at Anfield since 1981.

- Goalkeeper Scott Carson was on the Manchester City bench, 13 years after his final Liverpool appearance. He would also be on the bench for the 2021 Champions League final, 15 years after Istanbul.

- Standard ticket prices now ranged from £37 to £59, with discounts for over 65s and juniors.

2020s

Liverpool 2 Manchester United 0

19/01/2020 - Premier League - Anfield

The distant chasers hoped that Liverpool would be distracted by a trip to Qatar for the World Club Championship and Fabinho's injury. Actually, they came back stronger and more confident, with title rivals Leicester humbled 4-0 at home, and best of the rest Sheffield United and Wolves beaten at Anfield as Liverpool extended their lead to 14 points and a game in hand.

The home match with Manchester United was another major hurdle on the way to the title. With City only drawing the previous day, there was also another opportunity to increase their lead. Ole Gunnar Solskjær was manager now, spending lavishly on Harry Maguire, Aaron Wan-Bissaka and Dan James, who all played. For Liverpool, Fabinho was available again, but Klopp stuck with the same winning team, as van Dyke and Gomez continued their impressive defensive partnership.

Liverpool forced a series of early corners, and on 14 minutes, van Dyke jumped highest to power in a corner. United were overwhelmed, Mané was only denied for a corner. De Gea could not catch a skied Salah shot, and Firmino finished well, but VAR harshly gave a foul on the keeper, and Firmino also shot wide too. Wijnanldum also had a goal disallowed for offside after another stunning team move. Mané was put through, but DeGea saved with his feet. United's only real chance was when Peirira failed to connect from close range.

The second half followed the same pattern, Salah missed a glorious chance in front of the Kop from Robertson's cross, while Henderson smashed the ball against the post as United were struggling. Eventually, they managed to attack but Fred and Martial both could not hit the target. It also allowed Mané to break, but he scuffed his shot.

United pressed forward more in the closing minutes, but could not get past the resilient Liverpool defence. Deep into injury time, Alisson saved from a weak Wan-Bissaka shot. He didn't attempt to see out time, but quickly launched a long ball to Salah. The Egyptian ran from the halfway line, held off James, and slotted under De Gea. The Kop was in bedlam again, and Alisson ran the length of the pitch to be the first to celebrate with Salah.

There was barely time for United to restart, as the final whistle put Liverpool sixteen points ahead (and a game in hand). The Kop broke out into a chorus of "We're gonna win the league". Not a hope anymore, but a statement of fact. Nothing could stop Liverpool from winning the Premier League now. Apart from a global pandemic.

- Salah's first goal against Manchester United at the fifth attempt.

- Liverpool's 21st win of 22 league games (or 30th win out of 31 including the previous season). They would take 110 points from 38 games across two seasons.

- The last of seven consecutive clean sheets in the league.

- Liverpool would not lose in the Premier League for over a year, from January 2019 until February 2020 winning 40 of 45 games.

- At its peak, Liverpool's lead was 25 points, a top-flight record.

Liverpool 4 Crystal Palace 0

24/6/2020 - Premier League - Anfield

Liverpool were six points away from their first Premier League title, when football was postponed due to the Covid-19 virus outbreak. It would be over three months later, and in front of no fans that they returned to action, playing out a disappointing 0-0 draw at Everton.

An empty Anfield awaited Crystal Palace in midweek. They were managed by Roy Hodgson, and could be tricky opponents, having repeatedly taken points away at both Manchester clubs in the last two seasons. They were also on a run of four wins, with no goals conceded. Klopp chose from a full strength squad now, so Salah and Robertson came in after not featuring in the derby, and he could also select nine substitutes.

Liverpool started well, but could not score, Wijnanldum and Henderson shot wide from close range while a Firmino shot was saved. The breakthrough came after 23 minutes, as Alexander-Arnold bent a free-kick over the wall and into the net. The one-way pressure continued as Henderson hit the post, and van Dyke's rebound was scrambled off the line, while Salah later lobbed a shot over. Just before half-time, Fabinho chipped a perfectly weighted ball for Salah, and he lifted his finish over Hennessey.

Within 10 minutes of the restart, it was 3-0; Fabinho struck an unstoppable drive that flew into the back of the net. Liverpool were enjoying themselves, and in a quick break, Salah set up Mané, who guided a shot into the far corner. There could have been more; a Keita shot was deflected, a Salah cross was blocked, and Neco Williams' shot saved. Palace had been so dominated that they had not even managed a touch in the Liverpool penalty area.

Liverpool's lead was now up to 23 points, as all eyes turned to Stamford Bridge for Manchester City's match the following day. Chelsea duly won 2-1, and Liverpool were champions again, after a thirty-year wait.

- The first league match played at Anfield in June.

- Liverpool's title confirmation had the unusual distinction of being the earliest in terms of the fewest games played (seven games left) but also the latest date (25th June).

- Salah's goal was Liverpool's 100th of the season, in their 50th match.

- Jordan Henderson would be presented with the Premier League trophy by Kenny Dalglish on a stage specially constructed on the empty Kop, after the match against Chelsea.

- Crystal Palace had been the last team to win at Anfield in April 2017. In 2019-20 Liverpool won all the home league games, apart from a draw against Burnley.

- Salah scored 23 and Mané 22 goals in all competitions, while Firmino scored eight goals away in the league, but only scored his first at Anfield in the final match.

- Liverpool finished with a club record 99 points, and a league joint record number of home points and wins.

Crystal Palace 0 Liverpool 7

19/12/2020 - Premier League - Selhurst Park

The new season brought several difficulties with a shorter pre-season, transfer limitations and budget concerns due to the Covid crisis. The lack of a replacement for the departing Lovren led to an inevitable centre-back injury crisis, with van Dyke missing most of the season, as Gomez and Matip soon followed. The shock 7-2 defeat at Aston Villa was shrugged off with a characteristic run of one defeat in 15.

Beating Tottenham in midweek saw Liverpool back on top of the table, before a trip to Selhurst Park. Clyne was now playing there, but the other old boy Benteke was suspended. The champions' new signing Diogo Jota was out injured, and Salah rotated, so Takumi Minamino came in a rare start, while Fabinho was playing centre-back.

The changes worked quickly as Minamino opened the scoring after 3 minutes; with a precise finish after being set up by Mané. Ayew was clean through, but overhit his pullback to the unmarked Zaha, while Alisson saved from Milivojevic and Ayew.

At the other end, a Matip header was off target from close range, but the lead was extended after 36 minutes; Firmino played into Mané, who turned and finished powerfully. Before half-time, another break led to the third; Firmino released Robertson to gallop down the wing, and his cross was controlled by Firmino on the run and despatched sublimely.

Within 7 minutes of the restart, Henderson made it four, curling in from the edge of the area, after Alexander-Arnold set him up. Minimino missed a good chance when clean though, putting his shot past the post.

Klopp brought on Salah for Mané, and it didn't take long for him to make an impact against a ragged Palace. He split the defence with a ball to Firmino, who dinked over Guaita for his second. Into the last 10 minutes, and Salah himself scored, deflecting back a Matip header from an Alexander-Arnold cross. Three minutes later, he had another, Oxlade-Chamberlain found him on the edge of the penalty area, and he cut inside and curled on his left foot into the far corner.

Palace had not been that bad in the first half, but Liverpool were so clinical, with seven fine away goals from eight shots on target.

However, it was the high point of the season, as they would soon lose six successive home matches, and slip down to 8th place. The injury-hit squad managed to win eight of the last ten fixtures to rescue a creditable third place finish.

- Liverpool's record away win in the top-flight and Palace's biggest home defeat ever. It was also Liverpool's biggest league win since the 9-0 win against Palace in 1989.

- The goals were spread across five different scorers and seven different assists.

- Minamino's first Premier League goal for Liverpool.

- Mané also scored twice against Palace on the last day of the season, equalling the Premier League record for goals in eight consecutive matches against the same opposition.

- Alisson Becker became the first Liverpool goalkeeper to score, when he headed in a last-minute winner at West Brom in May.

- Salah scored over 20 goals for the fourth successive season, with a total of 31 in all competitions.

Bibliography

Websites

The ultimate source of Liverpool facts is the lfchistory.net website, a lovingly curated mass of meticulously researched information. It is also highly recommended to subscribe to their twitter feed for daily anniversaries and trivia.

The britishnewspaperarchive.co.uk website has a great selection of national and regional newspapers from the last century, available for subscription.

The lfcineurope.com website has a wonderful selection of facts and memorabilia from the European matches. Similarly, the Unoofical Liverpool Football Club Museum Facebook page has some great historical photos and items.

Books

A Season on the Brink by Guillem Balague - Weidenfeld & Nicholson (2005)

Allez Allez Allez by Simon Hughes - Corgi (2019)

An Autobiography by Kevin Keegan - Arthur Barker (1977)

Anfield the Illustrated History by Mark Platt with Williams Hughes - SevenOaks (2015)

At the End of the Storm by Gary Shaw and Mark Platt (2009)

A-Z of Mersey Soccer by John Keith & Peter Thomas - Beaverbrook Newspapers (1973)

Bill Shankly It's Much More Important than That by Stephen F. Kelly - Virgin Books (1996)

Bob Paisley - An Autobiography by Bob Paisley - Arthur Barker (1983)

Bob Paisley's Liverpool Scrapbook by Bob Paisley - Souvenir Press (1979)

Carra My Autobiography by Jamie Carragher - Corgi Books (2009)

Champions League Dreams by Rafa Benitez - Headline Publishing (2012)

Crazy Horse by Emlyn Hughes - Arthur Barker (1981)

Cup Kings Liverpool 1965 by Mark Platt - Bluecoat Press (1980)

Cup Kings Liverpool 1977 by Mark Platt - Bluecoat Press (2003)

Dalglish My Autobiography by Kenny Dalglish - Hodder & Stoughton (1996)

Eddies's Golden Years Scrapbooks 1959-60 by Eddie Marks - Marksport Publications (1986)

Ee-Aye-Addio We've Won the Cup by Brian Pead - Champion Press (1993)

Football on Merseyside by Percy M Young - Stanley Paul (1963)

Fowler My Autobiography by Robbie Fowler - Pan Books (2006)

Gerrard My Autobiography by Steven Gerrard - Bantam Press (2006)

Here We Go Gathering Comes in May edited by Nicky Alt - Canongate (2008)

Hunt For Goals by Roger Hunt - Pelham Books (1969)

I Did It the Hard Way by Tommy Smith - Arthur Barker (1980)

I Don't Know What It is, but I love it by Tony Evans - Viking (2014)

Into the Red by John Williams - Mainstream Publishing (2001)

Journey to Wembley by Brian James - Marshall Cavendish (1977)

King Kenny An Autobiography by Kenny Dalglish - Stanley Paul (1982)

Klopp: Bring the Noise by Raphael Honigstein - Yellow Jersey (2019)

Liverpool by Matthew Graham - Hamlyn (1985)

Liverpool Champions of Champions by Brian Pead - Breedon Books (1990)

Liverpool FC Official Annual 1977 by John Keith

Liverpool FC Official Annual 1978 by John Keith

Liverpool FC Official Annual 1981 by John Keith

Liverpool FC Official Annual 1982 by John Keith

Liverpool FC Official Annual 1983 by Michael Charters

Liverpool FC the Historic Treble - Official Celebration - Carlton Books (2001)

Liverpool FC: Ending the Seven-Year Itch by Steven Horton - Vertical Editions (2012)

Liverpool in Europe by Steve Hale & Ivan Ponting - Guinness Publishing (1992)

Liverpool Supreme - Cockerel Books (1985)

Liverpool The Complete Record by Arnie Baldursson and Gudmundur Magnusson - DeCoubertin Books (2014)

Liverpool The Official Centenary History by Stan Liversedge (1992)

Liverpool: My Team by Steve Heighway - Souvenir Press (1977)

Liverpool's 5-star Heroes - Sport Media (2005)

My Scrapbook by Ian Rush - SportsMedia (2013)

My Soccer Story by Billy Liddell - Stanley Paul (1960)

No Half Measures by Graeme Souness - Willow Books (1985)

On the March with Kenny's Army by Gary Shaw and Mark Platt (2011)

Phil Neal - Attack from the Back - Arthur Barker (1981)

Room At the Kop by Ian St John - Pelham (1966)

Rush: Ian Rush's Autobiography by Ian Rush - Grafton Books (1986)

Secret Diary of a Liverpool Scout by Simon Hughes - SportsMedia (2011)

Shankly by Bill Shankly - Arthur Barker (1976)

The Anatomy of Liverpool by Jonathan Wilson with Scott Murray - Orion Books (2013)

The Boot Room Boys by Peter Hooton - Virgin Books (2018)

The Ian Callaghan Story by Ian Callaghan & John Keith - Quarter Books (1975)

The Kop by Stephen F Kelly - Mandarin (1993)

The Liverpool Way by John Williams - Mainstream Publishing (2003)

The Liverpool Year by Kenny Dalglish - Willow Books (1988)

The Official Treasures of Liverpool FC by David Walmsley with Stephen Done - Carlton Books (2004)

The Real Bill Shankly by Karen Gill - SportsMedia (2006)

The Real Bob Paisley as told by the Paisley family - SportsMedia (2007)

The Shankly Years by Steve Hale and Phil Thompson - Ebury Press (1998)

Tosh an Autobiography by John Toshack - Arthur Barker (1982)

We Go Again by David E Usher (2014)

We Love You Yeah, Yeah, Yeah! by Steven Horton - Vertical Editions (2015)

When Football was Football Liverpool by Pete Hooton - Haynes Publishing (2009)

Who's Who of Liverpool 1892 - 1989 by Doug Lamming - Breedon Books (1989)

Index of Opponents

About the Author

David Plumbley was born in Chester, UK in 1966, and still lives there today. He worked in local government for twenty five years and more recently in banking, but taken sabbaticals to explore his love of travel. He has visited more than seventy five countries, and especially enjoys Asia and South America.

A passionate Liverpool FC supporter, he has been a season-ticket holder since 1978/9, and privileged to see so many of the Liverpool (and opposition) greats.

This is his second book after "Songs from a Quarantine" was written and published in 2020. He can be followed on Twitter at @dplumbley66.

"Songs from a Quarantine" by David Plumbley is now available on Amazon -

Join David in his lockdown journey through his 102 favorite songs, analyzing what makes them special, attempting to understand their meaning and supplying any history or miscellaneous trivia. Including 1950s rock 'n roll, 1960s legends, 70s & 80s classic pop / rock, and today's singer songwriters. Some you will love and some you can discover.

Printed in Great Britain
by Amazon

71605282R10200